"This book is a much needed, practical guide for teams and organizations looking to collaborate across differences. The authors' deep appreciation for diversity helps them deliver a research driven approach that I look forward to integrating into my own practice."

—Dr. Tiffany Jana, Founder of the TMI Portfolio of companies and
author of Overcoming Bias, Erasing Institutional Bias,
The B Corp Handbook, 2nd edition, and Subtle Acts of Exclusion.

"Whether your team is in the workplace or the classroom, *Intercultural Collaboration by Design* will empower you with design-based practices adapted for multidisciplinary use to build a world where people communicate across boundaries. The book's activities will enhance creativity, intercultural awareness, and team focus."

—Robin Landa, Distinguished Professor,
Michael Graves College of Kean University

"This is an extraordinary book! I have never seen anything so helpful in overcoming intercultural challenges across members of work teams. It is full of wisdom and helpful exercises. It is creatively written and easy to read."

—Jeffrey S. Harrison, University Distinguished Educator,
W. David Robbins Chair in Strategic Management,
University of Richmond

"I work across industry and academia with geographically and culturally diverse teams, and I can't wait to try the flexible tools and activities in this book. The Six Dimensions framework is already shaping how I think about guiding my students and colleagues through complex projects and team dynamics. The book is thoughtfully organized to give anyone the confidence to create welcoming collaborative environments. As our world becomes more globalized and yet more polarized, these are the skills we need to create a more inclusive and equitable world."

—Amy Bickerton, Design Researcher at Dropbox, Adjunct
Professor at California College of the Arts, and
Former Senior User Experience Designer at Amazon

"I feel very fortunate to have experienced these methods firsthand as a student—and now, with remote work becoming the new norm, I've been armed with a diverse toolset that will continue to enrich the collaborative thread that connects teams who are spread all over the world."

—Jessica Cook, Designer

INTERCULTURAL COLLABORATION BY DESIGN

Intercultural Collaboration by Design introduces a framework for collaborating across cultures and learning to use multicultural perspectives to address pressing global issues.

This handbook helps people work, learn, and teach across cultures. Through the activities highlighted in this book, virtual and intercultural teams will find a practical route for initiating and sustaining productive work across disciplinary and social barriers. Teams can craft a plan to achieve their goals by selecting the activities that best meet their needs and interests. First-person anecdotes from the authors demonstrate how the activities encourage teams to embrace diverse perspectives in order to create innovative solutions.

With over 30 hands-on activities, this book will be of great interest to diverse teams from a variety of disciplines who want to enhance intercultural learning and co-working. Whether in the classroom or workplace, the activities are appropriate for a variety of collaboration contexts, without a need for background in art or design.

Kelly M. Murdoch-Kitt is an Assistant Professor at the University of Michigan's Penny W. Stamps School of Art and Design. She believes in integrating visual communication, interaction design, and service design with global and social responsibility.

Denielle J. Emans is an Associate Professor at Virginia Commonwealth University School of the Arts Qatar. She is passionate about collaboration, storytelling, and empowering teams to build strong relationships to fuel creative action.

Their ongoing research, which supports diverse international teams in addressing sustainability topics, has been recognized by the Design Incubation Teaching Awards. They have co-authored chapters in the *Routledge Handbook of Sustainable Design*, the *Handbook of Sustainability and Social Science Research*, and the forthcoming *Collaboration in Design Education*.

INTERCULTURAL COLLABORATION BY DESIGN

Drawing from Differences, Distances, and Disciplines through Visual Thinking

*Kelly M. Murdoch-Kitt
and Denielle J. Emans*

Routledge
Taylor & Francis Group

LONDON AND NEW YORK

First published 2020
by Routledge
2 Park Square, Milton Park, Abingdon, Oxon OX14 4RN

and by Routledge
52 Vanderbilt Avenue, New York, NY 10017

Routledge is an imprint of the Taylor & Francis Group, an informa business

British Library Cataloguing-in-Publication Data
A catalogue record for this book is available from the British Library

Library of Congress Cataloging-in-Publication Data
A catalog record has been requested for this book

ISBN: 978-0-367-21932-1 (hbk)
ISBN: 978-0-367-21931-4 (pbk)
ISBN: 978-0-429-26882-3 (ebk)

Typeset in Bembo
by codeMantra

To Jim & Tilden
      —KMMK

To Jordon
      —DJE

CONTENTS

ACKNOWLEDGMENTS

We extend our gratitude to the many people who helped make this work possible: The hundreds of students, representing dozens of nationalities and residing in Qatar, the United Arab Emirates, and the United States of America who have contributed to our research since 2012; our families for their support and understanding; our colleagues, mentors, and readers for their encouragement and feedback.

We are thankful for our amazing support team who helped us bring this work to life:

Illustrator	Tammi Heneveld
Graduate research assistants	Ashley Moon
	Bruna Oewel
Undergraduate research assistants	Sanya Verma
	Abigail Ziemkowski
	Anusha Bohra
	Summer Nguyen
	Louise Malmgren
Writing feedback	Hilary Levinson
	Delia DeCourcy
	Whitney Wilkes-Krier
	Sabrina Harrison
	Cathy Lee
	Amanda Goldman
	Mindy Magyar
	William Temple
We thank our institutions for their generous support:	Penny W. Stamps School of Art & Design, University of Michigan
	The University of Michigan Office of Research
	Virginia Commonwealth University School of the Arts in Qatar.

GLOSSARY

You will find several different terms throughout this book referring to the various people you may engage with on your collaborative journey; we introduce them here to help orient you to their meaning. Like different cooks in a kitchen, each member of your collaborative intercultural team plays a unique role in the team's activities, projects, and personal growth as you work together across cultures and learn to use various cultural perspectives to address pressing global issues.

Teams are more than two people engaged in an activity or a project sharing responsibility to achieve shared goals.

Remote teams, also called **intercultural** or **diverse teams**, are small groups of people from different cultural and/or disciplinary backgrounds, such as classmates or work colleagues, who intentional bring their varied perspectives together through collaborative learning and working. Our research deals with intercultural teams that work together **remotely**, communicating and collaborating through digital tools. However, diverse or intercultural teams could certainly exist within the same geographic location, and in-person teams could benefit from many of the activities in this book.

Teammate(s) refers to the individual people who come together to form a **team**.

Partners are two team members engaged in an activity together. Because some of the book's activities are more appropriate when conducted one-on-one, individuals will sometimes need to identify one specific partner within their diverse team to work with for a particular activity. Infrequently in the text, connections established with community members outside of the team may be referred to as partnerships.

Collaboration is the process of two or more people, i.e. *collaborators*, working together to co-create something through joint decision-making, in which everyone takes part in the process and responsibility for the outcomes.

Intercultural collaboration involves teammates with two or more distinct cultural backgrounds. Intercultural collaborations can occur between teammates in the same physical location or separated by distance.

Collaborators are people you work with to co-create something through a joint decision-making process in which everyone takes part in creative decision-making. Depending upon the context or situation, they could be remote or local to you. Collaborators could be part of your diverse team or external to the team, such as stakeholders and community partners.

Local colleagues are people who are in the same physical location. They may or may not be part of your diverse team. Several activities within the book recommend working with local colleagues in order to gain perspective or understanding prior to discussing certain topics or participating in activities with your remote teammates.

Group refers either to three or more people working together in person or a larger collection of remote teams. A classroom or workplace that incorporates multiple teams could be considered a "group" when all of the teams are involved in a particular activity together—e.g. A large group discussion or critique.

Participant refers generally to someone who takes part in collaborations and describes those who have been involved in our research.

Team building is an ongoing process that helps teammates learn about themselves and each other in order to establish the requisite trust to effectively and innovatively work together.

Activities involve creating, sharing, editing, and interpreting different Tangible Objects: Thought Objects, Progress Objects, and Dialogue Objects as manifestations of visual thinking. Making and sharing these objects facilitates learning, understanding, commitment, and innovative co-creation. As an approach to team building, activities may result in sketches, prototypes, concept maps, calendars, writings, models, and a variety of in-progress artifacts.

Projects involve collective goal-setting and contributions from everyone on the team to achieve a mutually desired outcome. Projects are more complex and intense than the activities offered in early chapters. While the book's activities can be used to support or lead up to many different kinds of projects, some specific project ideas are offered in Chapter 6.

INTRODUCTION

Why we wrote this book

People are more mobile and more connected than ever before, but we could still become more interconnected. Geographically dispersed remote teams can communicate across time and international boundaries thanks to the ubiquity of internet connectivity, cloud-based communication, and collaboration tools. As opportunities to connect online increase, there is greater demand for intercultural communication and collaboration skills in professional and personal environments.

There is a higher need for these skills beyond adequately preparing people to enter the global workforce. Skills in navigating, communicating, and collaborating across cultures are critical for understanding the gravity of global challenges and in cooperatively mobilizing to find solutions for them. Big messy problems ranging from issues of social justice to environmental sustainability must be addressed across countries.

Learning to work effectively across global borders with teammates in other countries is now more critical than ever. In spite of this increasing need, however, only a small percentage of the world's most privileged people are able to travel, study, or work abroad to develop these competencies away from home. Obstacles to travel—including financial, academic, political, and social concerns—emphasize the need for locally accessible opportunities to gain skills in intercultural collaboration. In this book, we offer you the tools to create such an opportunity and provide new strategies for tackling global challenges together in the workplace, the classroom, and beyond.

This work is rewarding, but it is also hard. Remote teammates engaged in long-distance intercultural collaborations must establish mutual commitment and trust. People are inherently imperfect, and when we come from different backgrounds and ways of understanding the world, communication can be tricky. By using the *Six Dimensions of Intercultural Teamwork* (1.1) to your advantage and working through the participatory and visual intercultural learning activities in this book, individuals and teams can cultivate better global awareness and embrace diversity as a creative asset. The Six Dimensions of Intercultural Teamwork is a spectrum-based, actionable framework to guide teams toward:

1. Discovering Work Styles
2. Understanding Core Beliefs
3. Establishing Trust
4. Assessing Information
5. Decoding Communication Styles
6. Designing Shared Goals

How to use this book

No design degree required!

Although we, the authors, have a background in design, you do not need to be a designer to employ these approaches effectively. Practitioners, students, and educators from a variety of disciplines will find practical routes to initiating and sustaining productive intercultural work across disciplinary and social boundaries. Fancy hardware or software is also not needed—paper, pencil, and an internet-enabled device (for long-distance collaborations) are all that is needed in most cases. Although online collaborations are the basis of our studies, the activities and principles within this book are easily adapted to other team setups and collaborations.

Supporting equitable teams

This book supports teams who are making an effort to work together equitably, whether or not they have the benefit of facilitation. Some teams may wish to operate without formal facilitation, as hierarchies can affect their balance. Putting the responsibility on teams to manage themselves enables everyone to share power and authority. Therefore, we include as much detail as possible to provide the support you need for a productive experience.

Recipes for successful collaboration

Think about *Intercultural Collaboration by Design* as a cookbook with recipes sorted into chapters based on the different phases of a meal. You wouldn't prepare all of the recipes at once! While the chapters are organized sequentially, we invite you to browse and choose appropriate "recipes" for the different phases of your collaboration. Like a cookbook, this book also is not intended as a linear, cover-to-cover read. However, the first section of each chapter does explain the facets of collaboration from different perspectives.

Mix-and-match several "recipes" with your team

Still cooking along with us? The duration or intensity of your interaction may dictate the quantity and the type of recipes you select for your collaboration:

- *A quick snack: Short-term/3 weeks or less*
  An enjoyable way to get started! A newly formed team can try a few activities as a way to begin establishing trust between remote teammates. An established team might use an activity or two once in a while to stimulate fresh thinking or enliven its dynamic. Activities such as the Picture Story Shuffle (3.2) or Video Exchange (3.3) are wonderful ways to get to know each other or to enhance project ideas within a limited timeframe.
- *A multi-course meal: Medium-term/3–6 weeks*
  With more time, remote teammates might opt to begin a collaboration with the Belief Brainstorm (2.3), a foundational activity for broaching discussions of differences between cultures. Next, strike up a lively correspondence with the Perspective Exchange (4.3) to develop a collective understanding of a particular geographic location or topic. The Fictional Character Exchange (4.5) is another opportunity to learn about cultural nuances that might not otherwise come up during collaboration.
- *A glorious feast! Long-term/6 weeks or more*
  For those interested in building long-term relationships for co-working and co-creation, take the time to get to know remote teammates through some of the book's early activities. Ask and respond to cultural questions crafted through the Deep Dive (2.6a), share a personal Value Collage (2.2b), and come up with a team name, avatar, and Visual Origin Story (3.5). Working within an online Fourth Space (1.5b), co-creating and integrating a Shared Calendar (1.4), and completing the Goal & Role Tracker (6.3) will reduce roadblocks and steer your collaborative work toward shared goals. Creating a Collaborative Storyboard & Video Sketch (6.5) is a rewarding opportunity to channel *creative abrasion*—the opportunity to channel conflicts into positive outcomes—into a unified outcome that can be shared with a wider audience through Public Display (6.6).

High-quality ingredients in each activity

Each activity section includes an **overview discussion** that describes higher-level learning takeaways for the team, in conjunction with the **applicable dimension** associated with the chapter. **Helpful tips, step-by-step instructions**, and **discussion prompts** engage teammates in developing:

- *Lateral thinking*, an open, generative approach to exploring ideas and cultivating understanding.
- *Tangible Objects*, which build understanding, trust, and ideas among local colleagues and remote teammates.
- *Competencies* such as self-evaluation, critical thinking, analysis, visualization, ambiguity tolerance, communication, organization, and more.

Create objects for collaboration

Most of the book's activities involve creating, sharing, editing, and interpreting different *Tangible Objects* as manifestations of visual thinking. These objects help teammates explain or express their thoughts, elicit feedback, build on ideas, and account for multiple viewpoints in reaching consensus. We use the term "object" instead of "design" to accommodate a breadth of visual possibilities that may not fall under teammates' typical understanding of design. Unlike design, the word "object" takes the pressure off teammates to create something perfect. Imperfect Tangible Objects are more open to interpretation, hacking, remixing, and discussion. The point is not to reach perfection, but to craft objects that visually communicate ideas, foster team communication, or relay outcomes to people outside of the team. Making and sharing such objects facilitates learning, understanding, commitment, and innovative co-creation (Star and Griesemer 1989; Leonard-Barton 1995).

Better yet, Tangible Objects introduce multisensory learning opportunities for virtual teams, enhancing the "realism" of the project and team, which is particularly important when the team is virtual. The book's activities result in myriad objects: sketches, prototypes, concept maps, calendars, writings, models, and a variety of in-progress artifacts. To make things simpler, we divide these tangible manifestations of visual thinking into three basic categories based on what kind of communication they promote.

1. **Thought Objects** communicate ideas from an individual to the team and can also help an individual better understand their own ideas. They visually demonstrate an idea or process and help individuals and teammates better understand each other's thoughts, similar to *design schemas* (Nelson and Stolterman 2014). (See Chapters 1, 2, and 3.)
2. **Progress Objects** foster communication among teammates and are based on methods of *generative design research* (Martin and Hanington 2012). These objects prompt a reciprocal, generative engagement between two or more teammates, in order to move a process or idea forward. (See Chapters 4, 5, and 6.)

3. **Dialogue Objects** stimulate communication with people outside of the
team. They serve to stimulate critical thinking and provoke productive dialogue around a visual object or experience. They often connect different
types of people together. Much like a polished design concept, these function similarly to *discursive design* (Tharp and Tharp 2018). (See Chapter 6.)
Along with **Tangible Objects**, these terms are based on the sociological
concept of *Boundary Objects*. Boundary Objects are physical objects that generate shared understanding across diverse teams and disciplinary boundaries
(Star and Griesemer 1989). Design and other creative disciplines commonly
use different kinds of boundary objects as forms of visual thinking—to
explain or express thoughts, elicit feedback, build upon ideas, and reach
consensus.

Involving your local colleagues

Although not essential for every activity, we find that feedback, discussion, and
reflection with local colleagues enriches many of the activities. These are people
who are in your same physical location, but who may or may not be part of your
smaller remote team. In particular, working with local colleagues is an opportunity to explore your own cultural values, local communication patterns, and the
role of implicit bias. Unpacking these topics with local colleagues is a helpful way
to engage critical thinking and bias-awareness prior to interacting with remote
teammates.

If you want to get started immediately with a local colleague, jump ahead to
the Teamthink Constellation (1.2), any of the Chapter 2 activities, or the Practice
Critique (5.2).

About us

We were both raised in families that reinforced the value of cultural learning.
Our parents' careers and ideologies also affected our views of the world, relationships with others, and approaches to problem-solving. In addition to these influential childhood experiences, we have been fortunate to connect with amazing
people around the world and humbled by the generosity and hospitality we have
received on many continents. Without virtual tools for collaboration, our research would not have begun in the first place, nor would it have been possible to
engage in the intercultural exchanges that inspired this book.

Kelly M. Murdoch-Kitt

Kelly grew up in the southeastern United States, a region still coming to terms
with its history of social inequities. Perhaps this contributed to her parents' philosophy that everyone would be welcomed in their home, which enabled Kelly
and her siblings to learn firsthand from diverse experiences ranging from local
community gatherings to hosting exchange students. Kelly became an exchange

student herself at the age of 13, which further inspired her passion for intercultural learning. Down the road, an illness kept her from attending high school, and she completed courses at home—but Kelly found a silver lining in a different kind of intercultural learning. In those early days of public internet access, she built a community of friends around the world. "It's like you're going to school with the UN," her mother quipped. Since then, Kelly has channeled her passion for intercultural learning into various online and in-person experiences, traveling, collaborating, and teaching.

Denielle J. Emans

In spite of her American accent, Denielle comes from the "land down under," and yes, she does delight in eating Vegemite sandwiches. Those who enjoy Marmite, a lesser version of this salty spread, might bristle to learn that she was actually born in Great Britain but holds true to her Australian heritage. Adding yet another country to the mix, Denielle's parents moved to the United States in the early 1980s for an educational opportunity at Michigan State University. Although they never expected to make East Lansing, Michigan their permanent home, her parents built a thriving medical practice in traditional Chinese medicine and acupuncture in this small but highly international city. Growing up in a diverse university community expanded Denielle's thinking and set her on a lifelong trajectory toward social justice and intercultural learning. Beyond these formative experiences, Denielle has been immersed in the rich intercultural experience of living and working in the Gulf Arab Region of the Middle East since 2011.

Our research

Our goal in bringing people together to collaborate across cultures has always been to dismantle assumptions of otherness and build mutual respect and understanding by breaking down the barriers created by long-standing notions of power and privilege. Because of the many privileges we have experienced, it is especially important for us to address these issues and be allies for equity and inclusion in our work and personal lives. Additionally, our students are interested in developing intercultural skills firsthand, in spite of the myriad obstacles to travel.

Therefore, beginning in 2012, we began to develop the activities in this book through trial and error with our university students, arriving at the collection you'll find in these pages. When we began working on this project, Denielle was teaching at Zayed University in Dubai, United Arab Emirates, and Kelly was teaching at the University of San Francisco in California, United States. We have continued our study of intercultural collaboration as our careers have evolved. So far, over 230 participants have contributed to our research. We are excited to share their stories; we use pseudonyms to maintain their privacy. Currently, Denielle is an associate professor at Virginia Commonwealth University School of the Arts in Qatar, and Kelly is an assistant professor in the Stamps School of Art and Design at the University of Michigan.

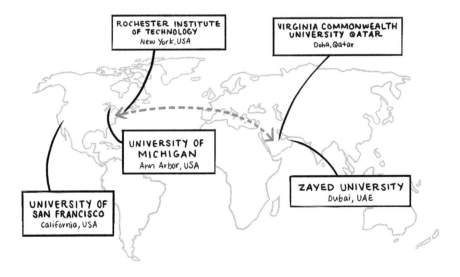

We acknowledge that our positions of privilege as university faculty enable us to conduct and share our research with you. Through the activities in this book, we invite you to join us in addressing the issues of privilege and social boundaries associated with identities and location; nationality and class; gender and race.

Connect with us

Please let us know how you use, adapt, and improve upon these activities. We would love to connect with you: orbit-project.com.

References

Leonard-Barton, Dorothy. 1995. *Wellsprings of Knowledge: Building and Sustaining the Sources of Innovation.* Harvard Business School Press. https://books.google.com/books?id=0oUoAQAAMAAJ.

Martin, Bella, and Bruce M. Hanington. 2012. *Universal Methods of Design: 100 Ways to Research Complex Problems, Develop Innovative Ideas, and Design Effective Solutions.* Digital ed. Beverly, MA: Rockport Publishers.

Nelson, Harold G., and Erik Stolterman. 2014. *The Design Way: Intentional Change in an Unpredictable World.* Cambridge, MA: MIT Press.

Star, Susan Leigh, and James R. Griesemer. 1989. "Institutional Ecology, 'Translations' and Boundary Objects: Amateurs and Professionals in Berkeley's Museum of Vertebrate Zoology, 1907–39." *Social Studies of Science* 19 (3): 387–420. doi:10.1177/030631289019003001.

Tharp, Bruce M., and Stephanie M. Tharp. 2018. *Discursive Design: Critical, Speculative, and Alternative Things.* Design Thinking, Design Theory. Cambridge, MA: MIT Press.

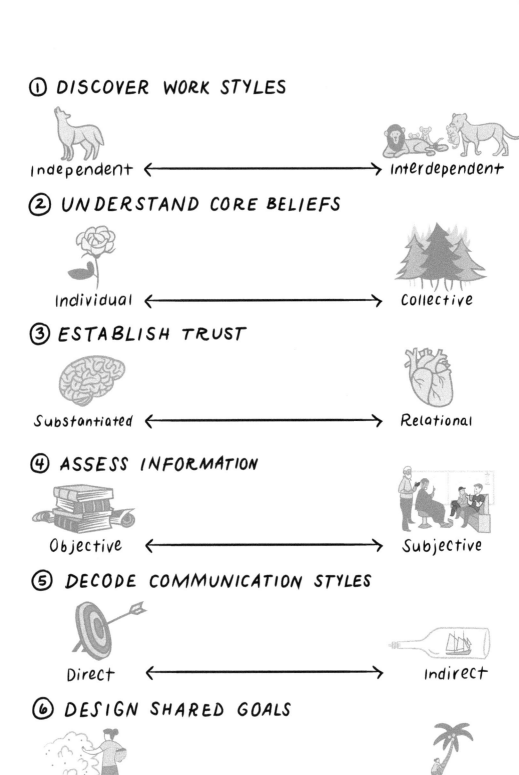

① DISCOVER WORK STYLES

Independent ⟷ Interdependent

② UNDERSTAND CORE BELIEFS

Individual ⟷ Collective

③ ESTABLISH TRUST

Substantiated ⟷ Relational

④ ASSESS INFORMATION

Objective ⟷ Subjective

⑤ DECODE COMMUNICATION STYLES

Direct ⟷ Indirect

⑥ DESIGN SHARED GOALS

Attainable ⟷ Challenging

1

DISCOVER WORK STYLES

Building interpersonal relationships through visual and tangible approaches

Independent ⟵————————————⟶ Interdependent

DIMENSION 1: Discover Work Styles

We contribute to team efforts in different ways.

For new collaborations, it is helpful to preview this chapter prior to beginning teamwork and then return to work through the activities together once the team is established. Existing teams can dive right in.

Chapter 1 introduces the Six Dimensions of Intercultural Teamwork (1.1), which help remote teammates better understand how to communicate, work, and relate to each other. The activities in this chapter delve into many work preferences and factors that can affect or impede teamwork if not proactively addressed. The related activities help teams build a positive foundation through understanding differences in time, discussing their work availability, and identifying tools and approaches to support productive communication. Imagine concentrating on a project alone in an office cubicle versus in a common workspace where people work together fluidly. Which feels more comfortable or productive for you? These ways of working parallel the "independence" and "interdependence" endpoints on the Work Styles Dimension spectrum and are just one consideration before getting started with teamwork.

| **INDEPENDENCE:** I work best when I can carve out dedicated time away from the team to work alone on a problem. I will return to the team to share what I've discovered or achieved. | **INTERDEPENDENCE:** I work best when I can find time to work with others to problem solve and find solutions together. I find creative energy in interactions with people. |

1.1

The Six Dimensions of Intercultural Teamwork: Collaborations and conceptions of community

Teams rely on relationship-building opportunities in order to coalesce and thrive. *Teamwork* means working in efficient cooperation with other people. Reducing uncertainty (Berger and Calabrese 1975) and promoting social exchange (Homans 1958) are crucial interpersonal skills for remote teams as they work together to achieve a collective goal. In this context, building interpersonal relationships is an essential component of intercultural learning and work.

Introducing the Six Dimensions of Intercultural Teamwork

The following *Six Dimensions of Intercultural Teamwork* are a spectrum-based, actionable framework designed to help teams enhance dialogue, spark creativity, and build consensus. Our assessment tool allows teammates to apply the framework to identify their individual learning and working preferences and then engage in effective teamwork by maximizing the similarities and differences they uncover. The Six Dimensions are a sequence:

1. Discover Work Styles
2. Understand Core Beliefs
3. Establish Trust
4. Assess Information
5. Decode Communication Styles
6. Design Shared Goals

During a collaboration, individuals can use their own positions along these spectrums as starting points to continually assess their learning and growth in relation to their peers (Magolda 2008).

Nobody falls neatly into the predetermined cultural categories proposed by anthropology. We've seen this firsthand through our studies of intercultural collaborations. To help teammates understand similarities and differences in a more nuanced way that specifically relates to teamwork, we developed and refined the Six Dimensions and the related Teamthink Constellation activity (Section 1.2). These have evolved over time, through practical application in intercultural student projects. We would like to take you into the heart of one of the collaborations which contributed to our development of the Six Dimensions.

In context: Discovering "in-between-ness"

Having completed their self-evaluations of the Six Dimensions, teams scribbled their numerical selections for one of the Six Dimensions, Communication Styles, onto sticky notes. These numbers served to quantitatively depict their different communication and preferences. As they worked, Denielle sketched two axes on the board and invited everyone to place their sticky notes along their matching coordinates. Soon, a cluster of people huddled around the board, excitedly positioning their numbers and exclaiming as they discovered their relationships with others in this scatterplot.

"Wow, Salma and I are right next to each other!" Maryam announced. "Maybe this is why we are such good friends?"

"I don't know," Alia countered. "Mohammad and Ahmed are on opposite sides from each other, and we all know how well they work together on projects."

"We are friends, too," Mohammad offered, "but I think being friends and working well together on projects are two different things. We have definitely figured out how to communicate with each other, though." This insight led to an enlightening team discussion about the necessary ingredients for functional collaborative teams.

At the conclusion of the team discussion, Sara finally asked aloud the question on everyone's minds. "I wonder where our teammates in the US will end up in comparison to us?"

When these teammates in Qatar sent the photo of their Communication Styles scatterplot to their teammates in the United States, there was similar interest in the visual relationships between people and their Work Styles. Then, they began to add an intercultural layer. They projected the photo of the scatterplot from Qatar on the wall and added their own sticky notes on top.

"Look at that," said Laura. "Maryam and I are really close to each other! But James and I are pretty far apart. And Ahmed is kind of in between me and Steve, but way further up on the Y-axis. I guess that means we have some communication differences to figure out as we work together."

After the US teammates finished positioning their own sticky notes on top of their teammates' scatterplot, creating the final phase of the Teamthink Constellation, they took another photo to send back to the team in Qatar.

"Based on what we talked about before doing this activity, I really thought we [US teammates] would all be on one side of the scatterplot and our [Qatar] teammates would all be on the other side," Katie said after completing the Constellation. "But really, everyone is kind of all over the place, and it is really about understanding where you are in relationship to everyone on your team. Teammates living in the same culture might be far apart in terms of their preferences. I guess everyone is a little bit 'in-between.'"

In our collaboration studies, participants in both cultures often express wonder as the bigger picture emerges. Their teamwork preferences for each dimension are depicted in a new way, and they are able to see relationships between themselves, collaborators, and friends.

Insights from the field

Reexamining cultural frameworks

Early iterations of the activity were based on the work of several western anthropologists, such as Edward T. Hall's continuum for understanding culture (1989); Geert Hofstede's differences in cultural values (2011); and Fons Trompenaars and Charles Hampden-Turner's framework for intercultural communication based on national differences (2011). Meanwhile, we recognized that these frameworks' absolute descriptions of cultural differences presented some challenges for teams. We realized we needed a system that worked against stereotyping and encouraged people to think of themselves and their teammates as inhabiting various positions within that "in-between" space. We began to experiment with different ways to promote teammates' individual discovery and expression of their own unique blend of characteristics. Over time, these discoveries evolved into the Six Dimensions of Intercultural Teamwork.

We all have multiple identities

We have found that, for productive intercultural teams, it is more valuable to assess how individuals work together and what peoples' work preferences are rather than to focus on supposed cultural differences. Similarities and differences exist regardless of nationality or geographic space. The goal of intercultural learning is to help teams understand that human beings do not fit into prescribed boxes based on their country of origin or residence. Rather, individuals are a blend of characteristics, and contrasts manifest even among people in the same workspace. Valuing that diversity is the ultimate goal of intercultural collaboration.

Building relationships

After our teams broke through cultural stereotypes and recognized that everyone is a blend of different values and Work Styles, they began to build interpersonal relationships. Throughout their collaboration, they found that building these relationships ultimately helped to make their work and project outcomes more equitable. The Teamthink Constellation activity prompted them to have open conversations about their differences in working styles early in the process, which enabled them to work through solutions together more honestly and transparently, sometimes before problems occurred.

Strategies for intercultural learning

Our Six Dimensions of Intercultural Teamwork took shape with these ideas in mind and are informed by theories of collaboration (Patton and Downs 2003; Rosen 2009); global learning (Mansilla and Jackson 2013); and intercultural communication (Martin, Nakayama and Flores 2002). The Six Dimensions seek to address the Council of Europe's strategies for intercultural learning (Sandu and Lyamouri-Bajja, 2018), outlined briefly here:

- **Equal status within a situation:** Despite the structural power dynamics at play in society at large, which make for inherently unequal relationships, the teammates in a given work situation should share power equally. In practice, that means actively working to address issues of power and privilege. This includes making sure that anyone perceived as "dominant" is not exerting power over—or in any way "instructing"—anyone typically stereotyped as less dominant.
- **Common goals:** Collaborators should work toward a primary goal defined by the team.
- **Intergroup cooperation:** Team dynamics should inspire cooperation rather than competition.
- **The presence of social norms supporting intergroup contact:** Ideally, the team will establish norms, guidelines, or rules for itself that govern participation and are arrived at via consensus. All teammates should know what these rules are.

As a tool for navigating intercultural learning and working, the Six Dimensions promote individual reflection, thoughtful team interactions, and improved interpersonal connections. Moreover, they offer flexibility that acknowledges the diversity within a culture or country, with respect to the time that it takes to build meaningful relationships between cultures.

Establishing common values

In *The Culture of Collaboration*, business strategist Evan Rosen asserts the importance of not only finding similarity, but of establishing difference: "The trick," he says, "is to build trust and bridge cultures so that collaborators can benefit from their differences rather than fail because of them" (2009, 50). Once we are able to see the ways we are similar and different from each other, we better adapt to relating to, and connecting with, our teammates, thereby working better together.

We all have teamwork preferences, including how we prefer to communicate, establish trust, and validate information. Patton and Downs (2003) describe the need to establish a set of common values as a condition for successful teamwork. They explain that common values lead to shared guidelines that can check teammate behavior when necessary and foster consensus about what kinds of conflicts or disruptions demand attention and formal resolution. Thus, during intercultural relationship building, teammates must first cope with uncertainty and then work to make sure that relationship expectations and contributions are equal.

After reading about the Six Dimensions and completing the assessment (in the next section) to reflect on your own preferences and tendencies, we challenge you and your teammates to see how far you can take your discussions around each dimension. As your team goes deeper, your path forward together will become clearer.

The Six Dimensions as a framework for this book

Each chapter of this book tackles one of the Six Dimensions in sequence. Corresponding discussion guides further your learning and your understanding of the collaborative concepts. As you become familiar with the Six Dimensions, you will notice that they guide the activities as well. In many cases, the activities are organized in ways that take you through the sequence: You will check in with yourself first, then think about your information sources, communicate with your teammates and/or offer feedback to each other, and work toward an end goal together. It is important to note that, although the chapters are organized sequentially with concepts that build upon each other, it is not necessary to complete all of the activities within each chapter—pick and choose those that will best serve your team and situation.

Enable diverse teams to create innovative outcomes

Research shows that diverse teams arrive at more innovative ideas and solutions together. Rosen makes precisely this point, arguing that diverse teams are able to operate from a more expansive viewpoint, giving them an advantage as they tackle complicated problems (Rosen 2009). When teams understand how best to communicate with each other, respect each other's work habits, and create opportunities for everyone to communicate, their diversity functions as an asset that facilitates shared outcomes.

Move from personal introspection to team discussion

When teams analyze themselves through the Six Dimensions, they understand the critical ways in which teammates are similar to and different from each other. This knowledge is particularly vital in intercultural collaborations. It is unlikely that teammates will enter a collaboration with identical values, particularly when they have different cultural backgrounds; using the Six Dimensions early in the collaboration allows teammates to pinpoint similarities and name key differences. This is a key ingredient for successful work outcomes down the road.

Use Tangible Objects in different ways

Alongside the Six Dimensions of Intercultural Teamwork, the creation of Tangible Objects guides communication in each chapter of this book. As described in the Introduction, creating Tangible Objects introduces multisensory experiences to virtual teams and enhances the "realism" of the project. These objects vary depending on the chapter theme and goal—for example, some are more geared toward building trust, as in Chapter 3, while interactions in Chapter 5 focus on decoding and using different Communication Styles.

Though the book is underpinned by the Six Dimensions, each chapter is a gateway to many related topics and issues. We touch on some of these related topics in order to stimulate your thinking; in this way, each dimension is its own starting point for both personal introspection and discussion. Using the assessment tool and the Teamthink Constellation activity (1.2) to apply the Six Dimensions of Intercultural Teamwork framework makes it easier to understand how we communicate, work, and relate to each other.

Discussing the Six Dimensions of Intercultural Teamwork

Independent ⟵——————————————⟶ Interdependent

1: DISCOVER WORK STYLES

We contribute to team efforts in different ways.

INDEPENDENCE: I work best when I can carve out dedicated time away from the team to work alone on a problem. I will return to the team to share what I've discovered or achieved.	**INTERDEPENDENCE:** I work best when I can find time to work with others to problem solve and find solutions together. I find creative energy in interactions with people.

General awareness of teammates' work style preferences helps teammates to feel acknowledged, included, and engaged throughout the collaboration. One fundamental aspect of organizing a project so that it runs efficiently is accounting for different peoples' preferences for how they best execute and contribute when working as a team. Most activities in this book are designed to address the full spectrum of Work Styles through combinations of independent work and teamwork.

When teammates embrace independent and interdependent approaches to work, all teammates feel a sense of both order and chaos over the course of their work together. This feeling promotes "collaborative chaos," which Rosen describes as "the unstructured exchange of ideas to create value" (2009, 12). Unstructured work time together—and alone—creates multiple opportunities for teams (and individuals) to develop ideas that they can share with each other.

In addition to our differences in Work Styles and how we perceive order and hierarchy, 1.4 provides further discussion about how issues of time difference and a sense of time can affect teams.

Individual ⟵⟶ Collective

2: UNDERSTAND CORE BELIEFS

Our values affect our sense of self-efficacy and belonging.

INDIVIDUAL: I feel that I have the ability to influence or change things that affect me. My personal values, principles, and their roots contribute to a sense of self-efficacy or ownership. I feel a responsibility to myself above others.	**COLLECTIVE:** I feel that my actions can directly contribute to or detract from team harmony. My personal values, principles, and their roots contribute to how I see my role in the community. I feel a responsibility to my community above myself.

Figuring out what you value is a challenging but important task. Learning whether your sense of self and community tends toward the individual or collective can help you understand team dynamics. Knowing that everyone on the team has engaged in this reflective process helps teammates to cultivate empathy for each other and a sense of belonging. For instance, after individual teammates do their own self-investigations, a team may need to discuss how they can hold values regarding individualism and collectivism that are different than those held by the individuals who make up the team.

Along these lines, recognizing one's own perspective in relation to teammates' perspectives (Mansilla and Jackson 2013) creates an opportunity to be proactive about team arrangement and structure. For example, will the structure be lateral or hierarchical? In this way, the Understanding Core Beliefs dimension intersects with the Work Styles and Communication Styles dimensions. Together, these dimensions raise questions about how we balance individual versus collective ownership and control or, as Rosen describes it, how we balance "consensus with expediency" (2009).

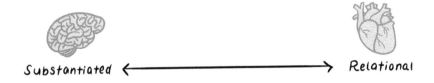

Substantiated ⟵————————————⟶ Relational

3: ESTABLISH TRUST

We recognize and establish trust and accountability in different ways.

SUBSTANTIATED: I demonstrate or recognize trust through specific actions. I hold people accountable to what they say they will do and take things at face value. I find written agreements to be helpful for ensuring accountability.	**RELATIONAL:** I demonstrate or recognize trust through emotion and intuition. My sense of others' accountability is based on my gut feeling about them and the history of our interpersonal relationships.

You and your teammates need to believe that all of you have a vested interest in your mutual success within your intercultural collaboration. This mutual belief in each other is called *trust*. Getting to know each other as people in order to build trust plays a big role in teammates' collective future success together. For long-distance collaborations in particular, part of the trust-building process involves learning to adapt to selected online communication tools. In that vein, it is especially important to understand the impact of various media on the way we—and our teammates—interpret and trust correspondence.

When it comes to building trust, delivering on promises and tasks, or personal accountability, is another driving force for successful teamwork. Just as increased self-awareness offers a foundation for learning about others' value systems, asking teammates to assess their own sense of accountability—whether, for example, it is internally or externally motivated—can prepare them to understand other systems for accountability. Once teammates are aware of how accountability works for them in their personal lives and work experiences, they can have a greater appreciation of, and respect for, the different types of accountability they will encounter within their teams as well as the role that cultural differences can play in terms of how people hold others (and themselves) accountable.

Accountability is also connected to how we give and receive respect. These differences can be influential forces in both professional and social situations. Therefore, understanding how respect is allocated is critical to managing expectations and establishing trust among teammates.

Objective ⟵————————————⟶ Subjective

4: ASSESS INFORMATION

Our individual and culturally informed patterns affect the ways we gather, understand, and verify what we know.

OBJECTIVE: I look to external sources for information, such as factual records, academic learning, or mass media in order to understand the world. I find personal affirmation in my educational history and employment record.	**SUBJECTIVE:** I look to my close-knit social circles for information, such as friends, family, and oral histories, in order to understand the world. I find personal affirmation in building relationships and my role within the community.

Objective and subjective information can be integrated to offer the team a unique perspective that helps increase knowledge around a topic or project. At various points in your collaborative process, your team will need different types of information in order to identify and understand a topic, start a project, get feedback, and move forward. Diverse teams can help each other understand the world through more focused disciplinary investigations or broader interdisciplinary study, thereby creating windows for exploration of the world beyond one's personal context (Mansilla and Jackson 2013).

For example, it takes a team effort to understand which sources to use for a particular goal; this process demands trust. Different cultures recognize different approaches to uncovering and confirming information. Use this as an opportunity for everyone to step outside of their comfort zones to discover a wider range of venues for uncovering answers. In a collaborative context, it is important to come to a consensus about what is acceptable in order to be able to trust that teammates acquire and find information, regardless of the source, with the understanding that what counts as valid may seem quite different to different people.

Direct ⟵⟶ Indirect

5: DECODE COMMUNICATION STYLES

We use language in different ways to relate to and communicate with other people.

DIRECT: I speak my mind and share my true intentions without sugar-coating things because I want people to know exactly what I think. While this straightforward approach may run the risk of offending some people, my clear communication style means that others are less likely to misunderstand me.	**INDIRECT:** I often use metaphors or sugar-coat my opinions in order to avoid tension because I don't want to hurt people's feelings. While my implicit approach may be less likely to offend other people, it brings greater risk of misunderstanding or misinterpretation.

Discovering communication differences enables teams to explore new forms of communication or to use different styles to the team's benefit. As you and your teammates compare your preferences, you may realize that you have very different ways of communicating. Communication Styles are often connected to the roles individuals typically play when working on a team as well as ways such roles might be perceived by other cultures. For example, someone with a direct communication approach may be best suited to informing the team, regularly and in no uncertain terms, of upcoming milestones and deadlines. Meanwhile, a person with indirect communication skills might be adept at facilitating discussions among teammates because their nuanced approach makes everyone feel included and welcome. To the indirect communicator, bluntly stating the point would feel rude and rushed, while the direct communicator may entirely miss (or misinterpret) the nuanced approach (Ting-Toomey and Dorjee 2018).

Regardless of Communication Styles or preferences, when working in a virtual collaboration (even when videoconferencing), it is easy for anyone to miss communications that take place primarily through body language, gestures, and facial expressions. Making an intentional effort to communicate in a way that your teammates can clearly grasp goes a long way toward building rapport. (See Chapter 5 for more information about decoding Communication Styles and intercultural critique.)

Attainable ← → Challenging

6: DESIGN SHARED GOALS

We use and develop our skills in different ways to create a shared sense of purpose in our work.

ATTAINABLE: I set goals that are easy for me to accomplish and within my skill set and comfort zone. Getting things done makes me feel like I am making a positive contribution to a project and/or team.	**CHALLENGING:** I set goals that are a reach for myself, which may be outside of my current skill set or comfort zone. Trying and learning new things during the process helps me grow and also brings more interesting insights to a project and/or team.

Because we respond to the intensity of goals in different ways, your team will ideally specify a combination of attainable and challenging goals in order to carry out work together (Latham and Locke 2007). Setting goals together helps teammates deal with different levels of *ambiguity tolerance*, which describes one's level of comfort with uncertain or potentially uncomfortable situations. Ambiguity tolerance promotes flexibility in thinking. Having an understanding of at least one aspect of the project can help teammates cope with other uncertainties down the line, such as people changing their minds, introducing conflicting ideas, and navigating the impacts of time difference. Ambiguity is an inevitable part of this process; one small thing your team can do ahead of time is to set some shared goals and agree to share responsibility for adhering to them.

Self-awareness and ambiguity tolerance also enable teams to anticipate challenges and work through conflicts to find productive paths forward in collective creativity (Hill et al. 2014). There is power in "reading from the same script" (Rosen 2009). Collaborative goal-setting helps teams set their sights higher to determine the actions they can take together. Teammates may realize they can work together to contribute to a larger issue in a way that they could not if they were working alone (Mansilla and Jackson 2013). Shared goals also give teammates a sense of purpose in terms of their personal relationships and responsibility to each other. Effective teammates want to see the project succeed because shared success also contributes to everyone's personal sense of fulfilment.

Parallels to the revised Bloom's Taxonomy and the design process

With a focus on active learning and engagement, the Six Dimensions support the activities in each chapter by enriching dialogue and decision-making among teammates. Generally referred to as "Bloom's Taxonomy," the original *Taxonomy of Educational Objectives* (1956), and its more recently revised version describe six different phases of learning, which build on each other. Both versions emphasize "learning by doing," (Bloom 1956; Anderson and Krathwohl 2001) which makes the taxonomy an ideal complement to this activity-driven book. This protocol for effective hands-on learning also maps onto the stages of the design process. The following table, on pages 24–25, shows how each dimension relates to the cognitive domains of the revised Bloom's Taxonomy. Parallel principles of the design process further enhance and drive these different ways of approaching collaboration, learning, and teamwork. With these principles in mind, you're ready to complete the self-assessment in the next section (1.2).

TABLE 1.1 Relationships between the Six Dimensions, Bloom's Taxonomy, and the Design Process

The Six Dimensions of Intercultural Teamwork	Revised Bloom's Taxonomy: The Cognitive Domains	The Design Process	Relationship
1. Discover Work Styles We contribute to team efforts in different ways.	**Remember** Recall previously learned information.	**Discover** Begin the process by exploring a broad knowledge base.	**Remembering** how teammates respond and contribute to the Chapter 1 assessment activities helps the team **discover each other's Work Styles**.
Chapter 1 lays an important foundation for future discussion and discovery; the team can reference these tools and activities throughout their working process.			
2. Understand Core Beliefs Our values affect our sense of self-efficacy and belonging.	**Comprehend** Demonstrate an understanding.	**Empathize** Understand and relate to the people involved.	**Comprehending** our own values and biases prepares us to **understand teammates' Core Beliefs**.
Chapter 2 introduces various opportunities for comparison as a useful tool in establishing comprehension. Teammates self-reflect and establish empathy by understanding opinions, facts, and core beliefs.			
3. Establish Trust We recognize and establish trust and accountability in different ways.	**Apply** Apply knowledge to actual situations.	**Define** Specify a problem to investigate and address.	**Applying** what we know about ourselves and our teammates helps us to **establish trust** with each other.
Chapter 3 encourages teams to connect through creating and exchanging different types of narratives. Establishing trust through sharing stories helps teammates define themselves and apply knowledge of each other throughout collaboration.			

The Six Dimensions of Intercultural Teamwork	Revised Bloom's Taxonomy: The Cognitive Domains	The Design Process	Relationship
4. Assess Information Our individual and culturally informed patterns affect the ways we gather, understand, and verify what we know.	**Analyze** Break down objects or ideas into simpler parts and find evidence to support generalizations.	**Ideate** Develop many different ideas or opportunities to intervene in a defined problem.	**Analyzing** teammates' contributions helps us appreciate the different ways we collect and **assess information**.
Chapter 4 brings information together to better understand the project and learning opportunities, which naturally leads to new ideas.			
5. Decode Communication Styles We use language in different ways to relate to and communicate with other people.	**Evaluate** Communicate feedback or defend choices based on internal evidence or external criteria.	**Critique** Engage with constructive feedback to actively and iteratively improve ideas.	Effectively **evaluating** each other's contributions relies on the ability to **decode each other's Communication Styles**.
Chapter 5 introduces activities and structure for evaluating work and providing constructive feedback with consideration for different Communication Styles.			
6. Design Shared Goals We use and develop our skills in different ways to create a shared sense of purpose in our work.	**Create** Bring ideas together into a new whole or propose alternative solutions.	**Prototype** Bring final ideas to life for further investigation and refinement.	**Designing shared goals** for productive and interesting outcomes prepares us to **create** together and synthesize everything we have learned.
Chapter 6 provides project ideas for intercultural teams to synthesize their learning.			

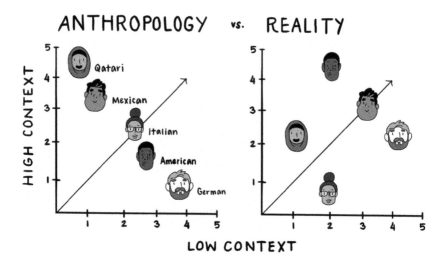

ANTHROPOLOGY vs. REALITY

LOW CONTEXT

1.2

Teamthink Constellation:
Putting the Six Dimensions to work

The Teamthink Constellation is a foundational activity for successful teamwork. In revealing how each teammate thinks about working on a team, the activity helps people understand how and why they might approach a project in different ways. The activity creates opportunities for intentional discussion about how to make the collaboration most effective. The Constellation is our term for the collaborative scatterplot created in the second stage of this activity, when remote teammates combine and plot their numerical selections for a particular dimension.

Through these conversations, the team can collectively approach project management while accounting for similarities and differences. As a foundational activity in this book, the aim is to promote self-reflection and, at the same time, acknowledge a wide range of working and learning styles. Ultimately, becoming aware of teammates' needs, methods, and working styles creates improved mutual understanding and compassion, which can promote peaceful and productive collaborations.

Creating a shared sense of teamwork

As outlined in 1.1, the Six Dimensions of Intercultural Teamwork can be applied as you work with your teammates on the Teamthink Constellation to better understand how you and your teammates communicate, work, and relate to each other. This activity has several possible phases, depending on how you proceed. First, complete the individual assessment. Then, combine your results with your teammates' results to create a Progress Object. Recall from the Introduction that Progress Objects serve to communicate and build understanding within the team.

Project management

Project management is the ongoing task of launching, organizing, accomplishing, and concluding work that addresses a team's specific goals, and our inherent cultural differences can affect how we work together to manage projects across a diverse team. In business settings, teams may already have a great deal of experience with project management, and thus take for granted that their approach may be influenced by their personal Work Styles and preferences. In some work settings, there are specific employees dedicated solely to managing projects. At universities, however, most undergraduate students have not yet had opportunities to cultivate formal project management skills. Students might assume this skillset is reserved only for business majors, but most people entering the professional realm benefit from some exposure to basic project management.

Particularly in digital environments, project management can be a challenging ongoing task. Differences in Communication Styles alone are enough to derail well-intentioned collaborators. In addition, scores of other challenges can develop, including differences in working styles, expectations, mental models of leadership, and visions of the final project outcomes or team goals. Developing a plan together is important to the success of any collaborative team, but it is particularly essential to intercultural collaboration (see Goal & Role Tracker, 6.3). Due to an array of unpredictable factors, it is also important for teammates to be prepared in case they find their original plans need to change.

Play a relational role

Keep in mind that everyone must simultaneously play a role in maintaining the team's relationships, communication, and trust. Some of these tasks could be assigned to a teammate filling a particular role, such as project manager. However, we have found that teams benefit from everyone contributing, to some degree, to the following duties:

- **Communicate regularly**: A friendly "hello" is always welcome! Discuss work as it evolves. Share ideas. Ask questions. Keep teammates informed about your progress through the communication tools you have mutually agreed to use.
- **Attend meetings**: Synchronous check-ins ensure the team remains on the same page. These can be done via videoconferencing or a live, text-based chat. It is important for everyone to attend and be present as teammates check in with each other. Regular meetings enable teams to discuss ideas, share progress, work through problems, provide feedback, and lend moral support to one another.

(Continued)

- **Share progress updates**: Beyond ticking off a "to-do" item on your shared task list, think about other ways you can communicate your progress to your team through synchronous or asynchronous tools. Accomplishing a task feels great in and of itself, so imagine fun ways to share that feeling with your team!
- **Take notes**: Even if there is a designated note-taker or if the meeting is informal, taking notes promotes active listening. This is particularly useful for remote teams in order to clarify potential miscommunications.
- **Provide feedback**: See Chapter 5 for more details on the various ways teammates can support the evolution of each other's ideas.

How the Teamthink Constellation works

Assess based on the Six Dimensions of Intercultural Teamwork

The Teamthink Constellation activity builds on the Six Dimensions of Intercultural Teamwork introduced in Section 1.1:

1. Discover Work Styles
2. Understand Core Beliefs
3. Establish Trust
4. Assess Information
5. Decode Communication Styles
6. Design Shared Goals

This is a two-part activity that walks both individuals (Phase 1) and teams (Phase 2 or 3) through utilizing the Six Dimensions as an individual and team assessment tool. The assessment tool also presents two contrasting examples, which helps teammates understand how better to manage their work process and projects based on an examination of their personal work preferences. Individuals complete the assessment by first reading the two examples for each dimension. Then, they select where on each spectrum their personal preferences fall.

While each dimension reveals a potential dichotomy (e.g., independent versus interdependent), the spectrums acknowledge that we are each a blend of characteristics. Unlike some of the classical anthropological frameworks for understanding culture, this assessment tool enables us to visualize the gray areas in terms of how we see ourselves and how we interact with teammates.

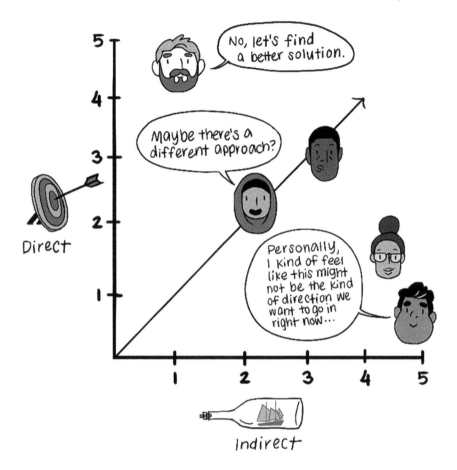

Self-reflect first, then discuss as a team

The Teamthink Constellation puts the responsibility on individuals to come together to co-create a positive team experience instead of acting under the direction of a specific leader or facilitator. Like a conductorless orchestra, this is
challenging, but not impossible! Outcomes of the assessment help teams:

- Reflect upon and interpret their own teamwork dispositions
- Compare responses to discover similarities and differences
- Begin a dialogue about how to maximize the potential of their different
  values around teamwork

Benefits & outcomes

- Prompt important conversations about teamwork preferences
- Depict the team as a diverse community
- Embrace inevitable differences
- Engage in multisensory learning

Activity

Teamthink Constellation

This engaging, empathy-building activity first enables you to evaluate your-self along multiple spectrums to gauge your learning and working preferences. Then, in the second stage of the activity, all remote teammates combine their selections by plotting them as coordinates along hand-drawn X and Y-axes. The resulting scatter-plot visualization, or Teamthink Constellation, enables teammates to see how they relate to each other along a particular dimension. It shows similarities and differences along a specific dimension helping teams hone in on specific factors that could become hurdles. The Constellation gives teammates a chance to talk through issues and possible solutions before differ-ences become problematic. Juxtaposing the results is exciting and helps teams envision themselves as a unit composed of individuals, each bringing a set of unique traits, capabilities, and perspectives. This sparks team building at the beginning stages of a project.

→ **People:** Individual/remote teammates
→ **Duration:** 30 minutes for the self-evaluation activity; 30 minutes to com-plete the subsequent team scatterplot
→ **Technology:** Camera, projector, videoconferencing software
→ **Other resources:** Paper, sticky notes, markers, whiteboard, projection screen

Tips

- **Map together:** When teammates combine their numbers for one of the Six Dimensions into a shared scatterplot, they can more clearly see their constellation of preferences. They can then directly address simi-larities, differences, and gaps in understanding. It is also an opportunity for individuals to start imagining themselves as part of one intercon-nected team, capable of accomplishing tasks and successfully working together.

- **Appreciating diversity:** This is an opportunity to compare your teammate's thinking to your own. Together, you will gain important insight into each other's communication and working styles, approach to relationships, and other important aspects that define you. Fostering respect and appreciation for these differences is not only a life skill but also cultivates *creative abrasion*—the opportunity to channel potential conflicts into positive outcomes (6.1).
- **Keep it positive:** Address cultural contrasts (and similarities) positively, so that teammates not only come to value diversity, but also understand how to better work with each other. Instead of treating differences in work habits or Communication Styles as insurmountable challenges, discuss these as positive features of your collaborative team.
- **Go analog:** We encourage everyone to do this activity "by hand." The sense of community generated by this activity is magnified by a non-digital output. Putting all teammates' results together onto one sheet of paper or a board creates a different relationship with the information than if this activity is completed solely on screen. This hands-on approach engages different parts of the brain, and intentionally reminds teams that the data points represent real people.

Self-assessment & reflection

Phase 1: Working individually

1. **Review:** Read Section 1.1 prior to engaging in this activity.
2. **Self-Evaluate:** Use the self-assessment on pages 34–35 to consider your preferences for working and learning based on the Six Dimensions. Answer as openly and honestly as possible. There are no right or wrong answers—simply state what you prefer in a collaborative work environment. For each dimension, score yourself in both of the categories. For example, for dimension 1, Discover Work Styles, select one number, 0 to 5, that describes your degree of independence and one number, 0 to 5, that describes your degree of interdependence.
3. **Reflect:** Use the following questions to think about your responses before meeting with your remote teammates.

Individual reflection guide

- What do you think are your own strengths and weaknesses with regard to working and learning?
- What forms of communication feel more or less effective for you personally?
- What situations have you been in that required you to step outside of your comfort zone or work outside of your personal preferences?
- What are some of your personal pet peeves when working with others? How can you bring these up respectfully with future teammates to eliminate?

The Constellation option

Remote teams could make constellations for all of the Six Dimensions in correspondence with the chapters of this book. Using this tool, teammates can become more comfortable talking about differences as a positive attribute to collaborative work, and approach each other with kindness and understanding.

Phase 2: With remote teammates

4. **Collect:** Gather your remote teammates' self-assessment selections in a shared document, if you have not done so already.
5. **Select:** Choose a specific dimension from the Six Dimensions to focus on (or decide to make a separate Constellation for each one).
6. **Plot:** Draw a horizontal and vertical axis on a whiteboard or a large sheet of paper with a range of 0 to 5 along each axis. Each teammates' selections can be translated as coordinates along these axes. For each teammate, align your left number along the vertical (y) axis and right number along the horizontal (x) axis. At the intersection point where the numbers meet, add a sticky note with the teammate's name. If completing this for long-distance teammates, add their notes until your Constellation is complete. If doing this activity in person, each person should add their own sticky notes.

Analysis

Phase 3: With remote teammates

7. **Discuss:** Take some time to discuss your experience with your remote teammates. Use the following guide for discussion.

DISCUSSION GUIDE

- What insights did you gain by mapping your cumulative findings together on to one shared visualization?
- What interesting insights came out of the discussion about these similarities and differences?
- Are there any personal aspects about yourself you want to share that were not addressed through the discussion?
- How will you use the information your teammates have shared to
  - discuss and make beneficial choices for your team?
  - understand similarities/differences across the team?

TEAMTHINK CONSTELLATION SELF-ASSESSMENT
Choose two options for each dimension by selecting one number from each side of the spectrum.
Scale: 0 = I strongly disagree/do not relate to this; 5 = I strongly agree/relate to this

1: DISCOVER WORK STYLES
We contribute to team efforts in different ways.

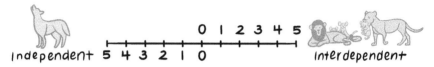

Independent 5 4 3 2 1 0   0 1 2 3 4 5   Interdependent

INDEPENDENCE: I work best when I can carve out dedicated time away from the team to work alone on a problem. I will return to the team to share what I've discovered or achieved.	**INTERDEPENDENCE:** I work best when I can find time to work with others to problem solve and find solutions together. I find creative energy in interactions with people.

2: UNDERSTAND CORE BELIEFS
Our values affect our sense of self-efficacy and belonging.

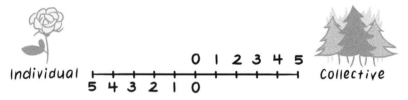

Individual 5 4 3 2 1 0   0 1 2 3 4 5   Collective

INDIVIDUAL: I feel that I have the ability to influence or change things that affect me. My personal values, principles, and their roots contribute to a sense of self-efficacy or ownership. I feel a responsibility to myself above others.	**COLLECTIVE:** I feel that my actions can directly contribute to or detract from team harmony. My personal values, principles, and their roots contribute to how I see my role in the community. I feel a responsibility to my community above myself.

3: ESTABLISH TRUST
We recognize and establish trust and accountability in different ways.

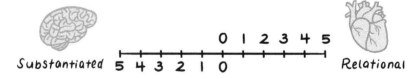

Substantiated 5 4 3 2 1 0   0 1 2 3 4 5   Relational

SUBSTANTIATED: I demonstrate or recognize trust through specific actions. I hold people accountable to what they say they will do and take things at face value. I find written agreements to be helpful for ensuring accountability.	**RELATIONAL:** I demonstrate or recognize trust through emotion and intuition. My sense of others' accountability is based on my gut feeling about them and the history of our interpersonal relationships.

4: ASSESS INFORMATION

Our individual and culturally informed patterns affect the ways we gather, understand, and verify what we know.

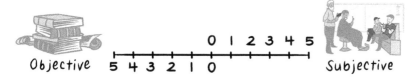

Objective 5 4 3 2 1 0   0 1 2 3 4 5   Subjective

OBJECTIVE: I look to external sources for information, such as factual records, academic learning, or mass media in order to understand the world. I find personal affirmation in my educational history and employment record.	**SUBJECTIVE:** I look to my close-knit social circles for information, such as friends, family, and oral histories, in order to understand the world. I find personal affirmation in building relationships and my role within the community.

5: DECODE COMMUNICATION STYLES

We use language in different ways to relate to and communicate with other people.

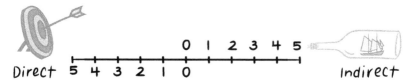

Direct 5 4 3 2 1 0   0 1 2 3 4 5   Indirect

DIRECT: I speak my mind and share my true intentions without sugar-coating things because I want people to know exactly what I think. While this straightforward approach may run the risk of offending some people, my clear communication style means that others are less likely to misunderstand me.	**INDIRECT:** I often use metaphors or sugar-coat my opinions in order to avoid tension because I don't want to hurt people's feelings. While my implicit approach may be less likely to offend other people, it brings greater risk of misunderstanding or misinterpretation.

6: DESIGN SHARED GOALS

We use and develop our skills in different ways to create a shared sense of purpose in our work.

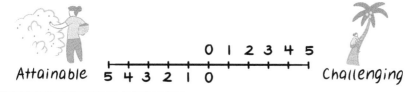

Attainable 5 4 3 2 1 0   0 1 2 3 4 5   Challenging

ATTAINABLE: I set goals that are easy for me to accomplish and within my skill set and comfort zone. Getting things done makes me feel like I am making a positive contribution to a project and/or team.	**CHALLENGING:** I set goals that are a reach for myself, which may be outside of my current skill set or comfort zone. Trying and learning new things during the process helps me grow and also brings more interesting insights to a project and/or team.

1.3

Success Sketches:
Drawing a positive future for your team

A Success Sketch is a visual depiction of possible futures for your team. These tangible Thought Objects offer you and your teammates the opportunity to express your aspirations for your work together and to get a sense of the different perspectives on the team before work begins. Framed around the idea that success should be the end result, this activity is designed so that your collaborative work proceeds from a positive place. The drawings you make can also provide context and motivation for working through differences revealed by the Teamthink Constellation results. Additionally, the post-activity discussion walks you through the factors to keep in mind as you consider how you will participate as a teammate in order to achieve positive outcomes.

What is a sketch?

A rough depiction of your ideas

Although artistic ability is actually *not* a requirement for sketching, sometimes the word "sketch" makes people feel self-conscious. In creative disciplines, sketches are rough depictions of ideas. Sketches are preliminary, unpolished, unfinished, and absolutely do not need to be fancy. Artists may use sketches to work out ideas before translating them into a finished piece. Designers use a similar process; they use sketches to translate abstract concepts into something visual or to figure out how a process will unfold.

No artistic skills needed

Whether or not you have formal "drawing skills" is irrelevant to sketching. The point is to share an idea, not to create something for a museum wall. Whatever materials or modes of expression teammates choose for their individual sketch are welcome without judgment. If sketching feels intimidating, try collecting images and arranging them to express your idea.

Ingredients for your Success Sketch

There are a range of ways you might decide to represent your feelings about an upcoming collaboration. You can use a range of creative materials and visual metaphors, such as representing excitement with the summit of a mountain or an explosion of confetti. Different approaches and materials can convey your ideas and show your personality.

Visual approaches for sketching

- **Expressive images** may include organic forms to represent emotions and hold multiple images in the same sketch. Instead of depicting a human form, for example, you might try to express feelings using different colors or line qualities.
- **Non-representational images** use shapes, colors, lines, and so on to build compositions that may express unseeable ideas, such as emotions or feelings. A non-representational human could be shown as a dot, squiggle, or purple blob with no direct correlation to human form.
- **Abstract images** strive to depict natural forms through more simplified visual approaches, such as geometric shapes, color fields, or lines. An abstracted human body could look like a stick figure or a circle on top of a triangle.
- **Representational images** portray natural forms and environments as realistically as possible. A representational human body would look as it does in real life. Representational forms are NOT necessary for this activity!

After selecting some sketching materials, refer to your Teamthink Constellation for ideas and also consider including some of the items on the following list in your Success Sketch. The activity at the end of this section provides additional details for employing this list so that you include many different facets of success.

The goal is to stimulate a multifaceted discussion and find ways to discuss abstract topics such as trust, time management, and accountability.

a. Goals
b. Relationships
c. Commitment
d. Communication
e. Growth
f. Compromise
g. Tools

Sketching facilitates knowledge exchange

Visual representations are an important aspect of collaborative projects because they facilitate the sharing of ideas, which leads to an exchange of knowledge and the creation of mutual understanding. The Success Sketch does not depict a project idea. Instead, it functions as a Thought Object to illustrate teammates' visions of how the team will grow or change together and what success will entail.

Finding ways to forge a bond can be difficult; you cannot exactly do a team-bonding ropes course activity together when some teammates are 8,000 miles apart. Instead, you will need to seek and create opportunities to make yourselves vulnerable, to listen, and to share with each other. Sharing Success Sketches is a starting point for each of these ventures, but only if you take the time to use your sketch to introduce yourself and your ideas about teamwork.

Sketching helps set expectations

Creating and sharing a Success Sketch brings everyone together by providing opportunities to discuss many of the anticipatory feelings teammates may have: excitement, concerns, and goals for how the team will function. Through the discussion of their tangible Thought Objects (i.e., sketches), teammates can come to a unified vision of their shared future. Teammates can then work together to figure out how to best guide the team toward success. The Success Sketch helps teammates to convey their excitement as well as begin to negotiate issues or concerns.

Much like other creative outputs in this book, sketches help teams get to know each other, branch out, and set shared expectations for collaboration. As such, this activity serves as a first opportunity to practice using visuals for individual knowledge construction and as a way to communicate with others.

Benefits & outcomes

- Give shape and form to your vision for the team
- Stay focused on future success
- Combine sketches into one to build a team trajectory

Activity

Success Sketch

This activity asks you to devote time at the beginning of a collaboration to recognize your teammate as an individual. This process can encompass exposure to—and validation of—a range of feelings and emotions. We each negotiate interpersonal situations through different strategies. Honoring these differences and knowing that each person has joined the collaboration to learn something new, is vital to team cohesion and success. Successful learning can look different for each person; using the Success Sketch to acknowledge those differences early on will help set reasonable expectations about what a fruitful journey entails for all teammates. If you have experienced a negative collaboration in the past, this is an opportunity for you to reflect on what you learned in those moments. Then, move forward by imagining an ideal team situation for this project as well as deciding how you will work to get to that place.

→ **People:** Individual/remote teammates
→ **Duration:** 30 minutes to complete the sketch, 1–2 days to share and discuss with teammates
→ **Technology:** Camera, videoconferencing software, chat/messaging software
→ **Other resources:** Whatever materials are useful for creating your sketch or physical representation (string, yarn, glue, paper cups, Legos, blocks, pipe cleaners, popsicle sticks, scissors, tape, colored paper, pencils, markers, etc.)

Tips

- **Stay in the present:** Do not dwell in the past. This activity is not about looking to the past or reliving a time when you experienced a negative collaboration. Instead, use this activity as a way to imagine an ideal situation and how you want to get there. What do you hope to gain for yourself? Your team? How do you envision your relationship with your team at the end of this process?
- **Make choices that feel authentic to you:** During the exchange of Success Sketches, try to step into the collaborative space as your real self. Doing so will not only ensure that you enjoy the goal-setting, but will be a first step toward building trust. Putting in the time to build trust as you plan your collaboration will pay off in successful outcomes over the course of your journey together.

(Continued)

- **Commit:** Engaging in intercultural collaboration is hard work and requires commitment from all parties. Be honest about your level of commitment to the process. Having an upfront discussion about your goals for the project will help teammates understand each other's motivations, interests, and level of commitment.
- **Be willing to compromise:** If you begin getting to know a new potential teammate, and then reach a point in your conversations that suggests a mismatch, don't despair! If you find that the two of you have drastically different ideas about working together (whether due to time constraints or your end goals), consider whether it is possible to negotiate a compromise. You could also consider alternative ways to support each other through shared research (see Chapter 4), critique (see Chapter 5), or simply offering an alternative perspective. (Read 5.7 for more conflict resolution ideas.)

Sketch

Phase 1: Working individually

1. **Think:** As you participate in this collaborative process with a team, how do you envision success? Use the following questions to help prompt and create visuals that represent your ideas about success in a collaborative environment. You will use this sketch as a discussion tool—or Tangible Object—to delve deeper into your preliminary ideas with your teammates and to listen to their unique perspectives.

   a. **Goals:** What kind of journey do you envision taking in order to accomplish certain goals for yourself and your learning? What do you think you will learn along the way? How do you hope the team will operate?

   b. **Relationships:** What does personal connection entail for you? How do you envision the connection(s) among your teammates? Would you like to get to know your teammates' friends and family or strictly keep things professional? What role will you play, if any, in creating or maintaining connections?

   c. **Commitment:** What does your level of commitment or enthusiasm look like? How would you demonstrate your approach to compromising or negotiating?

   d. **Communication:** How, or in what ways, would you like to communicate with your teammates, and how often?

   e. **Growth:** Ask yourself about the ways you might grow over the course of this experience. For instance, have you struggled with time management in the past? Do you want to agree on milestones for check-ing in and completing work at certain points during the process? Or will you follow individual schedules to work toward the ultimate goal or project deadline, with some communication in between?

f. **Compromise:** To what degree are you willing to compromise throughout the process? What are your non-negotiables during the collaboration?

g. **Tools:** What tools can you use to connect? Do you have a preference for talking with friends and family? Is it different than your tools for work or learning? Do you want to bridge these divides?

2. **Create:** Using whatever materials you like, create a sketch to illustrate how you would like to grow or change with your remote teammates over the course of your work together. This is not a visual project pitch or a depiction of your project ideas. What do abstract qualities—like trust, time manage-ment, and accountability—look like on paper? What do you hope to gain for yourself? Your team? At the end of this process, what do you hope for in terms of your relationship with your team? Refer to the previous descrip-tions of visual approaches for examples.

3. **Describe:** Write a few sentences to explain your sketch.

Present

Phase 2: With remote teammates

4. **Present to each other:** Ideally, present your sketch in real time during a video chat with your teammates. Alternatively, you can share in the online space (see Fourth Space, 1.5) or via email. If you are sharing asynchronously (e.g., via email), remember to include a brief written description with your sketch. You can also use your description as a conversation guide if you are sharing in real time.

5. **Listen:** Take great care to listen and pay attention to your teammates' re-sponses. What are they trying to communicate through their sketches? As visual Thought Objects, these sketches are tools that enable difficult conver-sations between teammates who are meeting each other for the first time. While you have spent time exploring what you want out of the collaboration through self-reflection and internal dialogue, the real skill is in listening and taking into account your teammates' perspectives, hopes, and fears as you move forward on a project or activity.

6. **Photograph & Upload:** Bring all of the sketches together into one place by photographing and uploading them to a shared folder or document, or by posting them to an online community (see Fourth Space, 1.5b).

7. **Merge Together:** Your new aim at this point is to reflect your team-mates' perspectives and concerns in one combined visual that represents

your shared vision for working together. A possible approach for this step is printing your teammates' sketches and setting them next to yours in order to consider how to merge the visualizations. A few options for merging your work include:

a.   Drawing on top of your existing sketch.
b.   Photographing and printing (or photocopying) the sketches, cutting them up, and collaging them back together as one.
c.   Redrawing something that takes into account all teammates' options.

Analysis

Phase 3: With remote teammates

8.   **Discuss:** Take some time to talk through all of the sketches as a team, using the following guide for discussion.

DISCUSSION GUIDE

•   What have you learned about your teammates' preferences, and how do these preferences compare to your own? (These responses could be related to Communication Styles, time management, or family values.)
•   How can you work to create a positive collaborative environment while also respecting each other's differences and past experiences?
•   Describe your experience working with a visual Thought Object to help express your thoughts about the upcoming collaboration with your remote team.
•   What was it like to work together to create a shared visualization for the first time?
•   Were there any particular collaborative tools that were useful to the process? Why or why not? What aspects of the experience will you take with you into the next shared activity?

1.4

Shared Calendar:
Tackling time differences together

One of the biggest questions you might be asking yourself is how you can make a collaboration work when your teams are located in different time zones. To mentally prepare yourself, it is necessary to think about time, whether you are reading this prior to the start of a collaboration or in the midst of one.

The Shared Calendar is foundational in that it clarifies time differences. For any teams, local or remote, it is important to get on the same page in terms of how teammates are thinking about time and understanding how these ideas translate with regard to team goals. Teams can use the Shared Calendar during any of the relationship-building, discovery, ideation and project activities in this book. It is especially valuable in conjunction with the Goal & Role Tracker (6.3) for more complex projects.

After choosing from the range of available scheduling applications or shared documents to create the calendar, you can use this activity to develop a tool for the duration of your collaboration. The following considerations prepare teams to effectively co-create a Shared Calendar after reflecting on and discussing your ideas about time with teammates.

Consider logistical and cultural factors

Logistical considerations

Assess the implications of the time difference

Look up the time difference(s) between you and your teammates. When might be a good time of day to check in with your teammates or try to do some work together in real time? Is your teammate asleep when your day is just getting started, or vice versa? There are many online resources that can help you map out feasible working times based on two multiple geographic locations.

Understand business hours and waking hours

For virtual collaborations in particular, teams must embrace the reality that time differences between long-distance teammates present significant hurdles to effective teamwork. Teams working from different geographic locations will usually encounter differences in both business hours and waking hours. Business hours indicate the span of time when people generally conduct work business in a particular geographic location. Waking hours describe the span of time when people are usually awake. It is critical for teams to discuss and be mindful of cultural considerations related to time and how these affect communication and work-style expectations. As you walk through the following time-related factors, think about how you might address each in your team's Shared Calendar.

Just because they're awake doesn't mean they're ready to work

Some people are up early and go to bed early; some cultures start the workday later and end up going to bed much later. Many places in the world observe a mid-day break, particularly areas with hot climates. Check your assumptions: Your understanding of when the day starts and ends, and when the workday starts and ends does not necessarily map directly on to your teammate's culture. Instead, have a conversation about what your teammate's day actually looks like.

As an example from our studies, while many US-based students find evenings (after regular business hours, which generally run from 9 am to 5 pm) to be their best time for uninterrupted work, this part of the day is considered family time for many in Qatar. Culturally, evenings are a protected time when people do not work. Families in Qatar observe evenings as reserved for time to spend with one another. Since most Qatari students live at home with their parents and siblings, working after 5 pm is not an option, even though the time difference would make this an ideal time for their US teammates to meet and collaborate (i.e., within US business hours).

Cultural considerations

What counts as a weekday, and when does the work week begin?

Just as you will find variability in different cultures' business and waking hours, you may also encounter differences in what constitutes the workweek. Some countries begin their working week on Monday and end on Friday; the weekend is Saturday and Sunday. Some countries start their working week on Sunday and end on Thursday, with Friday and Saturday as weekends. These are the two most common interpretations of the workweek and weekends, but there are other variations. It is best to ask your teammates upfront and not assume their week is the same as yours.

Shifts in time difference

Think about whether or not the time difference between your locations will shift during the course of your co-working. For example, daylight saving time is observed in the United States but not in Qatar, so, when the time changes in the United States, time differences between teammates in these countries also change. There may also be a new time difference to consider if a teammate is moving or traveling to another location during the collaboration.

Holidays and seasons

It is also very important to consider national and religious holidays and other observances, as these can lead to lapses in communication or work that could otherwise be misinterpreted by teammates as disinterest or lack of engagement. Similarly, if you are collaborating with teammates in a different hemisphere, remember that your winter is their summer (and vice versa). Vacations, school, or other work breaks can also lead to lapses in communication. It helps to discuss these ahead of time, too. The timing of certain cycles, like the school year, can also affect the ability to collaborate.

Understand individual work and time attitudes

Independent versus interdependent Work Styles

Recall that the self-assessment for the Six Dimensions of Intercultural Teamwork asks you to evaluate your relative interest in working alone (independently) and with other people (interdependently). Think about your response to that dimension, as well as the responses collected during the Teamthink Constellation. Having a sense of our own Work Styles and our teammates' preferences enables the team to make the best use of time both when meeting in real time and in between meetings. If you are able to meet in real time, you will first have to figure out how to use that interdependent work time effectively. In addition, between regular check-ins—when teammates may be working independently—you will need to decide beforehand what needs to be done and who will do it.

For example, one teammate might be able to better concentrate and do their best work alone, so time during team meetings can be dedicated to having this person share their progress with teammates. Other teammates might feel most productive working on problems together, gaining energy from each other's ideas and contributions. Therefore, they might schedule a time to meet so they can work together between the team check-ins. No matter the individual preferences, communication between formal team check-ins keeps all teammates informed of each other's progress and helps people feel included as the collaboration develops.

Polychronic and monochronic interpretations of time

Teammates may also interpret time in distinctly monochronic (rigid) or polychronic (flexible) ways, which can affect time management. For example, a monochronic teammate's insistence on meeting internal, in-between "deadlines" may not hold much weight with a polychronic teammate. Instead, the polychronic teammate may prioritize other things they need to do, thereby getting around to their project contributions in their own time. That can be frustrating for the monochronic teammates, who are trying to communicate firmly that the milestone check-ins are important deadlines for the team's progress, not understanding that their persistence may actually be pushing their polychronic teammates away.

Bear in mind that polychronic and monochronic are only two ways of describing cultural relationships with time. Some cultures may have a much more nuanced approach, which is valid and worth discussing among the team.

When teammates find they have different interpretations of time, it can feel very frustrating and challenging for both parties. These feelings are especially intense during the phases of working together. However, creating the Shared Calendar can help prevent some of these challenges. The Shared Calendar enables teammates to discuss their different relationships to time and reflect these interpretations in one place. In addition, it reduces friction down the line by anticipating these differences before they manifest.

Use time differences to your advantage

Imagine a relay to cope with an extreme time difference

Depending on your team's various locations and the time differences, there may not be overlaps during business hours at all. It can be frustrating to find that your waking or working hours do not easily overlap. When we have had especially large differences in time, we encourage teammates to think about how they can use the time difference to the team's advantage. Imagine the work process as a relay race in which each teammate gets to "run" with some aspect of the total work during their waking hours. They leave detailed notes about what they have accomplished so they can hand off the work to their teammates, who can then pick up where they left off. It's nice to wake up to progress on a project that unfolded while you were asleep!

Be flexible about making schedule adjustments

For some teams, a bit of schedule flexibility can make meetings or work sessions possible. When you discuss working and waking hours, talk about whether or not teammates can make some individual schedule adjustments, such as being flexible with their business or waking hours. If possible, we recommend trading off on these adjustments so the same person is not always staying up too late or waking up too early. Alternatively, have an open conversation about whether or not a teammate is okay with routinely shifting their schedule for the sake of the collaboration.

Use communication tools to take advantage of time overlaps

The number of business hours or waking hours that do overlap should affect teammates' selection of—and therefore success with—various communication tools. Synchronous approaches, such as video and voice calls, are more effective in collaborations with overlapping business and/or waking hours. If you have some overlap in waking hours (but not necessarily business hours), you may need more flexible modes of communication, such as instant messaging, which can behave synchronously—as a real-time dialogue tool if both teammates are online and actively chatting—or asynchronously, to relay messages as thoughts occur to collaborative teammates, with the understanding that there may not be an immediate response. For collaborations with extreme time differences (12+ hours), teammates may need to rely heavily upon asynchronous methods.

Give your plan a personal touch

In addition to cultural considerations and time-based factors, it is important for teams to work together to create their own internal plan that takes into account each teammate's personal, professional, and/or academic commitments, schedule, and availability. This is an essential conversation for all teammates, as it helps you to get to know each other better as you discuss how to navigate your commitments outside of the collaboration. Learning to anticipate and openly discuss Communication Styles, work methods, and other challenges is essential to cultivating trust and enables teammates to give each other the benefit of the doubt when difficulties arise.

Benefits & outcomes

- Organize your team
- See teammates' schedules and available work time
- Gather availability, plans, and goals in one place
- Establish standing meetings, if time differences allow
- Identify which communication tools will work best for the team

---

Activity

Shared Calendar

Creating the Shared Calendar enables teams to tackle several related issues, including how their sense and use of time affects their role in the project; how they prefer to work; and how they envision their different Work Styles converging into a feasible project timeline. Prompted by the Teamthink Constellation, the purpose of this activity is to open a conversation around how each teammate understands and relates to time. Communicating these conceptions explicitly shows respect for your teammates' efforts—even if their orientations or preferences are different than yours—and thus helps build trust across the team. In particular, this simple activity builds awareness and respect for time zones and cultural differences. Together, teammates can reduce uncertainty by addressing these potential challenges and find ways to turn them into assets.

→ **People:** Individually/remote team
→ **Duration:** 1 or 2 hours
→ **Technology:** Shared scheduling application or spreadsheet
→ **Other resources:** Paper and pencil

Tips

- **Regular meetings:** Meeting on a regular basis is important in any collaboration. All teammates should be able to set and commit to a consistent meeting time; otherwise, it is unlikely you will be able to accomplish your work together. Discuss the format, duration, and expectations of your regular meetings.
- **Be realistic:** Every member of the team has their own unique obligations to family and friends, work-life responsibilities, and commitment to health and hobbies. Thinking about the demands on your time and how this affects your team early in the collaboration promotes setting realistic goals and expectations.
- **Time and spontaneity:** While many of our collaborations have required distinct and detailed plans in advance of a project introduction, some have been more spontaneous. Even if you do not have a lot of time to craft the perfect plan or itinerary, respecting and understanding time differences sets an important foundation going forward. The other approaches you learn in this book will also guide you as you go.
- **Accountability:** Creating a shared calendar that visually represents your time differences helps hold teammates accountable, but issues might arise that are not covered by the calendar. It is important to send each other updates along the way if personal obligations affect your ability to collaborate. Your teammates need to know if circumstances prevent you from being present for a team meeting or fulfilling a project deadline in time, for example, if you or a family member becomes ill, you have some kind of emergency, or are just too overloaded with other work (the amount of information you choose to share is up to you).

Create calendar

Phase 1: Working individually

→ *Refer to this activity's discussion guide throughout the process.*

1. **Understand:** Look up the time difference(s) between you and your remote teammates. Write out or print a timetable chart that shows your global time differences, and post it in your workspace. It is critical to understand your teammates time in relation to your time, so you can always keep it in mind. If you have a mobile device, you may also add their location in a global clock or weather application so you can easily check the time in your teammate's location.

Phase 2: With remote teammates

2. **Calendar creation:** Working with your remote team, create your Shared Calendar using a digital tool accessible to all teammates and that all teammates can add to (such as a shared scheduling or calendar application, spreadsheet, or document). This prevents frustration by reminding people that their business or waking hours and their teammates' do not necessarily overlap.

3. **Populate:** Begin to fill in the Shared Calendar by adding everyone's work hours, travel dates, and differences in workweek (e.g., some countries start the week on Sunday, others on Monday). Seeing teammates' schedules provides clarity around typical time-based collaborative hurdles and sets realistic expectations about availability. It also builds respect for teammates' work schedules and other commitments they may have.

4. **Holidays and travel:** Indicate any major national holidays, religious observances, or travel plans, particularly if they will affect the collaboration process or delay work contributions from a teammate. Be respectful of teammates' choices to give or protect their time.

5. **Regular meetings:** Seeing teammates' availability helps establish possible meeting times. Establish a routine meeting time to get together, share work, discuss ideas, and assess your team's progress. Choosing a consistent day of the week and hour to meet can make a huge difference in the cohesion and functionality of a team. Remain flexible to the needs of the team and keep in mind that finding a regular time to meet can be challenging across several different schedules and time zones. Some people may need to stay up late and others may need to wake up early to make regular meetings possible. Make sure the team balances the workload and preferences of each individual as you come to a consensus about the timing of these meetings.

6. **Use your time difference to your advantage:** The team does not have to work on everything simultaneously. With extreme time differences, some teams will find it beneficial to use their Shared Calendar to indicate who will be working when others cannot. Chart these periods of individual work as part of your process.

DISCUSSION GUIDE

- What is the most realistic way to manage the time difference between teammates?
- How might you match timelines to review or respond to work that has been completed in a different time zone?
- How does your Shared Calendar account for personal time, holidays, or other possible lapses in communication or work during the collaboration?
- What other obligations do you have that might detract from your contributions to this collaboration? Can you communicate these through the Shared Calendar in some way?
- How do you think your personal work preferences or interpretations of time might affect your team?

1.5

Collaboration Agreement & Fourth Space: Guiding team communication

Understanding Work Styles is important, but having a space in which to discuss and utilize a team's different Work Styles is critical for putting this understanding into practice. Enter the Fourth Space, a private online community your team will create together to support your collaboration. If you have not yet met your teammates, this section will help prepare you to create an equitable and welcoming space once your team has formed. After your initial meeting, be sure to walk through your Teamthink Constellations together, keeping your similarities and differences in mind as you collectively build your Fourth Space.

A Fourth Space can serve one remote team or several teams that are part of a larger group. Remote teams, also called intercultural or diverse teams, are small groups of people from different cultural and/or disciplinary backgrounds, such as classmates or work colleagues, who intentionally bring their varied perspectives together through collaborative learning and working. However, several intercultural teams could exist within the same workplace or classroom, and it can be useful to bring this larger group together in the same online environment. Depending on the situation, your team, and/or your larger group, decide what will work best to support the goals of your particular collaboration.

Third Place vs. Fourth Space?

The term "third place" comes from the fields of urban sociology and community building and is used to signify a place that is not one's home and not one's workplace. The third place is often a social center, a place for community connection. In American culture, many rely on coffee shops as third places (although an increasing number of people also use these as workspaces). In Middle Eastern culture, a *majlis* is an example of a third place where people gather to exchange news, discuss local issues, receive guests, and simply socialize. Regardless of the culture in which they are situated, one common characteristic of a third place is that their welcoming nature creates a sense of community and belonging.

Whether an intercultural collaboration is face-to-face or online, the idea of the third place as a community-oriented, welcoming space is useful for bringing teams together. In face-to-face collaborations, teammates are often faced with the reality of feeling out of place in the other culture.

Creating common ground

The potential for a friendly, inclusive environment that gives outsiders a sense of belonging is also true in virtual collaborations; although, it might be felt in a different way. When working together between the United States and Qatar, we face all kinds of bureaucratic restrictions in terms of inviting teammates who live far apart into our respective institutions' online learning management systems. Sometimes, it is not feasible, and, in some cases, it may even violate laws. In order to work together, we must create our own third place online.

A neutral virtual location

We refer to this virtual common ground as a Fourth Space. We distinguish between *place* and *space* in our definition of the Fourth Space because of the online nature of the virtual collaboration. Unlike a physical meeting place, a Fourth Space is a neutral location that is not geographically fixed and is open to all virtual teammates. The word "space" also acknowledges that the teammates occupy each other's mental space, and must also strive to keep their collaboration a "safer space" for sharing ideas.

These Fourth Spaces—like their tangible third place counterparts—are not culturally neutral zones. Instead, they offer an opportunity for rich cultural dialogues and a nurturing environment where both cultures can come together to do productive work. Creating an equitable and comfortable Fourth Space is a key ingredient in successful intercultural collaborations.

Key characteristics of successful Fourth Spaces

In our studies, we have found that establishing a welcoming and accepting environment, choosing a resource that can support a variety of media, and taking care with privacy/sharing settings are all paramount to the success of a Fourth Space.

Welcoming and accepting

First and foremost, Fourth Spaces should feel welcoming and accepting. These values are fostered by utilizing the Fourth Space as a dedicated place for project assignments and milestones related to sharing, discussion, and feedback. The following language guidelines help to build a community of trust and openness.

Multimedia friendly

In order to accomplish these forms of sharing, Fourth Spaces should ideally support multiple forms of media. Written communication and static images are the most common form, but it is helpful if the space can also support a variety of formats, such as audio and video clips.

Private to the team

Fourth Spaces should be private to the larger world and "public" only to those involved in the specific collaboration. This helps teammates feel safe and establishes the Fourth Space as a trustworthy environment. This can be enhanced by asking teammates not to share information from the Fourth Space outside of that space (or beyond the physical work environment or classroom).

Language guidelines for Collaboration Agreements and the Fourth Space

Ethical values of human communication

Communications scholars Kenneth E. Anderson and Paula S. Tompkins (2015) describes six ethical values of human communication that serve as helpful guidelines for exchanges within the Fourth Space. Keeping these values in mind in your team's written, visual, and spoken exchanges helps define a positive space for your team to build relationships. According to Anderson and Tompkins, these ethical values include:

- **Truth** and truthfulness help establish trust.
- **Justice** helps promote fairness.
- **Freedom** of communication acknowledges people as separate individuals with their own distinct ideas and feelings.
- **Care** demonstrates empathy and sympathy with others.
- **Integrity** is important for establishing a sense of consistency and ethical goodness across the team.
- **Honor** in communications demonstrates respect for others.

Plan ahead to address sources of tension

According to the research of Judith Martin, Thomas Nakayama, and Lisa Flores, there are six "dialectical tensions" that have an impact on intercultural communication (2002). Dialectical tension is the potential for friction, or opposing forces, that may show up when people discuss their ideas and opinions with each other. By examining these tensions, remote teammates can begin to understand how each tension influences their approach to communication and working dynamics. We discuss how these tensions might manifest in the Fourth Space, and explain how potential tensions can work to your team's advantage.

Six dialectical tensions

- Cultural/Individual
- Personal/Social
- Difference/Similarity
- Static/Dynamic
- Past, Present, Future
- Privilege/Disadvantage

Cultural/individual tensions

All people are unique, and their cultural background does not necessarily determine how they will communicate. In the Fourth Space, it is important to let go of cultural presumptions and stereotypes regarding the ways you or your teammates might choose to express yourselves. This is an opportunity for you to share thoughts, opinions, and feelings in a positive space. Acknowledging this point out loud and in writing reinforces trust.

Personal/social tensions

As part of a team, each person must fill certain social and/or functional roles. Consider how your roles influence the way you communicate with others, and vice versa. In the Fourth Space, some teams find it practical to develop a shorthand that indicates when they are making personal versus role-based contributions. A brief qualifying statement before communicating can help. An individual contribution could be "*Personally speaking*, I think we should go in this direction because..." A role-based communication could briefly remind the team of one's function within the team: "As *the person who took notes at the last meeting*, I am looking for some clarification about..."

Difference/similarity tension

Discovering similarities and differences is a constant within intercultural collaborations, but it is important to recognize that individuals within the same culture also have plenty of similarities and differences among them. In communication with your team in the Fourth Space and beyond, openly acknowledge these similarities and differences. Similarities feel more accessible by nature, so it is easier to linger there, but when you discover a difference, consider it a gift to the team. Push past potential hesitancy to discuss it together.

Frame the discussion with curiosity and a positive mindset in order to invite everyone to participate in productively exploring differences. "Isn't it interesting that you think this and I think that?" or "Can you tell me more about how you arrived at this idea? I'm so curious!" are great ways to begin positive dialogues around differences that help your team see sticky moments as opportunities for creativity and innovation.

Static/dynamic tension

Every culture has both values or other overarching patterns that will shift over time and other values or patterns that stay the same. Think, for example, about the political landscapes in some countries, which show consistency over time in certain ways (for example, the persistence of governmental institutions), while also reflecting major changes in other ways (such as the shift in accepted values and norms). These static and dynamic cultural patterns are a great opportunity for intercultural learning and represent information that is often not readily available from academic or popular sources. In fact, this is the type of knowledge best learned from someone who is living in the culture. (See Comparative Impression Maps, 2.5.)

Past, present, future tensions

We each have a culturally informed sense of the past, present, and future and how these interrelate. It is essential to realize that teammates from different cultures understand history in different ways, which affects their view of the present. Their view of the present, in turn, affects how they see the future. This viewpoint applies to a teammate's individual culture—and to the microcosmic collaborative team "culture." When teammates discuss their own views of the past, present, and future, they can begin to establish some understanding of each other's perspectives and how these might relate to the evolution of the team's work.

Privilege/disadvantage tensions

Differences in power can show up in many different ways within intercultural teams. Privilege, both within and outside of cultures, plays a role in the power structures function from social and political to patriarchal and colonial. Unpacking privilege with teammates can be a challenging discussion but is critical with teams that have differing access to resources or have been historically marginalized by society. Like culture, privilege can also blind individuals about the things they take for granted and understand but others do not, because they do not share that same level of privilege either due to race, religion, geographical region, economic status, or gender.

When teammates monitor their language and remove references that assume cultural dominance or cultural disadvantage, it helps establish equity among teammates. That means everyone feels their voice has value as part of the team and within the unique culture of the team—independent of whatever may be happening on the global stage. Along these lines, it is important for teammates to assess power differences in terms of the roles they assume on the team. Creating a space in which everyone's contributions, opinions, and feedback are welcomed and valued is an important step toward productive and positive learning. This kind of environment cultivates new ideas challenging the status quo because the team has agreed that the status quo does not apply to them.

Benefits & outcomes

* Agree upon guidelines for respectful communication and conduct
* Envision the team as a cooperative community
* Increase teammates' social presence with each other
* Establish a forum for discussions and visual interactions
* Find focus by gathering many ideas, images, and feedback in one place

---

a. Activity

Collaboration Agreement

Now that you've read about ethical values of communication and related dialectical tensions, it's time to draft a Collaboration Agreement. Do this as a preliminary step before building your Fourth Space so the team clearly outlines expectations for communication and behavior within—and outside of— its online space. These guidelines should respect the goals for the collaboration alongside teammates' cultural and personal preferences for digital interactions. If applicable, these could also refer to the requirements of your work project or course. (For more on articulating your goals for the collaboration, see 6.2, 6.3.)

→ **People:** Remote teammates
→ **Duration:** Allow at least 2 hours
→ **Technology:** Shared document
→ **Other resources:** Paper for note taking

Collaboration Agreement

Phase 1: With remote teammates

1. **Review:** Read through the following agreement points individually or as a team.
2. **Discuss:** Meet with your team to talk through responses and ideas for each of these agreement points. Take care to ensure that each teammate gets a chance to contribute and respond to ideas.
3. **Draft:** In a shared document, work together to address each point in writing. Even if one person is the scribe for the team, each teammate should contribute equally to the formation of the agreement.

Sign agreement

Phase 2: With remote teammates

4. **Print & Post:** Print the Collaboration Agreement. Sign, date it, and then hang it in your workspace. Having a physical reminder of accountability—to your team and the agreement you created together—can help create a deeper sense of connection with the team. It feels more "real" than something that is only represented in pixels.
5. **Update:** There will be opportunities to revisit and update your Collaboration Agreement as you work together. Use the same collaborative approach to agree on changes, then print and hang your newest version.

Agreement points

Discuss, decide, and write these together now:

1. **Title your shared document "Collaboration Agreement"**
2. Write a statement about **team structure** articulating equal status and authority for all, and defining particular roles if applicable (e.g., a note-taker to document all meetings)
   - Ask yourself: *"Do I want to play a particular role on this team, or would I be more comfortable with flexible roles?"* Discuss responses as a team so that you can agree on what should or should not appear in your shared space.
3. **Communication guidelines:**
   a. Topics to include
   b. Wording or phrasing to use
   c. Potential Dialectical Tensions you might encounter
   d. Topics, wording, or phrasing to avoid
   - Ask yourself: *"What kinds of content or topics would I find offensive?"* Discuss responses as a team so that you can agree on what should or should not appear in your shared space.
4. Expectations for **frequency/number** of contributions/posts to Fourth Space
5. **Permissions and restrictions** for sharing content outside of the Fourth Space
   - Ask yourself: *"How would I feel if someone shared my images or words with someone outside of our team?"* Discuss responses as a team.
6. **Duration** of the collaboration, if known
7. Process for **adding** new teammates or **removing** original teammates
8. Terms and conditions of **termination** of the collaboration
   For example, violating the team's contribution, communication, or permissions guidelines may result in removal from the Fourth Space and/or team

---

> *Discuss these together now, update Agreement later:*
> 9. Your team name and/or name for your Fourth Space (update after Visual Origin Story, 3.5)
> 10. Preferred approaches for resolving conflicts (update after reading 5.7)
> 11. Goals of the collaboration (update after reading 6.2, 6.3)
> 12. Protocols for exchanging constructive feedback (update after reading 5.2)

b. Activity

Fourth Space

A Fourth Space is an online community environment to facilitate discussion, collaboration, and other activities related to virtual teamwork. The online space should encourage teammates to share ideas, images, and new (collaboration-specific) content. It also represents a space for practicing ethical values at the heart of successful intercultural work and for addressing dialectical tensions that are likely to arise. Whether the team chooses to work together in discussion boards, social media outlets, or blogs, the shared space needs to feel inclusive and accessible to all teammates.

If participating in an online community together is not possible for one or more sides of the collaboration, then hang a large sheet of paper on a wall of a workspace in each participating culture. Your team can "post updates" by writing brief quotes, drawing sketches, and adding other contributions in order to create a visible, public record of your conversations and exchanges. Share these images with your team to make sure you are on the same page and even see how each teammate conceptualizes the goals and tasks of your work together.

> ### Tips
>
> • **Stay active:** Regularly sharing insight, information, and feedback with teammates in the Fourth Space can clarify perspectives, enable ongoing virtual dialogue, and serve as a wonderful record of your work together. Beware though—a Fourth Space can easily become stale from lack of use, attention, and meaningful interactions. Make a plan to encourage your team to use and interact in the space frequently.
> • **Private and password protected:** The Fourth Space needs to be accessible to all teammates. Make sure that whatever resources you choose can be password protected and accessible to teammates. Also, make sure that the settings or mode are set as "accessible to all" in the collaboration. Do bear in mind that not all websites and web apps are globally accessible. While the space may not be totally private, it should only accessible to those within the collaboration and not made publicly available.

(Continued)

- **Language use:** You may be discussing tricky topics during your collaboration and your shared space for the discourse must feel welcoming to all members of the team. Agree to use supportive, constructive language as much as possible. Consider if any language or images you post could potentially cause harm to your teammates, no matter your intentions.
- **Meetings:** Use the Fourth Space as a place to organize and document meetings. In a virtual collaboration, there are often meetings without all teammates present. Whenever there are discussions without the whole team present, you can start meetings by developing a collaborative agenda in the Fourth Space. A note-taker should document and share the discussion on behalf of all members. Another teammate should capture photographic documentation of sketches, whiteboards, or other analog forms of ideation to share.

→ **People:** Individual/remote teammates
→ **Duration:** The initial space can be created in 1–2 days, but the development and maintenance of the Fourth Space is ongoing for the duration of the collaboration, and sometimes afterward.
→ **Technology:** Many password-protected options are available for customized online communities, forums, and/or blogs.
→ **Other resources:** Paper, sticky notes, markers, whiteboard
→ *Teams who cannot create a Fourth Space due to bandwidth or other restrictions are encouraged to create team status boards in their workspaces. When receiving an email update from a remote teammate, reflect new ideas and developments by writing or sketching on a large piece of paper or whiteboard.*

Create online community

Phase 1: Working individually

1. **Research:** Explore the various options for private online communities, such as discussion boards, social media outlets, and blogs.

Phase 2: With remote teammates

2. **Discuss:** Meet with your remote team to share your ideas. Discuss the feasibility and accessibility of your favorite options.
3. **Initiate:** One person will need to take the initiative to set up the shell for the online community and then invite the other teammates. Give the space a creative name and choose an engaging image to represent the collaboration (see Visual Origin Story, 3.6).

4. **Populate:** Later in the collaborative process, once all teammates have access to the online community, everyone can start adding interesting and relevant content. This space becomes particularly important and useful when teams are working toward a shared goal. The content population should always be on-topic and relevant to the collaboration and/or to any cultural questions raised by the collaboration.

5. **Tag:** Once you begin posting content, you may find it helpful to organize your content by tagging research, posts, and images so that you and your team will be able to refer to your materials more easily at a later date.

Analysis

Phase 3: With remote teammates

6. **Discuss:** Take some time to discuss your experience with your remote teammates. Use the following questions to start your discussion.

DISCUSSION GUIDE

*   Do you currently participate in any online communities? Why, or why not?
*   How do you represent yourself online? (Or, if you do not currently participate in any, how do you think you would you represent yourself online?)
*   What questions or reservations do you have about interacting with a new person online?
*   How do digital interactions change the way we think and behave? Why? What can we do about that?
*   What ethical and dialectical tensions do you think might arise during this process? How will you address these tensions as an individual? And as a team?

References

Anderson, Kenneth E., Paula S. Tompkins, and Paula S. Tompkins. 2015. *Practicing Communication Ethics: Development, Discernment, and Decision-Making.* London: Routledge. doi:10.4324/9781315663159.

Anderson, Lorin W., and David R. Krathwohl, eds. 2001. *A Taxonomy for Learning, Teaching, and Assessing: A Revision of Bloom's Taxonomy of Educational Objectives.* Complete ed. New York: Longman.

Berger, Charles R., and Richard J. Calabrese. 1975. "Some Explorations in Initial Interaction and Beyond: Toward a Developmental Theory of Interpersonal Communication." *Human Communication Research* 1 (2): 99–112. doi:10.1111/j.1468-2958.1975.tb00258.x.

Bloom, Benjamin S. 1956. *Taxonomy of Educational Objectives.* Vol. 1: Cognitive Domain. New York: McKay, 20–24.

Hall, Edward Twitchell. 1989. *Beyond Culture.* New York: Anchor Books.

Hill, Linda A., Greg Brandeau, Emily Truelove, and Kent Lineback. 2014. *Collective Genius: The Art and Practice of Leading Innovation.* Boston, MA: Harvard Business Review Press.

Hofstede, Geert. 2011. "Dimensionalizing Cultures: The Hofstede Model in Context." *Online Readings in Psychology and Culture* 2 (1). doi:10.9707/2307-0919.1014.

Homans, George C. 1958. "Social Behavior as Exchange." *American Journal of Sociology* 63 (6): 597–606. doi:10.1086/222355.

Latham, Gary P., and Edwin A. Locke. 2007. "New Developments in and Directions for Goal-Setting Research." *European Psychologist* 12 (4): 290–300. doi:10.1027/1016-9040.12.4.290.

Magolda, Marcia B. Baxter. 2008. "Three Elements of Self-Authorship." *Journal of College Student Development* 49 (4): 269–84. doi:10.1353/csd.0.0016.

Mansilla, Veronica Boix, and Anthony Jackson. 2013. "Educating for Global Competence: Learning Redefined for an Interconnected World." *Mastering Global Literacy*, 5–27. New York: Solution Tree.

Martin, Judith N, Thomas K Nakayama, and Lisa A Flores. 2002. "A Dialectical Approach to Intercultural Communication." In *Readings in Intercultural Communication: Experiences and Contexts*. Boston: McGraw-Hill.

Patton, Bobby R., and Timothy M. Downs. 2003. *Decision-Making Group Interaction: Achieving Quality*. 4th ed. Boston: Allyn and Bacon.

Rosen, Evan. 2009. *The Culture of Collaboration: Maximizing Time, Talent and Tools to Create Value in the Global Economy*. San Francisco, CA: Red Ape Publishing.

Sandu, Oana Nestian, Nadine Lyamouri-Bajja, Council of Europe, and European Union. 2018. *T-Kit 4 Intercultural Learning*. Edited by Mara Georgescu. Council of Europe and European Commission: Council of Europe Publishing.

Ting-Toomey, Stella, and Tenzin Dorjee. 2018. *Communicating Across Cultures,* Second Edition. New York: Guilford Press.

Trompenaars, Fons, and Charles Hampden-Turner. 2011. *Riding the Waves of Culture: Understanding Diversity in Global Business*. London: Nicholas Brealey.

2

UNDERSTAND CORE BELIEFS

Creating visuals helps in understanding
values and biases

Individual ⟵——————————————⟶ Collective

DIMENSION 2: Understand Core Beliefs

Our values affect our sense of self-efficacy and belonging.

   **Select some of these self-investigation activities to do individ-
ually or with your local colleagues prior to meeting your remote
team as a way to prepare for future interactions with them.**

   Chapter 2 discusses personal values and core beliefs as critical to building
trust, respect, and care as part of teamwork. The activities help individuals
and local colleagues unpack topics such as cultural values and implicit biases
through the creation of visual Thought Objects. Later, working with your
remote team, this preparation can open the door for both enlightening and
practical conversations, from debunking cultural stereotypes to preferences
for team arrangement and structure. For example, will your remote team be
lateral or hierarchical? Deeper, more nuanced cultural questions will demonstrate your interest, curiosity, and sensitivity to your remote teammates.

| **INDIVIDUAL:** I feel that I have the ability to influence or change things that affect me. My personal values, principles, and their roots contribute to a sense of self-efficacy or ownership. I feel a responsibility to myself above others. | **COLLECTIVE:** I feel that my actions can directly contribute to or detract from team harmony. My personal values, principles, and their roots contribute to how I see my role in the community. I feel a responsibility to my community above myself. |

2.1

Creating visuals helps in understanding values and biases

All humans possess both biases and values, whether or not they are aware of them. It is important to acknowledge and come to terms with this, particularly prior to embarking on intercultural teamwork. This chapter focuses on creating several types of visual Thought Objects. When supported by digital technologies, these can promote bias-awareness by kickstarting your thinking about stereotypes and biases. In collaborative settings that involve working with someone from a different culture or context, discussing personal values and core beliefs is critical to building trust, respect, and care for your teammates. The activities outlined in this chapter help open a dialogue that extends to the collaboration itself, where each teammate incorporates their unique values in to the larger context of the project. When teammates agree to explore these topics together, using Thought Objects as a tool for dialogue, the process improves subsequent collaborations.

Thought Objects

As described in the Introduction, Thought Objects communicate an idea to oneself or from an individual to their team. These objects help individuals and teammates better understand each other's thoughts by visually demonstrating an idea or process. In the case of communicating about biases and values, the object acts as a proxy for depersonalized discussion of a deeply personal topic. Drawing upon this idea further, the weight of the discussion falls upon the artifact and its implications, rather than on a particular individual. The use of Thought Objects can also reduce some of the fears that individual teammates may have about discussing a topic that interests them which they are nevertheless embarrassed to propose or are concerned about discussing openly.

Lessons learned

Confronting bias in the way we have just described involves a great deal of work, and experience has taught us to frame these discussions with care. In some cases, individuals are concerned that something they say may highlight their inadequacies or bigotry. In other cases, concerns are tied to ego or being called out for subconscious or surface-level realizations about differences. In our initial efforts at intercultural collaboration, we unintentionally and implicitly asked teams to shoulder the huge challenge of confronting bias on their own.

Ever since, we have been working on creative ways to address this issue that comes up in a wide range of settings: in offices and classrooms, in international organizations, among travelers and hosts, and between countries discussing international policy. By providing some tools to integrate values and bias assessment into other intercultural collaborations, our aim is to cause a "trickle up" effect, bringing positive change to the way we approach international relationships on a global scale.

In context: Shouldering the burden of bias

During our very first collaboration, we asked remote intercultural teams to work together to create pairs of posters about their two cities highlighting similarities or contrasts. Architectural comparisons abounded in the visual outcomes, from San Francisco's Transamerica Pyramid tower and Dubai's Burj Khalifa to the Painted Ladies and the Souk Madinat Jumeirah. It seemed that everyone was having difficulty moving away from the built environment to explore other aspects of life in their respective corners of the world.

Of course it made sense, architecture—and the built environment—is everywhere, and it's a cultural force. The built environment was a safe way of exploring and sharing their worlds—one that would allow them to exchange a small taste of cultural nuance without the fear of treading into controversial topics; it was nearly impossible for us to reroute them from this path. We surmised that the discussions between the teammates, which took place primarily via email, were tempered by the relative safety of the images they shared. A pervasive sense of diplomacy emerged among teams; everyone was afraid to rock the proverbial boat. As facilitators, we felt stymied.

(Continued)

We had hoped to engage the intercultural teams in fascinating questions and dialogues that would give each class insight into their remote teammates' culture. And while juxtaposing two photographs of inner-city high-rise skyscrapers could potentially lead teammates to discussions of cultural differences, teams insisted, almost universally, on exploring formal and visual similarities.

We understood that discovering similarities or finding common ground could feel like a breakthrough for the teams. However, it was not enough. When it came time to exchange feedback, they fell flat. We were tempted to outlaw certain points of similarity that had turned into stumbling blocks—such as using architecture as photographic subject matter, or uttering the word "nice."

Perhaps the most telling moment occurred with the creation of books at the end of the collaboration, which included reflections from both teammates. Yet, when individuals realized that their teammates would see and read all of their content, they began to overzealously edit their written pieces. By the end, they all read as "go along to get along" submissions, with the personality, challenges, and even critical thinking redacted.

While the outcomes of this particular collaboration were visually beautiful, we, as facilitators, were left wondering where we had gone wrong and how we could have steered the teams differently so that they would embrace the more difficult work of finding and articulating differences and asking and starting dialogues about those differences. Our experience led us to develop the tools you will encounter in this chapter. These lay the groundwork for initiating and sustaining cultural dialogues that dare to venture—respectfully—beneath the surface.

The relationship between values and bias

If we want to retrain ourselves to acknowledge cultural similarities and differences consciously in order to have the sort of sustained dialogues that eluded us during our first collaborative experience, then *value introspection*—reflecting critically on one's own values—can be a helpful starting point. However, this form of introspection can also raise questions and concerns about cultivating bias awareness (Banaji and Greenwald 2013). For example, we might think, *"Based on the values I consciously hold, I think I am a good person—so how can I possibly also have negative biases or operate based on stereotypes?"*

Value introspection

When value introspection is tied to activities specifically designed to confront bias, it may affect the way you see yourself, possibly resulting in uncomfortable self-realizations. For instance, introspection can make us realize that there is a conflict between a value we hold dear, such as respect for others, and the idea that we might nevertheless fail to uphold that value consistently. It can be uncomfortable to recognize this gap, called *cognitive dissonance,* between belief and practice.

As we engage in value introspection, it is helpful to keep in mind that our values (and alongside them, our biases) change as we move through life. Child developmental psychologist Lawrence Kohlberg (1964) defines three stages of moral development. The stages provide some insight as to how our values can shift, whether we realize it or not.

1. We are first motivated by punishment and reward.
2. We come to understand that we must obey the law to be accepted in society, which Kohlberg describes as "conventional morality."
3. Many of us develop empathy, which gives us a sense of obligation to do good for others.

The relationship between values and morals is that values shape one's morals, or belief system, in deciding what is right or wrong. These developmental stages reveal ways our values may be influenced by extrinsic factors (e.g., the law) as well as intrinsic ones (e.g., a sense of obligation to help others). Expanding our value system in order to confront bias strengthens intercultural relationships. By examining these internal conflicts openly and honestly, we have an opportunity to learn new ways to embody values and then purposefully enact them with all people in good conscience.

Grappling with otherness

As feminist existential theorist Simone de Beauvoir once wrote, "Otherness is a fundamental category of human thought" (de Beauvoir and Parshley 1953). *The other* is that which is different from us. Because human brains are so good at categorization, we have a tendency to apply it to everything—including people. In working with teammates who have different cultural backgrounds from our own, framing one another as other is a natural tendency. However, there are benefits and risks embedded in this tendency. Assuming total and complete difference from one's self can make it difficult to forge a personal connection or build trust, both of which are essential elements for effective collaborative work.

On the other hand, acknowledging differences can be beneficial to collaboration in terms of helping diverse teams feel more open to sharing contrasting perspectives. This approach has been shown to lead to more innovative outcomes as teammates with differing backgrounds work together toward a common goal or solution (see Chapter 6 for more on this phenomenon). The human brain grapples with otherness in a variety of ways, particularly in the context of reconciling similarities and differences. A few particular ways the mind deals with difference are through *stereotypes, unconscious bias* and *confirmation bias.*

Stereotypes

Humans have a tendency to oversimplify and generalize descriptions of the categories our brains are so eager to create. A *stereotype* is a characteristic someone sees as applicable to everyone in a particular mental category, regardless of whether or not it is true. Stereotyping works hand-in-hand with unconscious bias in that implicit biases often make it difficult for people to see beyond stereotypes, even when they are clearly untrue. For example, if you have been told your whole life that all dogs hate cats, it can be hard for you to imagine a household where these creatures peacefully coexist.

Because of its roots in printmaking, stereotyping is also an interesting addition to the larger discussion of visualization throughout this book. As an ancient Chinese printing technology which was later given its western name by eighteenth-century typographer Fermin Didot, the physical process of stereotyping could reproduce fixed images without variation (Zhang 2017). Rapid reproduction helped to widely share these identical images. Once the mental picture created by learning a stereotype is imprinted in the brain, it is very difficult to forget.

Unconscious bias

We all carry ideas that inform the way we think about and see others. These ideas come from our own cultural contexts and upbringing and from our unique educational, workplace, family, and life experiences. For most of us, these experiences shape our feelings and reactions toward others in ways we do not consciously control—which is why this phenomenon is referred to as *unconscious bias*. While the word "bias" itself carries negative connotations, unconscious bias can include both positive and negative feelings toward a particular person or people. However, with some intention and effort, we can bring these biases to the forefront in order to become consciously aware of them and learn ways to work past them (Greenwald and Banaji 1995).

Confirmation bias

Biases abound in intercultural work, and confirmation bias can go hand-in-hand with unconscious bias. *Confirmation bias* describes a tendency to seek out information that is already aligned with one's existing beliefs or values or to interpret new information as being aligned with one's values. Ignoring or avoiding information that conflicts with one's value set is another component of confirmation bias. When working in intercultural teams, unchecked confirmation bias leads to a milquetoast celebration of sameness that impedes individuals from discussing and making the most of their different perspectives and approaches.

Becoming bias-aware

For many people, the word "bias" on its own evokes strong negative feelings. In order to do deep introspective work around biases, it is first necessary to come to terms with the prevalent knee-jerk (negative) reaction to the word. Talking openly about biases, both among ourselves and with others, enables us to shift our mindset and learn how to make less biased decisions by taking our prejudices into account. In turn, we can create an environment where we support each other in cultivating bias awareness (United States Department of Justice 2016). Another way to think about implicit bias is that if two things have never been put together for you before, it is very difficult to associate them with each other or imagine them together.

Confronting biases enables teammates to see each other as collaborators instead of as others. When teammates take the opportunity to recognize that they may be unintentionally basing their ideas or impressions of each other on generalizations learned from educational and family settings or derived from entertainment and media sources, the need to revise decision-making processes in order to take these layers of presumptions and stereotypes into account becomes clear. Moreover, individuals may be motivated to dig deeper and get to know their teammates as real people, rather than dwelling on the preconceived notions that can overwhelm and influence first impressions.

Getting started

The progression of visualization activities in this chapter will give you more personal insights into what you value and which of your own assumptions require you do to additional personal work. Working through these activities with local colleagues will help you build awareness and gain confidence to later talk about these issues with your remote teammates and in future team scenarios. By becoming aware of our existing biases and striving to live our own values while also respecting the values of our collaborators, we can improve our personal relationships and become better teammates in our professional or academic lives.

2.2

Value Collage:
Understanding personal and cultural values

Values are deep beliefs that guide our lives, whether we are aware of them or not. Values can manifest in the form of personal values or cultural values. *Personal values* are what we choose for ourselves as we determine how we want to live and what we think is right or wrong. *Cultural values* are contextual—they vary based on the particular beliefs and social patterns within different societies and are influenced by factors such as predominant religions or educational models.

Communicating our values

Cultural values are the core ideals, principles, values, or beliefs of a society or culture. These commonly held standards often relate to what a given society or culture considers right or wrong, acceptable or unacceptable, and important or unimportant. We communicate our values to others on a daily basis, through many direct and indirect choices and activities. Some examples of the ways in which we may unintentionally communicate our values include the clothing we wear and the food we eat, the way we commute to work and the jobs we undertake, the ways we treat others and the holidays we celebrate, and the media we consume and what we do with the information we learn.

Connecting the dots

There can be parallels or conflicts between one's personal values and cultural values as guiding principles for our life and work. Reflecting on personal values can be a useful starting point for considering broader cultural values and how personal and cultural values compare to the value sets of people from different contexts. Some people may have greater experience with value introspection, or working to understand and be aware of their values, than others. Those who have done local community-based work, or who have had opportunities to work, study, or volunteer abroad, may have a better sense of their own values as well as the connection between their values and the bigger picture. However, most people need a hand connecting these dots.

Daring to discuss differences

It is important to remember that the qualities people commonly value in your culture and in your smaller social circles are not necessarily the same in other countries and cultures. This is regardless of whether you are discussing values with a trusted friend, coworker, classmate, or working in the context of meeting a new teammate for the first time. Because similarities can create feelings of camaraderie and connection, encountering them across cultures may seem exciting at first. However, daring to discuss differences while suppressing our natural tendency to judge is critical to begin understanding teammates on a more profound level, and helps build trust.

Benefits & outcomes

- Explore and discuss personal and cultural values
- Foster awareness through self-investigation
- Build a foundation to later engage with mutual respect
- Cultivate healthy curiosity about similarities and differences
- Use critical thinking to analyze yourself in reference to local colleagues and remote teammates

---

a. Activity

Value Discovery

This two-part activity invites you to conduct a personal value assessment as a method for cultivating your own self-awareness about how broader cultural values relate to your individual personal values. This activity can be conducted with local colleagues or independently. If you do it independently, you can also take some time to share your individual results later with local colleagues to generate further discussion. In some cases, the outcomes of this activity might also be an interesting starting point for future discussion with your remote teammates, who may even share some similar cultural or personal values. Following this activity, explore your personal values and cultural identity through visually depicting them in the form of a collage or a composition that you create from im-agery, words, colors, and textures collected from a variety of physical or digital resources.

→ **People:** Local colleagues/individual
→ **Duration:** 30 minutes to complete the value assessment; 30 minutes of discussion
→ **Technology:** Black & white printer
→ **Other resources:** Paper, pens/pencils, markers/highlighters, whiteboard

---

Tips

- **Time and understanding:** The amount of time you devote to laying a collaborative foundation around personal and collective values may depend upon the start time and duration of the collaboration. There are a number of different approaches to choose from depending upon the amount of time available for preparatory work prior to embarking on the intercultural work.
- **Litmus test:** Your value lists and reflective writing can become refer-ence points throughout the course of a project. Your responses act as a sort of litmus test: Is the work you are producing aligned with their personal values?
- **Expanding values:** Are your values changing or expanding as a result of the work? Opportunities for reflection such as these can prime people to engage in discussions about choosing to do work that is aligned with one's values and about how to work with people who have different values.
- **Reflective writing:** This style of writing provides an opportunity to thoughtfully describe and analyze something in words. Because it can help you better understand complex topics or think about problem-solving in a new way, you may use reflective writing to probe more deeply into these topics and to think about your life experiences and val-ues with focused perspective. Initially ask yourself broad questions and progress toward more specific questions about your values and beliefs. Use the following questions to guide a personal written reflection:

  o **Broad:** In your opinion, what are examples of "good" and "bad" behavior?
  o **More specific:** Would your parents agree with your assessment? Why, or why not?
  o **Even more specific:** Would you ever, or have you ever, done these things? Why, or why not?

- ○ **Broad:** What qualities do you admire in others?
- ○ **More specific:** Who do you admire?
- ○ **Even more specific:** What do you admire most about that person? Why?

- ○ **Broad:** What frustrates or infuriates you?
- ○ **More specific:** What problem or issue makes you want to take action?
- ○ **Even more specific:** What do you most want to change about that problem? Why?

Value Discovery

Phase 1: With local colleagues

1. **Discuss:** Working with local colleagues, define your *cultural values*—the core ideals, principles, values, or beliefs of a society or culture—and discuss how you think these values are formed. What are some of the typical values associated with your culture or society? How are those values taught and learned? How do you see those values in action—even unconsciously—in your everyday life?

2. **Brainstorm:** On a whiteboard or large sheet of paper, generate a list of cultural values with your local colleagues that you believe are characteristic of the society or culture in which you live. Note that the cultural values you list may not align with your personal values; instead, the aim of this brainstorming activity is to think deeply about the impact of the broader culture on your beliefs, principles, and ideals. For example, the values you list might include equality, an obligation to others, harmony, self-criticism, collectivism, or appreciation for aesthetics.

Phase 2: Working individually

3. **Identify:** Assess the group's list of cultural values and then create your own list. You should also add new words to the list at this time. Which personal values are not yet listed? Do some of these differ from the status quo? Examples of such values might include playfulness, adventure, perseverance, humor, integrity, advocacy, or achievement. If these examples feel obvious to you, challenge yourself to dig deeper.

4. **Organize:** Do a second pass to review the selected words, and then organize your chosen words into clusters based on similarity. Finally, select one exemplary word from each cluster—or find a new, encapsulating word—to serve as a summary or label for that cluster.

5. **Summarize:** Use all of your summary words to write a series of short sentences that describe you and your life goals:

Examples:
- Approach others with **thoughtfulness**.
- Seek **joy**.

6. **Think:** In order to expand your thinking, consider the origins of these values and goals. Update your sentences—or write new ones—to show the connection between your personal and broader cultural values and where they come from.
   Examples:
   - Approach others with *thoughtfulness*. → My **religion** prompts me to approach others with **thoughtfulness**. I adopted my religion because of my family.
   - Seek *joy*. → In the United States, "pursuit of happiness" is a **political** value that encourages me to seek **joy** and help others find it. I think I first learned about political values in an elementary school class.

Discuss

Phase 3: With one local colleague

7. **Pair & Share:** Pair up with one local colleague. Briefly read your set of values sentences to each other. Thinking about the work that you do, the things you learn, and your daily interactions: In what ways do you currently address these values? How could you address them if you are not doing so already? What is possible in your cultural context? If you were to change your position on something, how would people in your world (friends, family, mentors, colleagues) react?
   Example:
   - I could be more *thoughtful* in the way I speak to my colleagues.

b. Activity

Value Collage

Where did your values come from? Are your values cultural, familial, generational, or social? Do you have a mentor, friend, or loved one who embodies certain values? Which cultural values do you identify with most? Try to determine the root origin or reason for each of your values. You will reflect your values through a collage.

→ **People:** Local colleagues/individual
→ **Duration:** 1 hour
→ **Technology:** Black & white printer
→ **Other resources:** Paper, pens/pencils, markers/highlighters, whiteboard, collage supplies (magazines, newspapers, food packaging, glue, tape, printed letters).

Phase 1: Working individually

1. **Familiarize:** If you have not previously created a collage, it may be useful for you to view some examples from the library or online to become familiar with the approach and possible outcomes.
2. **Collage:** Generate a physical or digital collage that reflects one or more of your selected value sentence(s) and its origin(s). Create your collage by taking pieces of your available materials (such as images and words ripped out of magazines or newspapers), arranging them on top of a piece of paper, and gluing or taping them into position.

Phase 2: With local colleagues

3. **Share:** With your local colleagues, go around the room and share the value statement that is most meaningful to you. To choose your value statement, you can select from your summary sentences, your collage, or both. Give a brief example of how that value or idea shows up in your life, or how you would like that value to show up, if it does not already.

DISCUSSION GUIDE

- What values were discussed that you had not considered as cultural or social expectations?
- What are the origins of your values? Are there some that are more related to experiences with your family, friends, or colleagues?
- Was there a particular incident in your life that you believe solidified a certain value for you?
- Did any values emerge during the discussion that you had not considered prior to doing this activity? Could any of these be considered unconscious values?

CHALLENGING ASSUMPTIONS AND OPINIONS

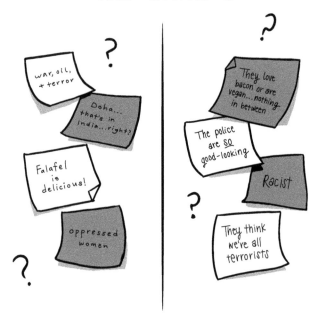

2.3

Belief Brainstorm:
Exploring facts, fakes, and feelings to confront bias

Like it or not, all humans carry baggage that affects our responses to the similarities and differences inherent in our interactions with other people (in terms of parameters like nationality, race, religion, and gender, to name some of the most obvious). These responses, and the belief systems that inform them, are influenced by many different factors, including our families, schooling, everyday interactions with people in our communities, religious practices, and the media. Now that you have had the chance to reflect on your personal values and those of your local colleagues in 2.2, the Belief Brainstorm & Diagram at the end of this section continues the examination of values, unconscious bias, and confirmation bias introduced in 2.1.

Distributed brainstorming, a form of lateral thinking

The Belief Brainstorm & Diagram uses *distributed brainstorming*, which means that everyone in the room has their own markers and pads of sticky notes or slips of paper for writing simultaneous personal responses (eliminating the need to say them aloud). This process helps to ensure that your group of local colleagues generates a sufficiently large collection of facts, fakes, and feelings based on your ideas of your remote teammates' culture. Distributed brainstorming is one form of *lateral thinking*, an open, generative, approach to cultivating understanding and solving problems. This particular approach to brainstorming also helps to eliminate the fear of judgment, particularly when many people rush to the same wall or whiteboard to post their notes in a flurry, and the possibility of anyone tracking an individual response back to its original author is far less likely.

Daring to discuss bias via diagramming

As discussed, *unconscious bias* unintentionally influences our response or behavior toward another person or situation, whether positively or negatively, due to feelings or beliefs that we do not consciously recognize. *Confirmation bias*, meanwhile, causes us to look for commonalities along value lines by encouraging us to interpret information or situations according to our own values and to ignore things that do not align with our values.

The idea of confronting bias can scare some people, particularly if they have never done collaborative or intercultural work. Just the word "bias" can make people feel defensive or uncomfortable. These feelings (and many others!) are completely normal. It is important to be aware of your own feelings and reactions as your journey begins and as you progress down the path of intercultural collaboration. Addressing your feelings throughout the process is an essential part of self-discovery and will help you pinpoint specific areas where you can focus your efforts in order to relate better to others.

Recognizing biases can improve collaborations

While discussing bias may feel uncomfortable, keep in mind that understanding and coming to terms with your own biases helps you to grow as an individual and as a collaborator. As noted in the first section of this chapter, the process of unpacking unconscious and confirmation biases is essential for effective intercultural work because it helps to alleviate potential tensions between people living in different cultural and social contexts. The group component of the discussion is critical: Working with local colleagues removes the "I" from the mix. Colleagues create the Thought Object together and then step away from their individual investment in the creation in order to discuss the thing itself.

The Belief Brainstorm & Diagram invites you to explore a range of biases and stereotypes that have the potential to create barriers to successful collaboration if they go unaddressed. The aim of this activity is to give you the tools for getting past those barriers **before** you begin working with a teammate from another culture. Because stereotypes and unconscious biases are often misaligned with one's conscious value set (Greenwald et al. 1998; Banaji 2018), this activity presents a valuable opportunity to gain additional perspective beyond the earlier discussion of values. The Belief Brainstorm & Diagram can help individuals, local colleagues, and remote teams take a closer look at their biases through the lens of their commonly held facts, assumptions, and opinions about your remote teammates' culture.

Facts, fakes, feelings

What is a fact? This may seem like a simple question with a straightforward answer. However, analysis-based judgment, or critical thinking, is required (Chaffee 2014). Information that we believe to be factual is often lumped together with information that is not necessarily factual. Once you begin talking with your local colleagues, you may quickly realize that the distinctions are sometimes murky between what you know to be true and what you feel or assume.

Prior to beginning the Brainstorm, we recommend using the following Tips section to have an open discussion about facts, assumptions, and opinions with your local colleagues.

Benefits & outcomes

- Examine your cultural contexts, upbringing, and life experiences
- Confront your own unconscious biases
- Investigate possible biases and stereotypes about the teammate culture
- Discuss and defuse preconceptions or prejudices
- Approach future team conversations with sensitivity

---

a. Activity

Belief Brainstorm

The Belief Brainstorm & Diagram is specifically designed to engage individuals in unpacking potential stereotypes *prior to* working with remote teammates. You will likely find that discussions, questions, and responses flow more freely among local colleagues, giving you the space to discuss and defuse preconceptions or prejudices that you might have overlooked. The ideas from your brainstorm and the categories from the diagram can be effective starting points for in-depth discussions about bias with your local colleagues. These offer opportunities for significant growth in critical thinking and global sensitivity. Working through biases and stereotypes in an internal setting will prepare you for more productive conversations later with your remote teammates.

→ **People:** Local colleagues
→ **Duration:** 1 hour
→ **Technology:** Camera or another photographic device for documentation
→ **Other resources:** Multi-colored markers; sticky notes or note cards; whiteboard, wall, or another vertical surface on which to post.

Tips

Facts

For example, talk together about how you define what a **fact** is, and attend to your local colleagues' responses. For facts, you should be looking for something along these lines:

- "*Facts* are things we know to be true, which come from reputable/believable sources." Or "A piece of information presented as having objective reality and therefore different from *opinion*."

Be cautious of who generated the particular resource, and be aware that political structures, histories, and relationships can influence content, such as which countries or borders are acknowledged on maps, or what kind of content is included in a textbook. Examples of sources for facts could include:

- Maps for geographic information
- Encyclopedias
- Textbooks
- Newspapers that practice fact-checking and are not censored
- One example of a fact that often comes up in our collaborations is that "Qatar produces a lot of oil." Inevitably someone in North America will mention this fact, which they usually attribute to national news media.

Fakes

Next, follow the same approach, this time asking the team to define **assumptions**. Collect ideas and examples from the team and write them down. The definition should look something like the following:

- "*Assumptions* are what others believe to be true, but are not necessarily based on facts."

Keep in mind that some of the examples of assumptions may indeed be factually true or contain aspects of truth, but they are assumptions because the information has not been derived directly from a factual source or because they are stated as blanket generalizations or stereotypes. Assumptions might stem from:

- Geographic location
- Exposure to foods that are "representative" of a culture (or not!)
- News media coverage
- Portrayals of a country or culture in movies, games, or other entertainment media
- People's responses to these items

(Continued)

- Based on the previous example of a fact, a related assumption that frequently arises on the North American side of our collaborations is that "everyone in Qatar is wealthy." (This false assumption comes from the combination of facts about oil production in Qatar shared by national news media, and because of the idea that oil production translates to wealth for the general population.)

Feelings

Finally, approach the topic of **opinions**: How does your team define this term? As with the other terms, someone from the team can combine your ideas into a team consensus definition along these lines:

- *"Opinions* are what people think or feel [about the other culture], which are not based on facts."

Sometimes it can be useful to frame opinion conversations in terms of "other people's" thoughts or feelings, rather than focusing solely on your own opinions. This approach can help people feel less self-conscious. For example, what would your weird relative at the family holiday dinner have to say about the subject? During the activity, write more stereotypical responses that you actually think or feel, but may be too self-conscious to contribute in earlier rounds of the brainstorming; this is also a good reason to consider saving opinions for the last round of brainstorming. In generating example assumptions at this stage, try these sentence starters:

- "I heard someone say that they think…"
- "My grandmother feels like…"
- "People think that…"
- "If I went there, my family would say…"

Brainstorm

Phase 1: With local colleagues

1. **Discuss:** Use the preceding Tips section to have a group discussion about facts, fakes, and feelings. Talk about how you would define a fact, an assumption, or an opinion, and give examples of each, including possible sources for these examples. Work through one concept at a time. Write responses and definitions on a board or a large sheet of paper where everyone can see them.
2. **Keep time:** Set a timer for 3–5 minutes for each of the following brainstorm sprints.
3. **Brainstorm sprints:** While thinking about your remote teammates' culture, each person in the group should write a series of personal responses to each of the following prompts. Free-writing involves recording whatever comes to mind. Avoid a "think-aloud" approach where each person responds audibly.

This often produces greater anxiety and results in generating fewer responses. This, in turn, will result in outcomes that are less productive in intercultural dialogues afterward. Similarly, do not identify which written contributions are yours. Use different colored paper or markers for each of the three sprints, or put a small "F" "A" or "O" in the corner of each paper to indicate its category)

a. **Sprint 1, Fact:** Begin by thinking of any **facts** you know about your remote teammate's culture, and whether you think that fact comes from a reliable source. List as many facts as possible through rapid free-writing, recording each one on individual sticky notes. All responses get posted on the board.

b. **Sprint 2, Assumption:** Next, consider your personal **assumptions** about your remote teammate's culture (what others think, say, or believe to be true about that culture, not necessarily based on facts). List as many assumptions as possible through rapid free-writing, recording each one on individual sticky notes. All responses get posted on the board.

c. **Sprint 3, Opinion:** Consider your personal **opinions** about your remote teammate's culture (what you think, believe, or feel). As with assumptions, it might be easier if you think about what other people's opinions might be. List as many opinions as possible through rapid free-writing, recording each one on individual sticky notes. All responses get posted on the board.

4. **Discuss:** With local colleagues, take some time to observe the collection of sticky note responses within each category (facts, assumptions, opinions). Use the following questions to guide discussion.

DISCUSSION GUIDE

- Are there things lumped in with your facts that are not actually facts? If so, how would you define these items?
- Are the assumptions and opinions based on your personal experiences and beliefs or not? Do any of these make you feel uncomfortable? Which ones? Why?
- Considering each category (fact, assumption, opinion):
  - Which was hardest for you to write, and why?
  - Which generated the most responses from the group? Why?
- How has this activity uncovered potential areas of unconscious bias that you may not have been aware of previously for yourself or your local colleagues?

b. Activity

Affinity Diagram

Following the brainstorming exercise, once all responses have been posted on a vertical surface in the classroom, diagramming is an important next step. Together, you will create an *affinity diagram* or visual clusters of similar items. This process helps designers understand and gain insights from large amounts of qualitative data by summarizing recurring themes. Working with local colleagues, look for patterns among the sticky notes and physically move similar responses into clusters. Then, write a descriptive title for each cluster. To use the outcomes of this activity to help you prepare for contact with your remote teammates, see Deep Dive, 2.6.

→ **People:** Local colleagues
→ **Duration:** 1 hour
→ **Technology:** Camera or another photographic device for documentation
→ **Other resources:** Sticky notes or small slips of paper from Belief Brainstorm (activity 2.3a); markers; tape; whiteboard, wall, or another vertical surface on which to post.

Phase 1: With local colleagues

1. **Assess:** After discussing each category (facts, assumptions, opinions), take a look at all of the contributions and look for patterns.
2. **Sort:** Begin to pick up and move individual sticky notes around to put similar items together into clusters.
3. **Review:** Communicate with local colleagues to ensure all categories are distinct and do not repeat (for example, two separate clusters of food-related notes).
4. **Label:** Create a label for each category using a sticky note/marker in a different color (or circle/underline to clearly indicate the title).
5. **Select:** Circle the clusters containing topics that might lead to interesting cultural questions to ask your remote teammates.
6. **Document:** Take photos and/or detailed notes of the final clusters and save these for future use and discussion.
7. **Discuss:** Take some time to observe the affinity diagram with your local colleagues. Use the following guide for discussion.

DISCUSSION GUIDE

• Review the affinity clusters. Which could you learn more about on your own?
• Which of the affinity clusters contain interesting topics for cultural questions that you cannot answer on your own?
• What do you want to ask the other culture now that you have completed this activity?
• Which topics would you feel most afraid to address with your remote teammates? Why?
• What do you think your remote teammates might say about your culture?

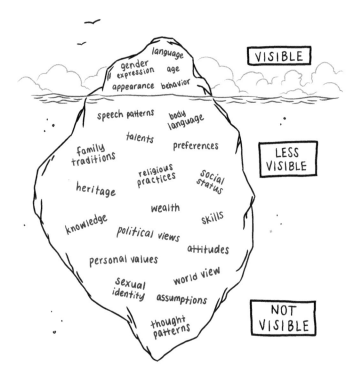

2.4

Personal & Group Icebergs:
Diagramming cultural characteristics

Probably the most famous iceberg is the one that sank the Titanic. The ship seemed fit to navigate the Atlantic's iceberg-ridden waters, but, ultimately, she was doomed by her collision with the massive ice mountain hidden beneath the surface of the water. In fact, that is why we often describe a small part of a much larger problem as "just the tip of the iceberg." The enormity and complexity of the problem—like the iceberg's mass—is invisible, hidden beneath the surface.

So it is too with culture and intercultural relationships; the characteristics that compose the enormity and complexity of any given culture are not necessarily visible to outsiders. Thus, exploring beneath the surface to become aware of those characteristics plays an important role in keeping intercultural relationships afloat. Indeed, to help explain the aspects of culture that—like the iceberg—can be hidden or visible, many researchers have aimed to understand the relationship between implicit and explicit cultural values.

The Iceberg Model: Implicit and explicit cultural characteristics

Noteworthy among this research is the Iceberg Model, a diagram created by American anthropologist Edward T. Hall (1976) and later refined from a workplace perspective by management and organization experts Cecil H. Bell Jr. and Wendell L. French. Through the visual of the iceberg, these models show which types of cultural characteristics are often visible, or *explicit* (e.g., physical or socially manifested values, such as fashion and music) and which tend to be invisible, or *implicit* (e.g., characteristics that may not be apparent, such as world-views, social skills, or company values). In the Iceberg Model, implicit cultural values are depicted as lying beneath a "surface of water" (Hall 1976; French and Bell 1995).

Diagramming cultural characteristics

In our experience, using the Iceberg Model as the basis for diagramming personal and group views of cultural characteristics helps individuals to address the anxiety they often feel when embarking on intercultural collaborations. This activity can tie into discussions with your local colleagues of implicit and socially manifested characteristics, as well as the biases and stereotypes these characteristics sometimes bring with them. Many times, our assumptions, facts, and opinions about people or cultures are above-the-surface characteristics. Understanding where these characteristics fall relative to the cultural Iceberg Model provides a useful opportunity to formulate questions for your future remote teammates (see Deep Dive, 2.6a). After creating Personal Icebergs, the recommended follow-up activity is to work to create a Group Iceberg.

Visual thinking through diagramming

In visual communication and information design, *diagrams* are representations of different types of information that generally rely on symbols or other visualization techniques. *Diagramming* is not just the process of creating one of these types of visual representations, but it is also a form of visual thinking. Diagrams serve a number of functions. They can communicate relationships between concepts or between data points. Diagrams also show how things work, distilling complex ideas into simpler parts, such as the components that constitute a service or experience (e.g., all of the analog, digital, and human aspects of something like an app-based ride-sharing service). Instructional representations of objects or structures are another type of diagram; examples range from the emergency exit route in a large building to an image in a user's manual with notes intended to teach a new driver how to use buttons attached to the steering wheel.

Visual metaphors in diagrams

Creating a diagram requires many levels of thinking and analysis. How components are depicted and where they are placed affects their ability to convey relevant information or ideas. To accomplish this task, communication designers sometimes employ *visual metaphors*. Just like their verbal relatives, visual metaphors serve to create associations between different things in order to rein-force a particular idea. The Iceberg Model is a visual metaphor that draws simi-larities between the abstract idea that there are visible and unseen characteristics of culture and the concrete idea that there are visible and unseen aspects of an iceberg. These associations reinforce the idea that there is always more to culture than we are able to see "above the surface."

Personal Iceberg

Diagramming personal ideas of cultural characteristics onto the Iceberg Model offers you an opportunity to examine your cultural background in relation to what is seen above or below the surface. It is very important to work as an individual before combining ideas with your local colleagues. When each person initially generates a Personal Iceberg diagram based on their own per-spectives, the later Group Iceberg often embodies more variety and cultural richness. This is because, during the Group Iceberg, you can use your Personal Iceberg as a Thought Object to bring your own opinions, ideas, and values into the discussion rather than simply going along with your local colleagues' contributions.

Group Iceberg

Following the Personal Iceberg activity (2.4a), convene with local colleagues to combine personal diagrams into one Group Iceberg (2.4b), then discuss the outcomes. Don't just dump the individual maps together! As the Group Iceberg forms, each person should take time to think about where to place each attribute while also taking into account the views of other local colleagues. Along with placement, carefully consider how characteristics relate to each other. When you discover similar characteristics, clump them together. After first thinking through these characteristics individually, the group dynamics of this activity require care as well in order to encourage contributions from local colleagues who prefer to work alone or who tend to fade into the background of larger group activities.

Benefits & outcomes

- Work individually (2.4a) and as a group (2.4b)
- Think visually about implicit and explicit cultural values
- Diagram implicit and socially manifested values
- Understand which values are especially important to you
- Uncover and consider the significance of hidden cultural factors

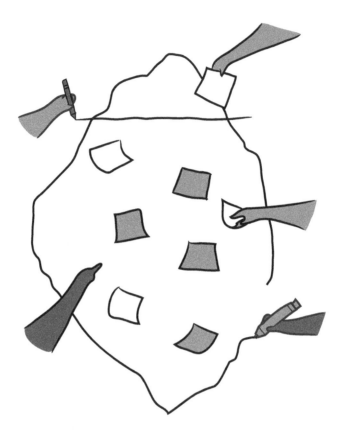

a. Activity

Personal Iceberg

Culture is made of many characteristics that lie below the surface. Reflect on your own culture by carefully diagraming the implicit and socially manifested characteristics and mapping them both above and below the surface. It is often easiest to think of characteristics that appear above the surface. Allow yourself to think visually as you diagram and consider which characteristics are especially important to you. In all likelihood, these characteristics will be somewhat different from those suggested by your local colleagues. Learning about these similarities and differences is a fascinating aspect of the next phase where you and your local colleagues will map your individual diagrams together into one larger Iceberg Model. This process is also a useful basis for discussion once you connect with your remote teammates, enabling you all to come up with meaningful questions for each other (see Deep Dive, 2.6a).

→ **People:** Individual
→ **Duration:** 1 hour
→ **Resources:** Paper, pens/pencils, markers/highlighters, whiteboard or another vertical surface

---

Tips

- **Think about culture:** Keep in mind that, unlike actual icebergs, culture is not a specific or defined physical object. It is always open to interpretation and can mean different things to different people. Learning to respect and value differences, as well as to see commonalities, is a critical component of this activity. The aim in this case is not to find a uniform voice but, instead, to recognize the value of all contributions.
- **Value difference:** Often our first instinct is to find similarities rather than to value differences. Similarity feels safer, so it is a natural starting point. While finding similarities and forging empathetic connections is an admirable way to see each other as similar human beings on this shared planet, celebrating our differences and valuing other perspectives is a true sign of intercultural learning and growth.

Working individually

1. **Read:** Prior to starting this activity, read the previous discussion about the Iceberg Model.
2. **Brainstorm:** Reflect on your own culture and what unique characteristics you think define it. Using the rapid brainstorming approach you followed with the Belief Brainstorm (2.3a), quickly identify at least 20 characteristics about your own culture. Come up with more if you can!
3. **Draw:** Create your own blank iceberg drawing on a piece of paper using the illustration as a reference.
4. **Diagram:** Consider which characteristics from your brainstorm lie above or below the surface and map them onto the blank iceberg drawing. When placing characteristics, think carefully about which should be placed above the surface of the water and which should be placed below the water line. Remember that visible characteristics are physically or socially manifested "above the surface" (e.g., fashion, food, music), whereas implicit characteristics (e.g., superstitions, work ethic, education) remain concealed "under the surface."
5. **Revisit Teamthink Constellation:** Reflecting on your selections for the second dimension, **Understand Core Beliefs**, which of the cultural characteristics on your Personal Iceberg could be described as individual or collective, and why? How do these relate to your own inclinations? Are there items that do not fit into either of these categories?

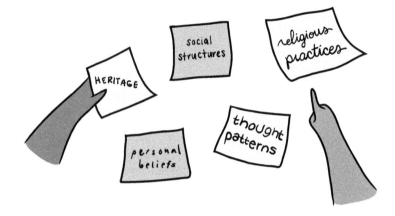

b. Activity

Group Iceberg

After completing the Personal Iceberg, this activity asks individuals to bring their personal diagrams into a Group Iceberg Model for larger discussion with local colleagues. As the characteristics come together in one iceberg, the learning really begins! You will find there is far more diversity, depth, and variety represented when ideas come together, compared to the diagram you created alone. Some commonalities across diagrams are likely, and you may find it useful to do some clustering or affinity diagramming on top of the Group Iceberg in cases of very similar or overlapping ideas. The process may also involve negotiation around placement and can provide an opportunity for local colleagues to discuss unique cultural characteristics that may appear unfamiliar to some members.

→ **People:** Local colleagues
→ **Duration:** 1 hour
→ **Resources:** Markers/highlighters, whiteboard or another vertical surface, sticky notes or individual pieces of paper, and tape

---

Tips

- **Avoid groupthink:** Rushing into the Group Iceberg prior to completing the Personal Iceberg can minimize your learning opportunities because individuals working in a group tend toward groupthink and agreement. There is plentiful diversity among individuals, even within a group of local colleagues living in the same culture.
- **Venture deeper:** Beware of lingering in your comfort zone. Is the group spending too much time negotiating and talking about things "above the surface?" Encourage deeper discussion by volunteering to talk about an item you contributed "beneath the surface."

Generate Group Iceberg

1. **Prepare:** Complete the Personal Iceberg (2.4a) prior to starting this activity.
2. **Review:** Look back at the Iceberg Model (2.4)
3. **Draw:** Draw a large iceberg shape on a whiteboard or large piece of paper. Remember to include the water line to indicate that there is a smaller portion of the iceberg above the surface and a larger portion below the surface. This iceberg will be the place where each individual will share their contributions.
4. **Present:** Open a dialogue about the list of characteristics that each person found interesting by presenting the Personal Icebergs. Decide if the characteristic should be placed above or below the surface on the Group Iceberg. Keep in mind that it is not necessary to agree on each attribute that is presented. Instead, discuss the *placement* of those characteristics. Does each characteristic belong above or below the surface?
5. **Be open:** It is important to value all ideas! Remember that your local colleagues may be bringing different backgrounds and views to the activity and these perspectives add value to the Group Iceberg. Be careful not to filter out conflicting viewpoints, as these represent your group's diverse perspectives.
6. **Transcribe:** Working with your local colleagues, transfer each set of characteristics to sticky notes or individual pieces of paper, making sure to keep track of whether you will place each note above or below the surface.
7. **Post:** Discuss the placement of each cultural characteristic and come to a decision about whether it belongs above or below the surface. Does the characteristic better reflect socially manifested values or implicit cultural values? Stick the characteristics to the appropriate place on the Group Iceberg Model to create a visual representation of everyone's contributions.
8. **Label:** If the group discovers related or similar characteristics when combining Personal Icebergs, use affinity diagramming to cluster these ideas together to avoid repetition across the shared diagram. Be sure to come up with a representative label for each cluster.
9. **Document:** After creating the Group Iceberg Model, document it for later review or discussion as the collaborative process moves forward.
10. **Discuss:** Take some time to discuss what you have learned using the following discussion prompts with local colleagues.

DISCUSSION GUIDE

- How did the group activity expand your thinking about your own culture and what you think lies above and below the surface?
- In what ways did you expand your thinking about culture overall and your impressions of your own culture's characteristics?
- Were there any conflicting viewpoints generated during the discussion that you found interesting or shed light on a broader view of your culture?

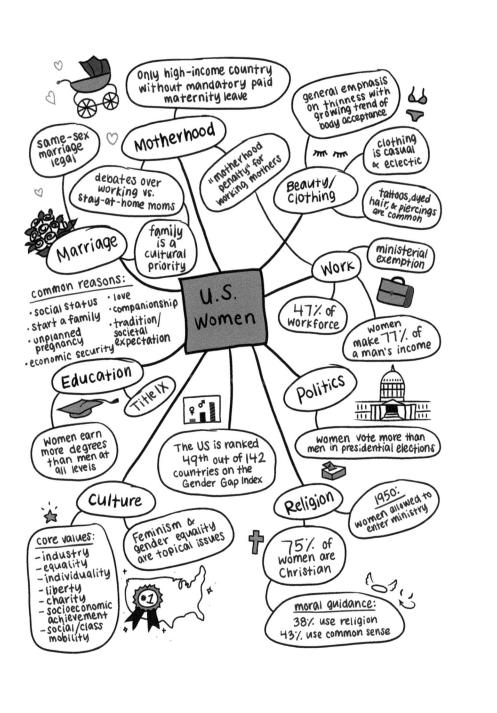

Only high-income country without mandatory paid maternity leave

Motherhood

same-sex marriage legal

debates over working vs. stay-at-home moms

"motherhood penalty" for working mothers

Marriage

family is a cultural priority

common reasons:
- social status
- start a family
- unplanned pregnancy
- economic security
- love
- companionship
- tradition/societal expectation

general emphasis on thinness with growing trend of body acceptance

clothing is casual & eclectic

Beauty/Clothing

tattoos, dyed hair, & piercings are common

Work

ministerial exemption

47% of workforce

women make 77% of a man's income

U.S. Women

Education

Title IX

Women earn more degrees than men at all levels

The US is ranked 49th out of 142 countries on the Gender Gap Index

Politics

women vote more than men in presidential elections

Culture

Feminism & gender equality are topical issues

core values:
- industry
- equality
- individuality
- liberty
- charity
- socioeconomic achievement
- social/class mobility

#1

Religion

1950: women allowed to enter ministry

75% of women are Christian

moral guidance:
38% use religion
43% use common sense

2.5

Comparative Impression Maps: Visualizing an issue across cultures

Comparison is a useful tool for learning more about a topic. People can be quick to point out inequities, biases, and flaws in other cultures before critically examining their own. This activity pushes against natural tendencies of cultural superiority by revealing how an idea or issue, such as gender inequality, can be interpreted in two different cultures. Deeply delving into a topic can give one the impression of learning a great deal about something. However, taking the opportunity to *compare* information, findings, and ideas can offer new insights and help mitigate confirmation bias by ensuring the consideration of multiple perspectives. Creating a set of Comparative Impression Maps provides an opportunity to dig deeper into one particular idea or topic by thinking further about an idea and related associations.

Mind-mapping

Comparative Impression Maps are based on an approach to graphical representation called *mind mapping*, a visualization technique that serves to loosely organize free-form ideas based on relationships and associations. Mind mapping usually starts by writing one word or phrase in the center of the map and circling it. Next, a line is drawn from the circled words to write a related word, phrase, or—in the case of Creative Impression Maps—a related image. This process continues until the paper or board is filled with a large "web" of words and ideas.

Comparing impressions through visuals

For this activity, you will create two culturally distinct maps using the same starting point. Unlike a typical mind map that explores one idea in a single cultural context, this variation of mind-mapping challenges you to create two different maps based on the same starting point. One map will be based on how you understand this topic and your own cultural perspective. The other map will be based on how you think this topic plays out in your remote teammate's culture.

By incorporating small sketches and thinking visually, rather than simply employing words or phrases usually associated with typical mind-mapping, the Comparative Impression Map activity will engage multiple channels in your brain and help you frame your thinking in ways that words alone might not be able to effectively describe. In this way, Comparative Impression Maps enable individuals to identify a specific topic from their Belief Brainstorm (2.3) and then think about it more deeply by visually depicting their own related ideas, associations, insights, and assumptions from multiple cultural perspectives.

Cross-cultural learning

These Comparative Impression Maps are specifically *cross-cultural*, meaning that this activity invites you to evaluate and compare your outcomes based on your view of your culture and your remote teammate's culture. Cross-cultural is not the same as *intercultural*, a word we have already used a lot, which refers to bringing two different cultures together. The comparison and evaluation will clarify your preexisting sense of differences (and similarities) as well as give you an idea of gaps in your knowledge that could provide further opportunities for individual research and catalyze conversations with your teammate(s).

Benefits & outcomes

- Think through cultural questions and concepts in multidimensional ways
- Promote lateral thinking through free-association
- Address unconscious biases that surface
- Express ideas visually by providing a mental snapshot of a particular idea
- Promote future clarifying conversations between remote teammates
- Recognize the difference between knowledge and assumption

Activity

Comparative Impression Maps

This activity engages you in creating a more visual version of a *mind map* to explore how your impressions of a selected topic differ between your home culture and remote teammates' culture. Recall that a mind map is a web of words, associations, memories, and images that explores a topic and all of its various relationships and threads. In this activity, you will create Comparative Mind Maps to explore a topic of interest that arose during the Belief Brainstorm activity (2.3). Each teammate will make two maps comparing their written and visual impressions of the topic from two different perspectives.

→ **People:** Individual/local colleagues
→ **Duration:** 1 hour
→ **Other resources:** Paper, pens/pencils, markers/highlighters, paper, whiteboard or another vertical surface

---

Tips

- **Individual diagram:** By working alone before working together, individuals have an opportunity to carefully consider their own specific set of cultural values. Working alone also enables individuals to do some introspection and exploration beneath the surface more comfortably, thus enriching the later group experience.

(Continued)

- **Step back:** After completing and documenting the first draft of your maps, taking a moment to think about each item and whether it represents a fact, opinion, or assumption is a great way to figure out where you might benefit from doing some additional research. Looking at the big picture, identify which aspects of the maps are based on assumptions or opinions.
- **Conduct research:** As you start to consult reliable resources, you will be able to fill in those missing details to help make your maps more comprehensive. You will also have begun to collect background material that you can use to develop questions for your remote teammates (see Group Iceberg 2.4b).
- **Make time to talk:** Although people might need a break or time to process what they experienced while creating the maps, it is essential to discuss what you learned from the process in order for the activity to be most effective.

Create two maps

Phase 1: Working individually

1. **Analyze:** Review the facts, assumptions, and opinions collected in the Belief Brainstorm & Diagram (2.3a and 2.3b). Use affinity diagramming to bring together similar ideas. Select three meaningful example topics (try to pick one from each category—fact, assumption, opinion—for a total of three) that you find interesting or relatable.
2. **Examine:** Choose one of these examples as a starting point for the mind map. Ask yourself: *Where did you learn this? Who says this? What aspects of the culture reinforce this idea? Why do you think people feel this way?*
3. **Map:** Create TWO comparative mind maps based on ONE of your selected topics. Your level of artistic skill is not relevant; any degree of sketching or drawing will add more personality to the map.
   a. Consider how this topic appears **in your home culture** and its various aspects and impacts, from political agendas and personal relationships to individual choices.
   b. Create a second mind-map of how this topic **might show up in your teammate's culture,** paying attention to the ways that media and other external sources may have influenced your thinking on this topic.

Self-reflection

Phase 2: Working individually

4. **Document and reflect:** Take a photo of each mind map. Then, carefully examine each map. Identify gaps in your knowledge and mark items that

reflect assumptions or opinions. Ongoing self-reflection prior to communication with your remote teammates is very important. Continue to confront your assumptions and opinions—and question your biases—before making contact with your remote teammates. Use the following Discussion Guide to jump-start your self-reflection process and help you identify gaps.

DISCUSSION GUIDE

- What knowledge gaps did you identify in your two maps?
- Why do you think these gaps exist?
- How will you go about filling in your knowledge gaps with facts?
- Which of these gaps would you like to learn more about from your remote teammates?

Knowledge gaps

Phase 3: Working individually

5. **Research:** Based on the knowledge gaps you identified, do some research (online, at the library, from firsthand sources, etc.) to try to fill in some of the blanks and update your assumptions, opinions, or questions with actual facts. Remember to include sketches or other visualizations among the written words.
6. **Revise:** Add to and edit your original mind maps based on your new information. You do not need to re-create your maps from scratch, just build on what you already have. Document your updated maps once you are finished.

Discuss

Phase 4: With local colleagues

7. **Discuss:** Have a conversation with your local colleagues about your experience in creating the maps. This conversation could occur immediately after the activity, or even a few days later, after people have had time to update their maps and process their thoughts. Keep in mind that it will naturally take everyone time to reflect upon and work through the insights uncovered by the Comparative Impression Maps.

DISCUSSION GUIDE

- What areas of each map are based on facts versus opinions or assumptions?
- How did you address the knowledge gaps in your maps, and how did you solve this? What were your information sources? What was the most interesting thing you learned while researching the knowledge gaps in your maps?
- What is one thing you learned from your research that changed one of the topics on your map in some way?
- In what ways did each map change after additional research and revision?

2.6

Deep Dive:
Creating structured dialogue to go beneath the surface

In our earlier collaborations, teammates were restricted by their fear of offending each other. As a result, their conversations rarely dared to venture toward topics like social structures, gender bias, or politics. However, many teammates want to know how their culture is perceived by their teammates' culture, or about the differences between their cultures. Left unanswered, these lingering questions or unchecked assumptions can make it challenging for teammates to build trust and later bond on a more personal level to produce the most effective work.

Intentional questions

These challenges inspired the Deep Dive, an activity that dramatically changed the tenor of teammates' conversations. Structured dialogues at the start of a collaboration set the stage for more complex and nuanced discussions between teammates. The activities in this chapter build to the Deep Dive. As a starting point for dialogue, the Deep Dive prepares remote teammates to formulate, share, and respond to *intentional questions*, the type of sensitive cultural questions that can lead to more in-depth discussions. Since we began implementing this activity, questions generated by the Deep Dive now prompt teams to discuss topics such as civil rights, gender equality, safety, worldliness, and religion. Because these kinds of conversations often bring up tough topics, such as cultural stereotypes, the structure of this activity relieves some of the stress involved in real-time conversations.

Real-life examples

Depending on the nature and duration of your collaboration, you might choose to engage in the Deep Dive by exchanging questions and answers via thoughtfully composed emails. The following are real-life examples of one intercultural team's questions with excerpted responses from teammates located in Qatar and in the United States. These examples were selected from many question-answer exchanges, several of which turned into more in-depth real-time discussions via videoconference.

In context: Example questions

On social structures

- **Question from US teammate:** Are social structures strict and/or binding? (i.e., How close do families remain, do the elderly live with their children/grandchildren? Are friendships generally limited to one gender?)
- **Combined answer from three Qatar teammates:** Family is a really important part of our culture. It differs from family to family whether they are strict or not. Most were strict in the past, but families have become more flexible. Most remain in close relationship. Many elders live with their grandchildren; even if they live in a separate house, they stay in contact. Also, family members visit elders weekly. Friendships are within the same gender. The other gender is preferred as a colleague relationship. So, working (job, projects, educational work, etc.) with the other gender is acceptable.

On worldliness

- **Question from Qatar teammate:** Are people in America generally not aware of the Middle East and/or Qatar? Is it true that not many people know where Qatar is and think that we live in a desert, in tents (houses), and use camels as the mode of transport?
- **Answer from US teammate:** I personally don't know much about Qatar, and I don't think many other Americans do either. I wouldn't say most Americans go as far as thinking about living conditions in the Middle East. Many just consume what the media reports.

Essential steps for building rapport

Creating questions is an essential step toward *structured dialogue*, an effective strategy for building rapport in intercultural teams. Structured dialogue creates the expectation that teammates on both sides will ask and respond respectfully and thoughtfully to intentional questions. Creating a structured opportunity to explore cultural curiosity helps defuse tension and worry. Teammates begin to push past stereotypes and assumptions to see each other as unique people.

Writing intentional questions through iteration

As with many other activities in this book, we recommend that you work through ideas and practice sample questions with your local team first using an iterative process. In design, *iteration* means that you work on refining an idea in a cycle. This involves creating an initial *prototype* (a way to physically or visually show your idea), testing it, analyzing the feedback gained from testing it, and editing or improving the idea in order to test it again. The iterative process involved in developing intentional "prototype" questions for your teammate allows you time for critical thinking, revisions, and/or rephrasing questions before you introduce them into the conversation with your intercultural teammates.

Choose words with care

Connecting with a teammate in an online space may give the impression that you are working in a more fluid or open environment. Be attentive that this sense of fluidity does not lead to carelessness in your language choices. Especially in the early stages, the relationship you are building is fragile. Treat it as such, and be aware of how the virtual environment affects this sense of fragility. At the same time, teammates should continually remind themselves that they are each speaking from a personal perspective and not on behalf of an entire nation or culture.

Opportunities for ongoing dialogue

Remote teammates should expect to continue asking each other a multitude of questions throughout the collaboration, whether related to the project at hand or part of a continued effort to delve into questions of culture, stereotypes, and biases. There are many ways to continue your conversation and correspondence beyond the initial dialogue generated by the intentional questions. The Fourth Space (1.5b), email, and even mobile chat can offer opportunities to build trust and delve deeper into the topics that interest the team.

Benefits & outcomes

- Compose substantive questions to encourage rich dialogue
- Realize that preparing for meaningful dialogue is a two-way street
- Transform amusing assumptions and mental images into icebreakers
- Converse at a more profound and meaningful level
- Create opportunities to exchange personal perspectives

a. Activity

Deep Dive

The Deep Dive incorporates an *iterative* process to refine the idea in a cycle that involves creating an initial *prototype* by testing it, analyzing the feedback gained from testing it, and editing or improving the idea in order to test it again. Your first set of draft questions is essentially your prototype. Asking the questions to your local colleagues enables you to test your first iterations of them before asking these questions of your remote teammates. Thinking about how your local colleagues reacted to your questions and incorporating any suggestions to improve or change them is the analysis stage. You are refining questions through editing and rewriting. You could engage in this process several times with your local colleagues in order to test and improve your draft questions before finalizing them to send to your remote teammates.

➜ **People:** Local colleagues/individual
➜ **Duration:** 30 minutes
➜ **Technology:** Camera, projector, videoconferencing software
➜ **Low-bandwidth version:** Black & white copies of the Iceberg template, pen/pencil to fill in categories in the appropriate places
➜ **Other resources:** Paper, sticky notes, markers, whiteboard, projection screen

---

Tips

- **Answer:** When answering questions, try to elaborate beyond simply "yes" or "no" responses. Provide details about your reasons for thinking a certain way. To generate a more detailed response, challenge yourself to answer the "why" behind an idea, even if you were not asked to do so.
- **Suspend Judgment:** When your teammate responds to a question, try to *suspend judgment* by withholding automatic conclusions; accept their contributions at face value and do not bring your own internal commentary into what they are saying.
- **Ask:** Challenge yourself to ask more questions during a conversation with the goal of learning about someone else's life, experiences, and unique insights. A focus on asking (rather than telling) is an opportunity to consider your own personal biases, values, and build cultural sensitivity.
- **Lag-Time:** In a virtual discussion, you may experience a lag in image or audio transmission. Sometimes the delay of bandwidth can result in

---

(Continued)

someone feeling as though they are getting cut-off in a conversation or do not have a chance to interject in a conversation. Pausing can be a useful way to enable each person to listen and to analyze carefully. Take your time with speaking and responding so as to use the potential pitfalls of the medium to your advantage.

Creating questions

Phase 1: Working individually

1. **Reflect:** Think back to your Group Iceberg (2.4b) and the groups of sticky notes placed "beneath the surface," as well as any areas you found most interesting in your Comparative Impression Maps (2.5).
2. **Narrow:** Identify three to five keywords or sticky notes that interest you and that have the potential for generating interesting cultural questions. Your choices should provide an opportunity to gain firsthand insight into your teammate's culture through dialogue. If you are drawing ideas from the Iceberg, keep in mind that you can choose from any of the team's contributions; you do not need to select your own. From the topics uncovered through the Iceberg or Comparative Impression Maps, consider what you already know, if anything. It is fine (and expected!) to choose topics you know nothing about.
3. **Document:** Photograph your selections from your Group Iceberg and/or Comparative Impression Maps for later use. You will share these photos with your teammate to help them understand what prompted your line of questions.
4. **Think & Write:** Take some time to think about your selections, considering how you can turn them into questions. You may wish to do some online research on your chosen topics. Keep in mind that if you can easily find answers online, the subject might not make for a compelling conversation. Draft three to five cultural questions for your remote teammates based on your selections. Avoid questions that can be answered with a simple "yes" or "no." You will also want to create questions that invite opportunities for follow-up questions; this can be a way to deepen the conversation and get to know each other better.

Phase 2: With local colleagues/individual

5. **Review:** Test your questions with your local colleagues, giving each other feedback on the way questions are written and phrased. If asking a particular question makes you feel uncomfortable, work together to consider ways that it could be rewritten, while still addressing the same topic.

6. **Revise & Update:** Based on feedback, make edits to your questions.
7. **Discuss:** Now that you have formulated your questions, take some time to discuss your overarching ideas and thoughts with local colleagues. Use the following guide for discussion.

DISCUSSION GUIDE

- How do you feel knowing that your remote teammates are also participating in these activities and will reciprocate with cultural questions for you?
- Did you learn something unexpected or surprising about yourself in the process?
- What question(s) are you most eager to ask? Why?
- Which questions or topics make you curious yet uncomfortable?
- How can we phrase questions to be culturally sensitive?

Exchange

Phase 3: With remote teammates

8. **Exchange:** Share questions with your remote teammates in your Fourth Space or via email first, so that everyone can preview them and consider their responses. Post the original photographs of the selected sticky notes along with questions you have developed. Your remote teammates will reciprocate.
9. **Choose tools:** Figure out which communication tools will work best for your team. Consider a hybrid approach where you first exchange and reply to questions via email, then follow up with a conversation via video chat. Regardless of the format, this is a great opportunity to use your prepared questions from Phase 1 as a starting point for understanding your teammates' cultural perspectives.
10. **First introductions:** Introduce yourself to your remote teammates with some basic conversational questions. Exchanging small talk can be a common starting point toward understanding each other.
11. **Challenge your tendencies:** If you are participating in a video chat, take care with your communication habits (1.5, 5.1). If your tendency is to talk a lot, challenge yourself to take your time and really listen to what your teammate has to say. On the other hand, for quieter types, challenge yourself to speak up. Real-time discussion also punctuates responses with gestures, facial expressions, and tone of voice. These important details humanize the exchange by making responses more engaging, and invite the possibility of follow-up questions or comments.
12. **Suggested structure:** The structure of the intentional question-answer session enables teammates to share cultural insights from their own individual perspectives.

    a.   After introductions, one teammate asks a question and allows time for the other teammates to pause and consider a response.

    b.   In responding to the question, think first about whether or not you have a personal story (or something that has happened to someone you know) that you could share as an example in your response to the question.

    c.   If you do not have a specific story to share, think about how to answer the question based on what you know based on your geographic location and unique perspective. If you do not have personal experience in the area being discussed, explain to your teammate that your response is based on observations, impressions, or opinions.

    d.   In either case, consider that your remote teammates may need explanations about certain aspects of the cultural context of your response.

    e.   The respondent should also consider how their specific response to the question connects back to their personal values or to broader cultural values. Also explain these connections to the teammate who asked the question.

    f.   Leave time for follow-up questions or additional dialogue. Perhaps there are multiple positions to consider on an issue. Maybe your remote teammates have more questions about some of the culturally specific details within your response.

    g.   When discussion on a particular question winds down, switch roles. The respondent asks the next question.

13. **Discuss:** Use the following guides for discussion and follow-up questions.

DISCUSSION GUIDE

Ask remote teammates:
- What is your favorite food? (Everyone loves to talk about food.)
- What hobbies do you enjoy?
- What are some of your interests (outside of this specific topic/project area)?
- What are you working on right now that excites you?
- Have you visited places outside of your hometown? If so, what is your favorite place to visit?

Follow-up question starters:
- That's so interesting! Please tell me more about....
- Why do you think that is?
- What led you to think this way?
- What did you enjoy most about....?
- What did you enjoy least about...?
- What would you do if... (hypothetical scenario based on a teammate's response)?
- Where does this idea come from? Is it your own idea, or does it have social or cultural roots?

b. Activity

Deeper Dive—share icebergs & impression maps

This advanced step is for those who are planning to work together over a longer period of time and/or aiming for a deeper cultural learning exchange. Complete activities 2.4 and 2.5 prior to the Deeper Dive.

Phase 1: Working individually

1. **Send/Receive:** Exchange your Thought Objects—the completed Group Iceberg (2.4b) and Comparative Impression Maps (2.5)—to your remote teammate via email or Fourth Space.
2. **Analyze:** When you receive your teammate's Thought Objects, look through the characteristics that appear above and below the surface, thinking about how your personal assumptions or opinions might have originally affected your beliefs about the other culture.
3. **Identify gaps:** Take the time to read through the Thought Objects (your own and teammates') in a sensitive way. Don't put pressure on yourself to know all the answers. This activity is about identifying and addressing gaps. It helps illuminate possible unconscious biases and can help you address some of your blind spots by updating your own Thought Objects with information from your teammates.

Planning your Deeper Dive

Phase 2: With local colleagues

4. **Analyze:** With your local colleagues, discuss areas in the Thought Objects that you find interesting or do not understand. What differences or similarities do you see between the ones you created and what your teammates shared?
5. **Create questions:** During the group discussion, help each other generate three to five questions to ask your remote teammates based on their Thought Objects. Expanding upon your Deep Dive, focus on writing "beneath the surface" questions to help you get to know each other.
6. **Discuss:** Use the following guide to discuss your experience comparing and contrasting the Thought Objects.

DISCUSSION GUIDE

- In looking at your remote teammates' Thought Objects, do they help fill any additional gaps in your own Thought Objects?
- Which of your own cultural characteristics are unlikely to appear on the Thought Objects from your remote teammates? Why?
- Now that you have exchanged Thought Objects and initial Deep Dive questions with your remote teammates, what would you most like to ask them?
- What are your questions for your remote teammates? How can these be improved for depth and cultural sensitivity?

Learning from afar

Phase 3: With remote teammates

7. **Convene & Converse:** Meet with your remote team to ask and answer the questions you have prepared for each other. Use the following guide for discussion.

DISCUSSION GUIDE

- What did the comparison of Thought Objects reveal that you might not have discovered otherwise?
- What similarities did you notice between various exchanged Thought Objects? Did any similar ideas appear in them?
- What are some of the differences between the Thought Objects, and what do you think these reveal about each culture?
- How did this activity help you to self-reflect about your own culture?
- How did this process (visualization, reflection, and revision) change your perception of the topic overall?
- What is the difference between what you can learn from online resources and what you would like to learn more about regarding a topic from someone based on their lived experience in a particular culture?

References

Banaji, Mahzarin. 2018. Mahzarin Banaji on Implicit Bias Interview by David Edmonds. www.socialsciencespace.com/2018/08/mahzarin-banaji-on-implicit-bias/.

Banaji, Mahzarin and Anthony Greenwald. 2013. *Blindspot: Hidden Biases of Good People.* New York: Delacorte Press.

Chaffee, John. 2014. *Thinking Critically.* 11th ed. Boston, MA: Cengage Learning.

De Beauvoir, Simone. 1953. *The Second Sex.* Translated by Howard Madison Parshley. New York: Vintage Books.

French, Wendell L., and Cecil Bell. 1995. *Organization Development: Behavioral Science Interventions for Organization Improvement.* 5th ed. Englewood Cliffs, NJ: Prentice Hall.

Greenwald, Anthony G., and Mahzarin R. Banaji. 1995. "Implicit Social Cognition: Attitudes, Self-Esteem, and Stereotypes." *Psychological Review* 102 (1): 4–27. doi:10. 1037/0033-295X.102.1.4.

Greenwald, Anthony G., Debbie E. McGhee, and Jordan L. Schwartz. 1998. "Measuring Individual Differences in Implicit Cognition: The Implicit Association Test." *Journal of Personality and Social Psychology* 74 (6): 1464–80.

Hall, Edward Twitchell. 1976. *Beyond Culture.* New York: Anchor Books.

Kohlberg, Lawrence. 1964. "Development of Moral Character and Moral Ideology." *Review of Child Development Research* 1: 381–431.

United States Department of Justice. 2016. "FAQs on Implicit Bias." Office of Public Affairs. www.justice.gov/opa/file/871121/download.

Zhang, Yuning. 2017. "Stereotyping and Communication." In *Intercultural Communication,* edited by Ling Chen. Boston: Walter de Gruyter GmbH & Co KG: 529–562.

3

ESTABLISH TRUST

Storytelling using rich and lean media

Objective ⟵————————————⟶ Subjective

DIMENSION 3: Establish Trust

We recognize and establish trust and accountability in different ways.

Whether your team chooses to do one or many, this chapter's storytelling activities provide fun ways to learn about each other through Thought and Process Objects that help to develop greater trust.

Chapter 3 introduces several terms and theories that describe how various characteristics of media (e.g., synchrony, richness, and social presence) impact how stories are transmitted, received, and interpreted by audiences. Through various forms of visual storytelling, you will learn to believe and trust your teammates while cultivating their belief and trust in you. Building a personal connection will help as you negotiate cultural differences and can inject empathy into situations that might otherwise cause conflict. Learning about each other on a personal level also improves the quality and frequency of communication between teammates. In turn, enhanced communication often leads to more creative and in-depth project outcomes.

SUBSTANTIATED: I demonstrate or recognize trust through specific actions. I hold people accountable to what they say they will do and take things at face value. I find written agreements to be helpful for ensuring accountability.	**RELATIONAL:** I demonstrate or recognize trust through emotion and intuition. My sense of others' accountability is based on my gut feeling about them and the history of our interpersonal relationships.

3.1

Storytelling using rich and lean media

Connecting audiences to diverse narratives through visual storytelling helps them learn to value differences by exposing them to unfamiliar perspectives and experiences. We define *diverse narratives* as any kind of story that presents values, topics, and ideas outside of our typical purview or expectations. The primary principle of this chapter is to understand how narrative structure and visual storytelling can connect people together to exchange diverse narratives. Stories and storytelling have been used throughout human history to convey information, perpetuate moral frameworks, and evoke emotion. Researchers Robert Kosara and Jock Mackinlay (2013) explain that stories help us to hold onto and transmit information as well as remember facts. In this role, they describe them as "connective tissue." Through the activities in this chapter, you will also think about how stories can connect and establish trust between teammates.

Intercultural collaboration through storytelling

Embrace different communities through stories

Visual storytelling can also be a way to underscore the value of diversity for team-mates as they use narratives to connect with people different from themselves and learn about their experiences. Creating this sense of connection through visual story-telling holds resounding promise for intercultural learning, understanding, and team-work because it a compelling way to represent the array of cultural identities found across the world. In exposing audiences to diverse narratives they might not other-wise encounter, there is an opportunity to begin confronting pressing issues such as xenophobia and implicit bias, as well as to experience the beauty of other cultures.

Meaningful participation of diverse voices

In collaborative scenarios, understanding and connecting with the guiding prin-ciples behind narrative structure offers teams an opportunity to imagine team-work as part of a larger story—an experience that itself involves a beginning, a middle, and an end. Through creating, sharing, and interpreting different types of visual narratives, individuals engage in opportunities for introspection through the exchange of stories about their unique lives, dreams, and experi-ences. This process fosters trust between teammates as they get to know each other through personal stories.

Storytelling reveals a variety of disciplinary perspectives and provides insight into the ways these disciplines create and interpret culture. Indeed, in our studies of intercultural collaborations, we have found that visual storytelling and narrative con-struction can expand conceptions of physical space, deepen interpersonal interactions and improve interpersonal skills. In this way, exposure to diverse stories enables us to begin to embrace different communities. Stories can help cultivate a genuine respect for and an understanding and appreciation of cultural and social values.

Narrative structure, visual storytelling, and signs

Narrative text and structure

Narrative structure involves both the content of a story and the structure that the story follows. In film studies, the content is commonly referred to as the *story* or *plot*. The narrative structure can take many forms and contain multiple *story arcs*, or continuing storylines, and does not necessarily proceed chronologically. Have you ever seen a film or read a book that starts at the conclusion and traces back to the beginning? Other stories, meanwhile, might take a more conventional approach and work in a linear progression. While there are several schools of thought regarding narrative structure and elements, cultural theorist and video artist Mieke Bal's broad interpretation of a narrative text is particularly relevant to this chapter. Bal defines *narrative text* as anything that tells a story to an audience (Bal and Van Boheemen 2009).

What are signs?

Visual storytelling is a communication form that predates human literacy. Since the early days of cave paintings, visual storytelling has expanded to include both static and moving images, which can range from basic sketches to polished illustrations, photography, video, and video games. Many different types of *signs*—that is, something that can be interpreted in ways other than its literal meaning—can be used in visual storytelling and are not restricted to images alone.

The words on this page are signs, as are the words you speak to your friends and colleagues, the photographs you share, symbols and icons you see as you walk down the street, and even emojis embedded in quick communications. We are so flooded with signs that most of us interpret them fluidly and fluently, without giving them much of a second thought (Hall 2012). For the purposes of this chapter's activities, signs are *any type of visual*.

Interpreting signs through semiotics

The interpretation of signs is called *semiotics*. Although the contemporary discipline of semiotics is attributed to Ferdinand de Saussure, a Swiss linguist, and Charles Sanders Peirce, an American philosopher, humans have long been interested in how signs (images, ideas, words, etc.) can mean something other than their literal interpretation. Understanding signs is essential to how people communicate with each other (Hall 2012).

Just as signs can be understood differently across cultures and people, so too can stories be interpreted differently based on the sender's and receiver's contexts (Bal and Van Boheemen 2009). Narrative constructs offer insights about who is telling a story and who is reading a story, and their analysis can be steeped in bias and stereotypes but also in insight and discoveries.

Reading narratives

Learning to interpret—or read—narratives is as much a self-revealing activity as it is an opportunity to respond to and challenge embedded socio-cultural norms. However, when considering how teammates might interpret your narrative, it is also important to take into consideration certain cultural factors such as the direction in which people literally read a page of text (e.g., top to bottom, right to left, left to right). Text-reading direction could impact interpretations of an author-driven visual story or interactions with a reader-driven story.

Author- and reader-driven approaches to visual narratives

In support of these ideas, the various genres of visual storytelling must take into account the intentions of the author as well as the response from the reader

(Segel and Heer 2010). We must, therefore, assess the degree to which a narrative visualization employs author- versus reader-driven approaches as part of our analysis. *Author-driven* approaches may not offer much interactivity, but they provide linear paths for the audience. *Reader-driven* approaches, on the other hand, are more open to interpretation and interactivity because they do not offer a strictly defined or linear experience. There is a historical tendency to compartmentalize and separate author-driven and reader-driven approaches in other media shifts in the context of contemporary visual narratives (Segel and Heer 2010).

Media and presence in storytelling

Terms and theories to know

Most of us are familiar with a wide range of storytelling techniques and media due to their widespread consumption and impact. Consider for a moment how you would feel about reading a story via email. There are no images. You have time to read it at your own pace, and your mental images might accompany the words; however, text-on-screen does not convey much social presence or information. Your response might change if the email's author attached several complementary images. You would likely respond differently to an entire tale shared with you via video recording. So how would your response differ if your team exchanged stories via videoconferencing or even in person? These examples connect to several intertwined terms and theories that describe how various characteristics of media (e.g., synchrony, richness, and social presence) impact how stories are transmitted, received, and interpreted by audiences.

Asynchronous and synchronous storytelling

The receiver's ability to respond or interact with content depends on whether stories are transmitted *synchronously* or *asynchronously*.

- **Synchronous** or "real-time" communication (synchrony) occurs when people communicate simultaneously.
- **Asynchronous** communication (asynchrony) is not simultaneous; it depends on the back-and-forth relay of information via tools such as email, shared documents, and blogs.

Social presence in media

Asynchronous and synchronous transmissions often carry different levels of *social presence*.

- **"Social presence" in media** describes how certain media are better able than others to convey the physical presence of people (Short, Williams, and Christie 1976).

    ○ *Low social presence media* include asynchronous forms like email or posts in the Fourth Space.
    ○ *High social presence media* include synchronous videoconferences, telephone conversations, and in-person meetings.

Media richness theory

Some forms of media are inherently more information-dense, or "richer" than others, and, therefore, more capable of conveying social presence (Dennis and Kinney 1998). When trying to establish trust through shared stories, understanding media richness can provide helpful insights. It impacts how people use communication tools, and how they respond to different kinds of communication.

- *Media richness* describes the amount of information generally conveyed via different forms of media.
  - *Rich media* conveys more information (e.g., videoconferencing).
  - *Lean media* conveys less information (e.g., email).

"Information" refers to a specific subject matter as well as additional content and communication that inform the receiver's interpretations and experience. These include indications of social presence, such as facial expressions and tone of voice, as well as contextual cues, such as lighting and audio.

Social presence, media richness, and interpretation

The stories we tell about ourselves are linked to the medium in which we tell them and by extension to the technologies that enable those mediums (McLuhan and Fiore 1967). When teammates are exchanging stories, this means they must consider which format works best for their purpose and whether or not the format itself will contribute to (or detract from) the experience. There are pros and cons to media characteristics that impact how teammates send, interpret, and respond to communication and storytelling (Robert and Dennis 2005). Here are a few to keep in mind as your team exchanges stories:

Asynchrony & lean media considerations

- More time encourages concentration and reflection.
- Teammates' motivation may **decrease** due to lower social presence.
- Asynchronous doesn't necessarily mean "lean."
- Asynchronous Video Exchange (3.3) provides rich benefits: facial expressions, gestures, tone of voice, and personality.

Synchrony & rich media considerations

- Synchrony enables immediate, conversational feedback
- Teammates' motivation may **increase** with higher social presence.

- Synchronous communication promotes spontaneous dialogue through rich, "high social presence" media
- Synchrony and richness are not perfect.
- There is less time for developing well-formulated responses through critical thinking.
- Varying degrees of second language proficiency may impact how comfortable people feel speaking in real time, resulting in hesitation and additional information processing time.

Visual information boosts comprehension

Visual information boosts comprehension as well as retention in both synchronous and asynchronous formats. Most of the activities in this chapter offer a blend due to Robert and Dennis's (2005) suggestion that when you have complicated activities, the best option is generally to combine high and low social presence media. While the Picture Story Shuffle (3.2) benefits from the time and reflection that accompany asynchronous approaches, the Video Exchange (3.3) is designed to simulate some virtues of synchronous transmission. When possible, we suggest synchronous check-ins to support all activities.

In context: Sharing narratives is an emotional journey

Storytelling in visual and verbal forms has been crucial to the success of our collaborations since the very start. As time has passed and online access and resources have flourished, our storytelling activities have expanded to encompass a range of asynchronous and synchronous communication methods. These each come with their own sets of benefits and challenges.

A scene from an asynchronous visual narrative exchange:

"Is everything okay over here?" Denielle asked one of her Qatar-based students, who was frowning at her laptop screen.

"I keep hitting refresh" the student explained, "but I still don't have any images or a story or anything from my teammate in our shared folder. Everyone else has theirs and I am really looking forward to hearing back from her. Do you think she forgot me?"

Fast-forward to a different type of asynchronous narrative in another collaboration:

"I'm redesigning my avatar across social media. I was getting ready to send some of my links to my teammate, and I realized that I had different drawings of myself across my various social media. I didn't want her to

(Continued)

get the wrong impression of me, as if I am disorganized or childish. So I'm making a new one that is more up-to-date so I can use it consistently across everything."

A Video Exchange among teammates introducing higher "social presence":

"I see you are grinning at your screen," Denielle commented to another student.

"Oh, yes! Her video to me was all about her passion for women's rights, and it's exciting to know that there are young women my age all around the world who care about this topic as much as I do. I can't wait to talk more about this!"

As you can see, the process of sharing stories can evoke a range of emotions. There are both highs and lows that come along with the experience of trying to work across great time and distance with someone you have never previously met. By interacting with and learning from each other's visual narratives, this process can be an exciting, frustrating, and rewarding journey.

The emotional meta-narrative of teamwork

Promote social exchange and reduce uncertainty

The delights and frustrations of working with narratives are not media-specific; static-image exchanges can be enjoyable for everyone who follows their agreed-on submission deadlines. On the flip-side, Video Exchanges can sometimes be nerve-racking and difficult to manage. This unavoidable duality of intercultural collaboration wraps each intentional, curated story inside of a meta-narrative: The arc of the experience is a narrative in and of itself, and you and your teammates are characters in your story. The role you play in the story of your collaboration will have an impact on how your teammate views and interprets the stories you deliberately share. Ultimately, your shared goals in exchanging stories in various forms are to promote social exchange and reduce uncertainty.

Building narratives

Narrative structure affects how readers understand the beginning, middle, and end of a story, whether in written or visual form. For example, a series of still images (photographs or illustrations) can tell the tale of a person, place or event, while filmic tools convey plot and character through multimedia experiences that combine moving images or animations with music and other dramatic devices. In both cases, creators can alter a story's chronology to increase audience suspense—by starting at the end of a story, for instance.

In our increasingly digital world, people also construct narratives about themselves in personal, professional, and online environments. These identities, real and imagined, come to life through written and visual content that takes many forms. The way someone organizes their resume, the choice to participate or not in online public spaces and social media platforms, are the types of decisions people make that add to their personal narrative.

What kind of meta-narrative will your team build? High and low social presence media both play a role in teammates' motivation and emotional reactions, but personal accountability, follow-through, and a little bit of luck (especially when it comes to technology!) are important, too. Whether you do all of the activities in this chapter, or select just one or two, be sure to consider the level of social presence you bring to the work, the cultural factors in play, and how media selection affects the reader's interaction with your story.

3.2

Picture Story Shuffle:
Cultural moments in five frames

Everyone loves a good story. People worldwide enjoy sharing a good story as much they enjoy listening to one. There is ample historical evidence that humans have been exchanging visual narratives with each other for thousands of years. Images convey large amounts of information in compelling ways; when combined with spoken or written words, as discussed in Chapter 5, images and words work together to help our brains better retain information.

The Picture Story Shuffle is a guessing game that invites your team to experiment with different configurations of visual signs in order to produce an array of meanings. You will write down a true story about yourself to share with a teammate and create a series of images to accompany it. First, however, you will only share your images, leaving it up to your teammate to try to make sense of them. It is always amusing to hear other people's interpretations of our own visuals! After sharing some laughs over your teammate's version of the story and exchanging some questions, you will finally reveal your actual tale. Then, you will switch roles and repeat the process.

Sharing stories visually may sound simple and straightforward, but in order to appreciate the inner workings of how we create and interpret visual stories, it is useful to dip a toe into semiotics, the interpretation of signs. While semiotics does not deal exclusively with the visual, for the purposes of better understanding of how to make and decode visual narratives, we will discuss semiotics through a visual orientation.

Intercultural interpretations

The act of visual storytelling engages both author and reader in a formative journey toward a shared mental landscape. Imagery creates a compelling meeting point for discussion, interpretation, and investigation of meaning. In the context of intercultural communication and collaboration, intercultural semiotic scholar Juming Shen points out that both author and reader bring their own cultural contexts to the creation and interpretation of signs. Thus, cultural background plays a significant role in how we derive meaning from signs.

Decoding the visual narrative

Interpretation of signs can vary according to peoples' cultural backgrounds and physical locations. There is a rich opportunity to learn about teammates by working together to decode signs. The Picture Story Shuffle invites you to decode and interpret a series of signs, that comprise a story, with your teammates. You will serve in the role of author (creating a series of distinct signs to tell a story about yourself) and reader (as you interpret a story your teammate has constructed for you). As you move through the activity, there are wonderful opportunities for cultural dialogue and discussion about the different readings of the story.

   Giving your teammate a chance to order the visual story for themselves before hearing the real story builds curiosity. Curiosity not only piques interest but also promotes attentive listening (or reading) when the tale is revealed. Research supports that this approach, on a cognitive level, also engages your teammate's memory through their multiple interactions with your images and the meanings associated with them (delivered in writing and/or in speech).

   At the core of the Picture Story Shuffle are the ideas that signs create meaning based on their interdependence on each other and that meaning varies by context. Though your initial guesses will likely be different from each other's actual stories, the process invites you to engage in understanding the unique aspects of a story. It's exciting to see how similar or different your guess might be from your teammate's actual tale!

Openness to learning about others

Perhaps paradoxically, an asynchronous approach can facilitate investment in understanding your teammates' perspectives in a more profound way than if you were to share your stories synchronously. By putting yourself in someone else's shoes, you can begin to understand their experience. Additionally, because you are not obliged to critique the story or idea, this form of discussion removes the burdens of criticism, so you can share and guess in an imaginative manner. With this point in mind, you can start familiarizing yourself with the process of using visual and verbal storytelling to share anecdotes, as detailed in the next section of this chapter.

Benefits & outcomes

- Understand the value of visual storytelling
- See a different perspective through your teammate's eyes
- Gain insight into how teammates communicate using images and words
- Deepen connections and interpersonal relationships between teammates
- Learn more about teammates and their respective cultural contexts

---

HALA

NATHAN

Activity

Picture Story Shuffle

The Picture Story Shuffle puts a lighthearted twist on storytelling and cultural learning. To play this game, teammates will each think of a story to share with each other through simple pictures you create. These pictures are the basis of the game. You will brainstorm ideas for stories with local colleagues before creating and shuffling these pictures to share with a remote teammate. But do not disclose the actual story in oral or written form just yet! After the authors share their initial images—without revealing the story behind them—the fun begins! Teammates attempt to rearrange the pictures they have received and create a story from their own arrangement. The guessing game encourages each teammate to invest in the other's story content. After sharing humorous and inevitably incorrect interpretations, each original author shares their original version of the story. The process of uncovering cultural elements that require further explanation is all part of the fun!

→ **People:** Local colleagues/remote teammates/individual
→ **Duration:** 1 hour to brainstorm; 1–3 days for the guessing game
→ **Technology:** Camera or scanner, email
→ **Other resources:** Paper, pen/pencil, sticky notes, markers

---

Tips

• **Image Quality:** Do not let poor imagery get in the way of telling your story. While this activity is not about being a perfect illustrator—you nevertheless want to make sure the image is understandable and communicative. A good way to confirm the legibility of your images is to check with your local colleagues before sending them to your teammate. Ask if they are clear and can be understood in the manner you intended.

(Continued)

- **Got questions?** Follow up with each other to ask questions and provide further explanations; if you do not hear back from your teammate, consider that they might be stumped. Ask if they would like some hints or if there are any questions you can answer for them while they are putting together their version of your story.
- **There's no right answer:** You might guess incorrectly, but that's okay. Your teammate will likely guess incorrectly too. There is no right or wrong. Your teammates will be excited to tell you the right order because they have invested time in deciding what they want to tell you, and they will find it interesting to hear how you have "messed up" their stories!
- **Use non-blaming language:** This activity is an opportunity for you to practice using non-blaming language in describing your actual story as compared to your teammate's guess. Remember, this is fun! You might say, for instance:
    - That was such a great way to piece together my story... I wish it had gone that way... What actually happened was...
    - What a cool way to have read my images...My actual story went like this...
    - Wow, I would have never thought my story could sound so funny, it was actually a lot scarier than that...Here's how it went...

Phase 1: With local colleagues

1. **Brainstorm:** On paper or sticky notes, brainstorm ideas for personal cultural stories based on different holidays or traditions. This is an opportunity to hone in on special moments reflecting your culture and to teach your teammate something new. In turn, you will learn about their ways. Some of the most memorable stories contain visceral emotional components; funny, scary, or embarrassing experiences can make for engaging narratives. Write down all ideas; do not eliminate any at this stage!
2. **Discuss:** In pairs or small groups, discuss story options with your local colleagues. Think aloud together about how your stories are connected to local traditions, values, or other aspects of your culture that you might otherwise take for granted. You may find it helpful to refer to the work you did during the Affinity Diagram (2.3b) and/or Iceberg Model (2.4a & 2.4b) activities. Which aspects of the story, specifically cultural elements, might require further explanation for your remote teammates?

Phase 2: Working individually

3. **Create:** Choose one idea from your brainstorm list and create at least five pictures that could represent key moments in your story. What images might

best represent the beginning, middle, and end of your story? These pictures could be photographs, sketches, illustrations, or collages representing different aspects of your story.

Phase 3: With a remote teammate

4. **Pair:** Teams of more than two people should select one partner to exchange images.

Phase 4: Working individually, via email or Fourth Space

5. **Exchange:** Shuffle the order of your images and email your pictures to your remote teammate. Be sure not to indicate the actual order! You and your teammate will invite each other to unscramble the pictures you each receive and to guess the story that goes with them.
6. **Guess:** Print arrange, and interpret your remote teammate's pictures. Can you piece together the full story? Write a short story based on your guesses. Don't worry about being correct—just have fun.
7. **Share:** Post in the Fourth Space, or email your version of the story to your remote teammate.

Phase 5: With remote teammate, via videoconference or SMS

8. **Reveal:** Once you exchange guesses, connect via videoconference to reveal your actual stories to each other. Show your images in their intended order. Describe particular cultural elements of the story and why you see it as funny, scary, or embarrassing.
9. **Interpret:** Follow up with at least one round of questions and explanations. Remember that follow-up questions can help to deepen your conversation. You might discover that an interesting dialogue emerges around the different ways each person reads and interprets the pictures in each story. Use the following guide.

DISCUSSION GUIDE

- How did this activity feel for you as the listener or reader versus as the storyteller or author?
- What kinds of cultural questions came to mind in discussing different interpretations of the pictures?
- What did you learn about local and/or cultural signs, pictures, and stories?
- Were there any pictures that you interpreted very differently than your teammate intended?
- How did this process impact your sense of trust when sending your images and shuffling your teammates' images?

3.3

Video Exchange:
Simulating synchronous connections

Video can shift our conception of remote teammates from abstract entities to actual people. This activity delves into breaking the ice personally with a remote teammate and "putting yourself out there" to build substantiated and relational trust. Exchanging and viewing personal narratives and informal introductions via pre-recorded video will help you see your teammate as a real person, living in a real place, even if speaking with them via audio or video chat is not possible. By sharing some kind of anecdote through video, you will reveal aspects of your life and who you are. Seeing teammates come to life makes them feel more real and makes them accountable. In addition, the emotional aspects of video create a relational connection.

Video fosters emotional connections

Time differences make real-time meetings difficult, if not impossible, for remote teams. In any type of collaboration (in-person or remote), video can play a significant role in facilitating introductions and shaping first impressions. In our early collaboration studies, the time difference meant that synchronous video chats were not really an option, so we primarily used asynchronous virtual platforms (with file size and storage capacity restrictions). We didn't even think about recording and sharing videos. We encountered challenges when our teams interacted without the benefit of high social presence media. Unable to see the team as a cohesive entity or to have concrete encounters with teammates made it harder for them to understand collaborative dynamics. In this particular case, our

Western and Arab teammates found it difficult to connect emotionally without high social presence media.

As our tools and resources improved, our tactics changed. During one Perspective Exchange (4.3) with still images, a teammate included one brief video among her static, photographic images. That little video snippet was captivating, informative, and, quite frankly, transformational. Before we knew it, the teammates were all recording and sending videos to each other. Suddenly, they had much clearer and more vivid glimpses into each other's lives.

Thus, the formal Video Exchange emerged organically and out of a real need. It is now a deliberate personal storytelling activity that we have frequently introduced in subsequent collaborations. Now that most of our teams have access to video-sharing tools and cloud-based services, we have incorporated this high social presence technique into our collaborations, especially where time and distance make teammates and projects feel very abstract.

Engaging with video

The prevalence of smartphones and the widespread use of other video-enabled devices make videography readily available. In addition, there are now even more ways to share videos than to create them. Static photographic images and text alone are unable to convey nuances that video communicates through visual and auditory data. As a rich, high social presence medium, video provides viewers with images and sound in motion, which can simulate the feeling of synchronous communication even when real-time communication is not possible. Written descriptions, music, sounds, or other audio effects can accompany visual media, engaging both readers and authors in multisensory experiences.

Non-selfie options

Creating introductory videos can also be an equitable experience for cultures in which people decline to share images of their faces. There are many ways to effectively tell a story about yourself by sharing details of your living and work environments from behind the camera. In this case, the emphasis is on showing spaces, not faces. By sharing aspects of your everyday life and providing accompanying commentary, your teammates with gain personal insights about you through high social presence media.

Benefits & outcomes

- Create and swap personal narratives through introductory videos
- Learn firsthand about a different culture
- Viewing narrative videos makes teammates seem less abstract and more human
- Use social exchange to reduce uncertainty about unknown teammates

Activity

Video Exchange

The Video Exchange enhances collaborations and helps teammates bond by adding an element of high social presence rich media. You do not need any special technical skills or tools beyond a phone or camera. This exchange is useful for capturing and conveying nuances of personality, daily life, and geographic or cultural contexts difficult to convey through static images or text. In long-distance exchanges, when time and distance prevent synchronous conversations via video chat, the Video Exchange helps make teammates, the project, and the collaboration feel more real. The duration of the collaboration is short, so you need to jump right in. This will provide a high-resolution—albeit condensed—idea of what life is like in the eyes of your remote teammates and help take your collaboration to the next level.

→ **People:** Individual/remote teammates/local colleagues
→ **Duration:** 2 hours maximum to record video (do not spend time editing); 1–2 days with a remote teammate, depending on the time difference.
→ **Technology:** Video-enabled device (phone, video camera, computer, etc.)
→ **Other resources:** Note paper, pen/pencil

Tips

- **Personal and cultural introductions:** It can be so much fun to experience a new city through the eyes of a teammate and get a taste of their favorite places, spaces, and food. Likewise, this is an enjoyable way to introduce your country or city to your teammates.
- **Recap unique characteristics:** Use your creativity to consider different aspects of yourself, your life, and your surroundings. Think about what details you can share that your viewer would not otherwise know.
- **Narrative:** Make sure to add an audio narrative to the background. Depending on your personal and cultural preferences, your video could take the form of a "selfie monologue" where you introduce and talk about yourself, or you could be behind the camera as a narrator and not show your face at all. If you are feeling ambitious or experimental, you could even thread different scenes together, perhaps with captions—or do something else!
- **Discuss sharing preferences:** Discuss and select how you will share the introductory videos with teammates (i.e., will the video be shared privately, with a team, or a larger group of people working together). Check the privacy settings as you upload and share videos, especially if you do not wish for your video to be visible outside of your team.

Phase 1: Working individually

1. **Introspect:** How would you share your world with your new remote teammates in one minute or less? Use your creativity to think about what aspects of yourself, your life, and your surroundings you wish to communicate. Although this is informal and unscripted, you may find it useful to make some notes beforehand to organize your thoughts and keep yourself on track while recording. Remember to relax and not overthink this.
2. **Create:** Create an informal video introducing yourself to the team. You can create it using whatever method you choose. It could be documentation of your workspace or room, something interesting you want to share with the team (think show-and-tell), a "selfie monologue," or different scenes threaded together through visual messaging apps with captions. Use your imagination! The duration of your video should be about one minute long.

Share with remote teammates

Phase 2: Working individually

3. **Upload:** Post your completed video online. Check your privacy settings if you do not wish for your video to be visible outside of your team.
4. **Share:** Send a link for your final introduction video to your remote teammates. Remember that your teammates will need a password to access private videos.
5. **Acknowledge:** Let your teammates know when you have received and watched their video, and thank them for sharing it with you. It's always nice to comment on a particular aspect of the video that you especially enjoyed or found intriguing.

Phase 3: Local colleagues

6. **Reflect & Discuss:** Recall the third dimension, Establish Trust (*we recognize and establish trust and accountability in different ways*). With local colleagues, take some time to discuss what you have learned about your remote teammates through the videos they have shared, and how this experience speaks to building substantiated and/or relational trust. Use the following guide for discussion.

DISCUSSION GUIDE

*   What aspects about yourself, your home, your workspace, or your culture were you most excited to share with your remote teammates?
*   Was there anything you felt shy or hesitant to share?
*   What format did you choose for the video? Were you in front of the camera or behind it? Why did you choose this approach?
*   What is your overall impression of your remote teammates based on their video?
*   What aspects of your teammates' videos did you find most interesting? Which of these things were new to you or were things you likely would not have learned elsewhere?

3.4

Digital Trail Trace:
Deciphering personal narratives in online spaces

Critical thinking about online representation

You and your teammates are able to collaborate because the World Wide Web
has been able to bring a wide range of people together in ways its founders
probably never anticipated. Now, it's time to take a look at its role in your
individual stories. The Digital Trail Trace invites you to take a step back to
examine, share, and understand your own patterns and those of your teammates. We define *digital traces* as social platforms, professional networking sites,
and links to a blog, portfolio, or resume. Over time, this activity has evolved
from sharing a few public links between teammates to a more critical analysis
of how our online presence shapes our personal narratives and, therefore, impacts teamwork.

The Digital Trail Trace is not about identifying correct or incorrect approaches to *virtual representation*, which we define as the way you deliberately

depict yourself in an online environment (through images, symbols, or words) and the way others interpret these depictions. Just as no two humans are exactly alike, no two people represent themselves in precisely the same way—intentionally or unintentionally—in the digital world.

Online identity as personal narrative

Your accumulated online identity is a personal narrative that encompasses everything you read, write, and do online—email, social media, blogging, maintaining a personal website, consuming news media, archiving your professional work, and even gaming. In some of these spaces, you leave some kind of visible trace—for example, posting a comment in response to a news article. Meanwhile, other spaces shape your online interactions, even if you do not interact with them in a public way. For example, you might privately send a link to a family member from a video-sharing site, but not comment on the video publicly.

Meandering versus crafting

Some of us meander the web in an unplanned fashion, engage in sporadic actions, and do not really have an underlying goal of making our online presence cohesive. On the other hand, some people are hyper-aware of their different online trails, carefully crafting virtual narratives about themselves through blog posts, comments, and so on. These people approach all of their online interactions in a structured way, ensuring they have visually (or verbally) depicted themselves in a cohesive way that fits with their online personality.

Some individuals have a different personality online than in their offline lives. For example, on their personal food blog, someone might write severe criticism about a local restaurant, even if they would never directly share their opinions with the restaurant staff. Sometimes it can be difficult to discern people's real personalities from their online caricatures, especially when dealing solely with their online representations.

Situating ourselves in networked publics

Depending on teammates' previous patterns of use and self-representation, working together in a collaborative space can enable insights about how each person creates and disseminates media as part of a *networked public*. This term is used interchangeably to define virtual spaces, as well as to describe common online affiliations (i.e., everyone who reads the same blog could be considered a part of that networked public) and the notion of the audience (everyone who interacts with your social media profile could be considered a networked public). Networked publics have both social and spatial connotations; they can be online gathering spaces and communities of people (boyd 2010).

Creating a visual landscape

Along these lines, social sites and other public information also usually contain strong visual and written components that assert a particular viewpoint or emotion. Many online platforms encourage users to share and interact with visual content, including imagery, videos, and emojis. Other people absorb, interpret, and read your visual information on conscious and unconscious levels as part of your narrative. For example, it is not about the meaning or content of one specific profile photo or illustration per se, but the entire collection of imagery one has chosen to share across many different platforms. Whether or not we do so intentionally, the visual landscape we create speaks volumes about us and creates a narrative about who we are and what we value.

Benefits & outcomes

- Learn more about teammates and self
- Explore and think critically about the digital traces we leave online
- Identify author- and reader-driven interpretations of online content
- Discuss how teammates portray themselves online

Activity

Digital Trail Trace

The Digital Trail Trace is an opportunity to examine the influences of online media in your life and that of others. By looking at how you currently represent yourself online, you will engage in self-reflection, and then expand this understanding by asking your teammates to share their impressions. This exchange helps build a more well-rounded understanding of teammates and of how the other culture interacts with and consumes online media. The bulk of this activity is done asynchronously; you and your teammate take turns gathering links and sharing your analyses. However, the degree of social presence involved in the media you share will vary depending on your level of participation online. Incorporating synchronous communication tools such as video chat or messaging at the end of the activity brings a higher social presence to the team's interactions as you come together to discuss findings in real time.

→ **People:** Individual/remote team/local colleagues
→ **Duration:** 2 hours
→ **Technology:** Internet access, web browser, shared document
→ **Other resources:** Pen and paper or word processing software

Tips

- **First impressions:** Think about the first impressions someone will have of you when they first encounter the collection of websites or apps you most often use. What do you think this collection says about you as a person in terms of your interests, your online footprints, and where you spend your time? After seeing this collection all together, is there anything that makes you want to (re)consider how you represent yourself online? Is there anything you want to alter in some manner?
- **Public content:** It is important to keep in mind that the internet can create a false sense of anonymity in some people's minds. However, much of the content we share online is public and not actually private in the ways we might imagine. Privacy filters have increased in social media spaces, but there remain large traces of our identities across the internet. Use this experience to consider ways you might clean up certain profiles or rebrand yourself.
- **External impressions:** The idea of engaging in this activity is for you to offer your teammates a digital pathway to help them learn more about you but, they may find other information that you might not expect. This realization can be somewhat daunting and may even feel like online stalking. Keep in mind that this is a natural component of conducting online searches and is the reality of the digital age.
- **Respect privacy:** One of the most important guidelines for sharing our public selves (for example, via social media sites or apps) is to share only what feels comfortable. If you have an account that is not already publicly visible, you can choose to add a teammate as a follower, but do not feel obligated to do so. By the same token, you do not need to make the whole account public for the sake of this activity.

Phase 1: Working individually

1. **Reflect:** Make a list of the ten websites or apps you use most often. Think broadly! You could include your inspirations; sources of entertainment, such as your favorite videos or online games; or task-based applications, such as email. What does this list say about you and your values, motivations, and needs? Write a few sentences to analyze your findings and how they represent you. Include descriptions of sites that may be inaccessible to your teammate due to language, censorship, and so on.

2. **Search:** Scour the web to see what traces you can find about yourself. For example, maybe you left a review on a travel site, had a conversation on a gaming forum, or were recognized by a local news source. If someone were to search the web using your name, what would he or she see? What does

your online presence say about you? Is this an accurate depiction of you? If you found nothing about yourself, how do you react to that? Write a few sentences to analyze your findings and how they represent you.

3. **Review:** Reflect on the first two steps: How do you use the web, and how does this impact your personality, working style, and life? How you have built your online presence (or not)? Write a few sentences discussing your personal philosophy of online presence.

4. **Interpret:** A picture is worth a thousand words. How do you represent yourself visually in these online spaces (e.g., avatar, illustrations, photos, consistent headshot photograph, or are you not visually depicted at all)? What do these visual choices communicate about you? Gather the various examples of your visual representations (profile pictures, avatars, etc.) into one shared document.

Exchange with remote teammates

Phase 2: With remote teammates

5. **Exchange:** After completing the previous steps, share your selections, written analysis, and visual representations from the "Review" and "Interpret" steps. Exchange with your teammates via email, messaging, or your designated collaboration space.

6. **Ask:** Create a list of curated questions about what you observed or learned from viewing your teammates' public personas. Once you have shared this list with your remote teammates, you will likely find that these lists can be a fascinating way for both of you to learn about the impressions your public links and materials give to others. For most people, this is a rare opportunity to hear this type of personal analysis from someone outside of their own culture.

Send analysis

Phase 3: With remote teammates

7. **Respond:** What was your first impression of the content your teammate shared with you? Think about how you felt or reacted to each of the links or resources they shared. How do those visual landscapes represent your teammate? How do you think the other culture interacts with and consumes online media? Send your impressions to your teammate.

8. **Connect:** Finally, determine at least one social space where you two can connect and follow each other.

Analysis

Phase 4: With local colleagues

9. **Discuss:** With local colleagues, take some time to discuss what you have learned about your remote teammates. Use the following guide for discussion.

DISCUSSION GUIDE

- Do you trust what you see online? How do you think online media has impacted your communication styles and access to a broader scope of ideas, opinions, and people?
- How would you characterize your teammate's personality based on their online habits, preferences, or affiliations? Do you trust this impression?
- What are ways that you and your teammates might become a "networked public" bound together by common goals, interest, or trust?
- After interpreting the resources your teammate shared with you, what conclusions can you draw about these resources. What do these conclusions mean?

3.5

Visual Origin Story:
Adventures in collaborative storytelling

Joining a team means learning about new people. Taking the time to weave together imagery can make a team feel more cohesive and complete, even when they're located on opposite sides of the earth and have never met in person. The Visual Origin Story activity evolved from one of our first forays into using visual narratives for the purpose of team-building prior to starting work on the actual project.

This activity strikes a balance between author-driven contributions and reader-driven co-creations, with the aim of merging visuals to create one representative team image, or *avatar*, and constructing a narrative about it. Teammates create their own individual avatars first, then work together on the team avatar and story. As with structured dialogue, we found that these teams benefitted from a structured opportunity for positive and upbeat personal interactions before rolling up their sleeves to dig into a challenging topic together.

Collaborative storytelling

The process of telling and crafting stories through the creation of characters, settings, and situations as part of a storyline can take many forms and utilize many kinds of creative mechanics. *Collaborative storytelling* is determined by the shared contributions of a team and can be co-created in a variety of ways. Narrators might build on each other's contributions by adding new elements to the end of a sequence without altering the previous contributions. Another approach might be to craft a story together through parallel contributions, which enables editing of prior contributions, and can be done synchronously or asynchronously. Multiple stories can also be shared simultaneously within collaborative spaces, such as the Fourth Space, virtual worlds, or games.

You have likely participated in some form of collaborative and/or interactive storytelling at one point in your life. New digital tools have increased collaborative and interactive storytelling formats from online spaces to video gaming worlds. These evolving formats continue to blur the lines between author-driven and reader-drives approaches in terms of who plays the role of narrator or listener.

In context: Visual narratives and teambuilding

"What do a robot, a horse, an insect, and an outgoing personality possibly have in common?" One of our teammates wondered this aloud as she browsed through the array of images she had received from her teammates.

As she read their explanations, though, she started to imagine how the positive characteristics of the individuals represented in the images could come together into a single entity that could illustrate the team. She printed out the images, cut them out of paper, and began assembling them into different configurations. A smile crept across her face as she said, *"I can't wait to see what they are creating with all of these different parts!"*

As she documented and shared her creation with the team, along with a short story about this fantastical beast, she asked her teammates to chime in with suggestions, additions, and changes.

"I was feeling hesitant about this project because the topic seems so tough," she explained to them in writing as she posted her image in the shared online community, *"but now I feel really motivated to get started and to work with you all."*

Cultural roles in storytelling

We have found that remote teams who engage with collaborative storytelling build feelings of unanimity, mutual understanding, trust, and a sense of community. Professor of Sociology Donna Eder (1988) points out the social constructs of "narrator" and "listener" are variable across cultures. Some cultures embrace the idea of a single storyteller and attentive listeners, while others challenge this notion. In Mayan culture, for example, there was a clearly defined "responder" among the listeners whose role included asking important questions, making comments, and sometimes completing sentences. This type of engagement transforms storytelling into a more collaborative activity and reinforces friendship and solidarity. Showing agreement, providing additional information, and offering opinions inherent in these practices can also help guide conflict resolution.

> **Benefits & outcomes**
>
> • Create a team name, avatar, and origin story
> • Participate in playful lateral thinking as a team
> • Remember characteristics of your team by manipulating visual information together
> • Imagine and co-create a shared world for your work together

Activity

Visual Origin Story

Origin stories exist in every human culture and are used to offer explanations about how something came into existence. Creating a Visual Origin Story combines lateral and visual thinking to as your team envisions its collective capabilities and imagines a positive trajectory together. For example, the team's co-authored origin story might describe teammates' superpowers and how they work together to "fight the evils of the world." The activity involves both asynchronous components with low social presence (your independent work) and synchronous moments with high social presence (coming together with your team to discuss and create). Working together synchronously at the end stage of this activity is recommended, if possible.

→ **People:** Individual/local colleagues/remote teammates
→ **Duration:** 1 hour (plus 1–2 days to combine avatars)
→ **Technology:** Internet access & web browser
→ **Other resources:** Pen, paper, or word processing software
→ **Low-bandwidth version:** Printer, photocopier, scissors, tape, pen, paper

> **Tips**
>
> • **Individual avatar:** Have fun creating your own individual avatars first, then share them with your team to describe your personality or things you love. The avatar can be as quirky and strange as you want it to be, as long as you can speak about how it connects to your personality. Robots, horses, insects, objects, humans, and more are all welcome to the party!
> • **Combining avatars:** Think of interesting ways to combine the avatars together. Don't just make a matrix of fragmented parts and call things done. Instead, think about how the parts fit together in interesting new ways. What new creatures could you create? What hybrid object might be constructed to represent the team?

- **Brainstorming:** Throughout the process of working together, think about the different collaborative storytelling techniques that might help your team brainstorm together. Perhaps one person adds an element to another person's contribution or you might have an open back-and-forth discussion where multiple stories take place in a shared world. Have fun and share ideas!
- **Stay playful:** This does not need to be a serious activity and, in fact, keeping the mood light will build positive feelings among your team. If you will be working on a serious topic later in the process, activities such as this one provide a useful emotional counterpoint to relieve some of the stress and tension that can result from working with challenging topics.

Personal avatar

Phase 1: Working individually

1. **Brainstorm:** Create an *avatar*—an image that will represent your personality—to share your new teammates. Feeling stuck? This exercise in lateral thinking will help you come up with some imaginative ways to represent yourself. First, grab a pen and paper to write down your responses to the following:
   - A verb for an activity that you like to do, ending in -ING ("flying," "jumping," etc.)
   - Favorite color(s)
   - Your favorite snack food
   - An adjective that best describes you
   - Your favorite creature, real or imagined
   - Favorite musical artist
   - Favorite board or video game
   - A particular hidden talent of yours
   - Name of the street or town where you grew up
   - Name(s) of your pet(s) (if applicable)
2. **Imagine:** Next, combine any number of selections from the previous list to develop a fun description of yourself. Perhaps you are a superhero who can make tacos appear with the snap of your fingers? Or do you feel you embody a hybrid of your two favorite animals? Come up with two to four options for yourself by combining answers, adding descriptive features, or editing as needed.

   Examples of how you might describe your new superhero self:
   "I'm a..."
   - Flying Kimchi Horse
   - Laughing Aqua Robot
   - Yodeling League of Insects
   - Bouncing Extroverted Cheeto

3. **Visualize:** Continue to working individually to create a visual representation of yourself based on what you have imagined, making sure to connect to any personality or skills you might bring to the team. Some ideas to get you started include:
   - Draw on top of a photograph
   - Create an illustration or caricature (a bowl of kimchi wearing sunglasses, a Cheeto with a face, etc.)
   - Collage together items from magazines or newspapers
   - Develop other creative representations, such as a hand puppet constructed from fabric or other materials

Unified team visual

Phase 2: With remote teammates

4. **Discuss:** Meet via video or messaging to share all of your fun individual avatars in a shared document. Make sure to explain all the qualities and elements you have embedded in your creation. Ultimately, your goal will be to combine these images into one team avatar.

Brainstorm different ways you might combine your individual images into a single team avatar.

Examples of how to discuss combining avatars into a single team image:

> *"What do a robot, a horse, an insect, and an outgoing personality possibly have in common? What about a mythical robot-insect-horse, driven by a miniature lady?"*
> *"Yes, let's draw it!"*
> *"Here's what I think the body could look like…"*

5. **Combine & Document:** Working together, combine the individual avatars together to create one unified team visual. Depending on the chosen materials, you may need to photograph, photocopy, or scan the results in order to share them with your teammates.

   Some options to combine your images include:
   - **Analog collage:** Print several copies of the individual images. Cut them out and then tape the images together to make a new composite image; consider bringing other physical materials (fabric, paints, etc.) into the process to make the experience more lively, multisensory, and exciting.
   - **Analog drawing:** Studying each person's individual contribution, consider how could you bring elements from each individual avatar into a single image? Sketch some ideas on paper to document and share.

- **Digital table:** Insert a table into your shared document (the number of rows should correspond to the number of teammates. Place selected images side-by-side. Experiment with different placements and orientations.
- **Digital composition:** Use free or paid image-editing software to combine images digitally into a single composition.

6. **Merge together:** Work in rounds to discuss each person's visuals. This process may require multiple rounds of discussion, selection, and revision.
   - For larger teams, you might vote to select one person's creation to visually represent your team.
   - Smaller teams might experiment by combining elements from all teammates. Discuss preferred approaches with your teammates.

7. **Name your team:** Give your unified team visual a name. This name should capture the spirit of the team as reflected in the visual itself.

Team origin story

Phase 3: With remote teammates

8. **Write:** Based on the narrative elements of your new unified team visual, use a similar approach to co-author a brief fictional origin story about the team, including key strengths and possible adventures.
9. **Finalize:** For the duration of your time working together, the final team name, avatar, and origin story will represent your team in group critiques and other forums.
10. **Discuss:** Take some time to discuss what you have learned about through this collaborative storyboarding experience. Use the following guide for discussion.

DISCUSSION GUIDE

- What did this activity teach you about collaborative storytelling?
- What kind of cultural content or meaning is embedded in your team name and combined image? Ask teammates to clarify or explain elements of their images.
- Did learning about your teammates during this process make you feel closer to them?
- How did this process help your team establish trust and build a relationship?

References

Bal, Mieke, and Christine Van Boheemen. 2009. *Narratology: Introduction to the Theory of Narrative.* 3rd ed. Toronto; Buffalo: University of Toronto Press.

Boyd, Danah. 2010. "Social Network Sites as Networked Publics: Affordances, Dynamics, and Implications." In *A Networked Self*, 47–66. London: Routledge. doi:10.4324/9780203876527-8.

Dennis, Alan R., and Susan T. Kinney. 1998. "Testing Media Richness Theory in the New Media: The Effects of Cues, Feedback, and Task Equivocality." *Information Systems Research* 9 (3): 256–74. doi:10.1287/isre.9.3.256.

Eder, Donna. 1988. "Building Cohesion through Collaborative Narration." *Social Psychology Quarterly* 51 (3): 225–35. doi:10.2307/2786921.

Hall, Sean. 2012. *This Means This, This Means That: A User's Guide to Semiotics.* 2nd ed. London: Laurence King Publishing. http://laurenceking.com/product/This+Means+This,+This+Means+That:+A+User%27s+Guide+to+Semiotics.htm.

Kosara, Robert, and Jock Mackinlay. 2013. "Storytelling: The Next Step for Visualization." *Computer* 46 (5): 44–50. doi:10.1109/MC.2013.36.

McLuhan, Marshall, and Quentin Fiore. 1967. "The Medium Is the Message." *New York* 123: 126–8.

Robert, Lionel P., and Alan R. Dennis. 2005. "Paradox of Richness: A Cognitive Model of Media Choice." *IEEE Transactions on Professional Communication* 48 (1): 10–21. doi:10.1109/TPC.2004.843292.

Segel, Edward, and Jeffrey Heer. 2010. "Narrative Visualization: Telling Stories with Data." *IEEE Transactions on Visualization and Computer Graphics* 16 (6): 1139–48. doi:10.1109/TVCG.2010.179.

Short, John, Ederyn Williams, and Bruce Christie. 1976. *The Social Psychology of Telecommunications.* London; New York: Wiley.

4

ASSESS INFORMATION

Learning from multisensory collective wisdom

Objective ⟵——————————————⟶ Subjective

DIMENSION 4: Assess Information

Our individual and culturally informed patterns affect the ways we gather, understand, and verify what we know.

Your remote team may progress through these exploratory activities in a sequence, or select from them in order to find a topic of mutual interest or to see a problem from another perspective.

Chapter 4 engages teammates in multisensory activities to explore and discover new ways of gathering and understanding information beyond their typical habits and perspectives. When teammates combine different approaches to truth-seeking, they can gain a well-rounded perspective on a topic. Research indicates that differences in this area present some of the greatest challenges to teams and that tolerance is key to integrating diverse practices and preferences, particularly in regard to assessing information's reliability and usefulness.

| **OBJECTIVE:** I look to external sources for information, such as factual records, academic learning, or mass media in order to understand the world. I find personal affirmation in my educational history and employment record. | **SUBJECTIVE:** I look to my close-knit social circles for information, such as friends, family, and oral histories, in order to understand the world. I find personal affirmation in building relationships and my role within the community. |

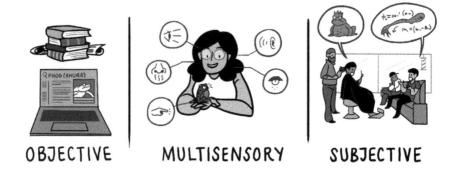

OBJECTIVE   MULTISENSORY   SUBJECTIVE

4.1

Learning from multisensory collective wisdom

Activating a range of senses positively impacts the way humans learn. The activities in this chapter encourage teammates to explore and understand information through multiple senses while respecting different Work Styles. Our ability to collect, comprehend, and assess information is informed by cultural patterns and norms. Even when there are significant differences, recognizing and respecting those patterns is important for preventing unproductive conflict. Through these activities, teammates learn how to best assess information together while addressing the potential obstacle of differing approaches.

At this stage in the collaborative process, your team is likely grappling with preconceived ideas of each other's cultures. At the same time, you are working together to define a specific rallying point, an area of mutual interest for further exploration. Neither task is particularly easy, especially when you are struggling to understand abstract ideas about culture and geographic location. While online environments can enhance learning and make remote collaborations across cultures feasible, they are also limiting. It is therefore important to think about how to extend your learning beyond the digital channels you have already established and to engage in a range of multisensory activities, which can yield richer learning and information-gathering experiences (Willis 2006).

Multimedia learning theory and sensorimotor modalities

The premise of multimedia learning theory is that when people encounter visual and verbal information in combination, they are able to learn more effectively than when they encounter them separately. In this theory, the visual includes pictures, drawings, photographs, animations, videos, or immersive environments, while the verbal includes any kind of spoken or written words. Multimedia learning occurs when the learner combines visual and verbal information to arrive at an understanding, or "mental model" (Mayer 2002).

Expanding on this, we have found that incorporating additional senses (smell, taste, and haptics—movement and touch) are instrumental to project development, intercultural learning, and teambuilding. Research supports that such multisensory activities, which include more than one of the five senses, boost engagement and learning (Willis 2006). Our multisensory activities take collaborative pursuits beyond the screen in order to understand various phenomena in the physical environment. In addition to gathering information to share with the team, we find multisensory and multimedia learning encourages teammates to see their own culture objectively as they begin to understand and appreciate each other's unique experiences.

Enhancing communication and "realness"

In some cases, remote teammates might not speak the same language. Or teammates may be able to communicate in one shared language, but they end up brainstorming in their native languages. In these types of situations, combining low-stake visuals (such as sketches) into these activities can help teammates understand each other more, even if they can't read each other's original sticky notes. Regardless of shared language proficiencies, we have found that multiple types of learning create richer experiences and deeper understanding. Seeking opportunities to create multisensory learning opportunities for each other will enhance communication and engagement among remote teammates.

In our experience, when teammates become involved in relevant activities beyond the screen, they consistently report that the collaboration feels more real to them. So, in addition to increasing your cultural and topical learning, incorporating a range of multisensory activities into your collaboration—such as traveling around town to take photos of your community or engaging in a hands-on data visualization—will bring you and your teammates together.

In context: Creating an experiential exhibition

Who could predict that a video of bread would inspire a multisensory exhibition? During one collaboration, Denielle traveled with a small group of young women to Abu Dhabi. The travelers eagerly documented and shared their journey with their teammates in the United States as part of their Perspective Exchange (4.3) and their ongoing efforts to learn about each other. One of these exchanges included a video of the group dining outdoors at the Emirates Palace sharing a loaf of multi-colored bread.

The US teammates watched and re-watched the video, poring over the details: the sunny setting, the vivid pink watermelon juice poured into tall glasses, and the meticulously manicured fingernails. But it was the bread—which they dubbed "rainbow bread"—that captivated their attention. They were mesmerized as their teammates tore off chunk after chunk of this bread, revealing new colors. Perhaps some of the appeal had to do with the fact that they received the video during lunchtime in the United States.

(Continued)

Ultimately, though, the video was compelling because of the vast number of cultural nuances embedded in it, and because it gave the US teams the feeling that their teammates were including them in a quiet, intimate moment. The Abu Dhabi luncheon video created an appetite for more than just rainbow bread. It sparked an idea for the US teammates; perhaps there could be some opportunities for sharing these fascinating and beautiful aspects of Middle Eastern culture with a wider audience.

The US teams ramped up their Perspective Exchange (4.3), asking their teammates in the Gulf to send more photos, videos, and commentary and sharing more of their own in return. The images and videos they shared were scenes of daily life, not things a person would encounter in a guidebook or on a postcard rack: stroking a beloved pet cat, preparing a cup of hot cocoa, or stumbling upon a heated discussion.

From this point, the US teammates decided that the outcome of their intercultural exchange with their Qatar-based teammates would be an experiential exhibition to share some of what they had learned. They wanted to create opportunities for others to become aware of their own biases, reflect on their own culture, and think about how to communicate and find common ground with people who have completely different backgrounds.

The resulting exhibition space comprised several multisensory interactive stations that made an effort to replicate the key stages of their journey toward a topic of interest and a common project goal. One station invited an exploration of biases using invisible ink and blacklights. Another incorporated VR headsets to immerse visitors in several Doha locations, including a local *souq* (an outdoor market), the seaside, and a historical area. Before exiting the exhibition space, visitors passed through an empathy-building game designed around navigating an environment in which one does not speak the language.

Combined with their multisensory learning experiences, the team's ongoing multimedia exchange of photographs, voice notes, text messages, emails, and videos made this collaboration and their resulting exhibition a success. Together, the stations invited introspection about biases and beliefs, piqued cultural curiosity, and built empathy around intercultural exchanges.

Divergent and convergent design research approaches

Using various multisensory learning inputs alongside divergent and convergent approaches to collaboration helps teams see problems in new ways. This combination is particularly important at the early stages of collaboration, when you are getting to know your teammates. In his book, *Change by Design*, Tim Brown and Barry Katz (2009) discusses these two approaches in detail. In summary, *Divergent* approaches encourage individuals and teams to broaden their exploration of ideas, prototypes, and so on. Some of the divergent work will happen independently, outside of team meetings, with teammates bringing their ideas back to the team for discussion.

Divergent phases, which inherently present a range of choices, are followed by *convergent* opportunities, which focus on decision-making and narrowing choices down to a few specific ideas; thus, convergent approaches help to consolidate and bring teams' thinking together. Across the design disciplines, convergent and divergent approaches are often done in a cyclical manner. In various design disciplines, conjoined divergent and convergent approaches are often described as aspects of a model called the *Double Diamond*.

What is the double diamond?

This model begins at a point of convergence at a particular problem and diverges as the team explores the problem from all different angles (often referred to as the *Discovery* phase). From this broad exploration, the team then works toward convergence in *Definition,* the second phase. This means they define a specific area of focus, bearing in mind the unique aspects of their problem, audience, and context. At this point, they often write a specific definition for their problem. The next phase, *Development*, is a second opportunity for divergence; it is here that the team generates as many different design concepts as possible in response to their problem definition.

The final convergent phase is often the product of many cycles of idea generation, testing, and refinement. Critique and feedback are important at this stage (see Chapter 5) and help move rough prototypes toward finalized solutions by pinpointing issues and/or making constructive suggestions for improvements. The Design Council is a great resource for more information on the Double Diamond and the various design methods that can comprise it (2015a, 2015b).

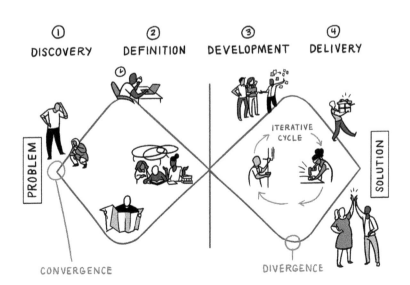

Use multisensory approaches to find a rallying point

Combined with divergent and convergent approaches, the multisensory activities in this chapter will help guide your team toward shared interests and passions through different ways of gathering, sharing, and understanding information. Through this process, you may identify a *rallying point*—a common interest, concern, or goal worthy of further exploration, around which you might later develop a project (see Chapter 6). In doing so, you will deepen your cultural understanding and your exploration of the topic at hand, while remaining mindful of the individual and cultural differences that affect information assessment and verification. These skills are particularly useful if you choose to tackle complex "wicked problems," such as issues of environmental sustainability or social justice.

Benefits & outcomes

- Visually depict teammates' thinking and ideas
- Integrate ideas to find combinations of interests
- Practice low-stakes discussion, decision-making, and cooperation
- Determine a shared topic or focus for further exploration

4.2

Focus Quest:
Finding a topic through divergent and convergent approaches

In a multimedia learning environment, teammates use emails, text messages, voice notes, photographs, and videos to communicate, maintain motivation, and identify topics that all members are excited to work on together. The Focus Quest activity guides teammates in determining a rallying point that they can discuss together. If you are interested in pursuing a project together, the Focus Quest and resulting rallying point will help you later identify common values and goals to address this interest (see Project Generator 6.2a).

This multiphase activity combines several *divergent* and *convergent* steps to help teams think about a number of different ways to approach the subject beyond what might immediately come to mind. Remember, while divergent approaches help you to explore widely, convergent approaches help you narrow down and make choices. Examples of convergence and divergence within the Focus Quest:

- *Convergence:* You first work with local colleagues as a way to start defining a broader topic. This approach establishes a common understanding and language and agreed upon vocabulary that will be used later when sharing with remote teammates.
- *Divergence:* Remote teammates then bring these topic ideas into a brainstorming session to generate as many ideas or thoughts as possible.

Activity

Focus Quest

The ultimate goal of the Focus Quest is to determine a shared topic or focus for the remote team to further explore or work on together. Brainstorming, mapping, and collaging encourage idea generation and moments for collaborative exchange and dialogue. In the end, bringing these ideas together into a collaborative collage encourages teammates to find and observe harmonious combinations of interests and to literally see what others are thinking. Recall that a *collage* is a composition created from combining and arranging many small images, image fragments, color swatches, samples of textures, and even typographic (word-based) elements. To reach this point, however, each teammate will first work through a series of steps with their local colleagues, then bring the resulting topics to brainstorm with the remote team.

→ **People:** Local colleagues/remote teammates/individual
→ **Skills:** Critical analysis, ambiguity tolerance, free association, consensus building
→ **Duration:** 1 hour
→ **Technology:** Camera, projector, videoconferencing software, shared document and/or visualization tools
→ **Other resources:** Paper, sticky notes, markers, black or whiteboard, projection screen

---

Tips

- **Values:** Use the brainstorming and sharing aspects of the Focus Quest to get in touch with how the project can connect to both personal and cultural values, while also discussing shared values of remote teammates. Discuss the difference between which values you distinguish as personal versus cultural and why. Keep in mind which topics might resonate with other members of the team.
- **Umbrella topics:** Some large topics will take your team into an abstract territory, opening a range of opportunities for discussion. Prior to discussion, reflect on your feelings and formulate your thoughts so they are clear for discussion.
- **Visual thinking:** The visual aspects of this activity help teammates show and share their thinking. Viewing your teammates' visual contributions may also give rise to questions you may not have otherwise considered, or lead to new ways of understanding their perspective.
- **Learning opportunity:** The collage is a small task that invites the team to work together and invites low-stakes discussion, decision-making, and cooperation. Hopefully is also provides some practice and sets the stage for more in-depth collaborations to come. Look for opportunities to compromise, find similarities, or run through a series of "what if" scenarios with a range of wildly different options.

Identify focus

Phase 1: With local colleagues

1. **Reflect:** Think back to your Belief Brainstorm & Affinity Diagram (2.4a & 2.4b), Group Iceberg (2.4b), and Comparative Impression Maps (2.5). You can use these to identify topics and/or use the methods you learned in these activities to think through new possibilities.
2. **Vote:** Shuffle sticky notes into clusters or write lists to organize the group's interests. Each person can vote for one of these topics that interests them the most. The three topics with the most votes will be the starting point.
3. **Define:** Continue working together to break down the starting point topic into sub-topics, discussing how the topic is defined in society, culturally, and on an individual basis. Appoint a note-taker to capture insights from the team on a whiteboard or large piece of paper.
4. **Local brainstorm:** As a team, assess micro and macro perspectives on the topic, along with concepts that are traditional, mainstream, predictable, or cliché. What are the first things that come to mind? Conversely, what are the unexpected, unconventional, or more nuanced aspects? If a topic seems "easy," that likely means you need to dig deeper. The note-taker should record responses, or, as an alternative, you can write each idea on individual sticky notes and post them on the board or wall. By the end of this activity, the team should have generated a large number of interrelated points of interest.
5. **Narrow:** Identify and remove three ideas the team thinks are too obvious. Identify three topics that strike you as culturally or locally specific. Visually distinguish these: circle them, add a star to them, illustrate or sketch them, and so on. In some cases, you might be curious to know whether your remote teammates have a cultural equivalent to some of your locally oriented selections.
6. **Document:** Photograph the documentation from the brainstorming session with your local colleagues to share with your remote teammates.

Share

Phase 2: With remote teammates

7. **Meet/Post:** Share the outcomes of the local brainstorm in a videoconference with your remote team or by posting images and a written summary in the Fourth Space. In either venue, take time to describe and explain the following:
   - The top three topics from the local brainstorming session
   - The culturally specific/local selections
   - The selections which were eliminated as "too obvious."

   If videoconferencing, you can use screen-sharing functions to show your brainstorming documentation.

8. **Remote brainstorm:** After discussing all topics, you will do another brainstorm based on these as a remote team to find your area of focus. You can accomplish this through videoconferencing with a note-taker keeping track of ideas in a shared document, or by posting ideas in the Fourth Space and commenting on each other's favorites. Repeat the brainstorm if you still need to narrow these down. Document and post the final topic(s) in a shared folder or Fourth Space. This is your rallying point!

Analysis

Phase 3: With remote teammates

9. **Collect images:** Each teammate will find three to five images related to your team's rallying point to create one topic collage together.
10. **Topic Collage:** Set up a shared document or a visual workspace in which you can work together or individually. Gather your images in that space, and work them into a harmonious composition that reflects your team's shared interest in your specific area of focus. Create a title for the piece related to your rallying point, and work together to write a specific sentence describing your topic of mutual interest. Some teams may wish to craft this in the form of a problem statement, pitch statement, or research question.

Analysis

Phase 4: With remote teammates

11. **Discuss:** Using the following guide, discuss what you have learned together through this process.

DISCUSSION GUIDE

- How did the process of brainstorming help your ideas evolve? How did ideas change between the local group brainstorm and the remote team brainstorm?
- What ideas or values were difficult for you to let go of during the process? Why?
- In what ways did the discussion with your team change your ideas about possible topics?
- Were there any unexpected ideas or perspectives that came from the discussion?
- How did the collaging process impact your thinking?

4.3

Perspective Exchange:
Two sides of a topic

The Cultural & Geographic Perspective Exchange enables teammates to share different perspectives about a team's chosen *rallying point*—a mutual interest, question, or concern. The team's rallying point will come to life through the multisensory learning embedded in this photographic exchange which gets teammates away from the screen and out into their communities. The photographic essays that you create will help to shed light on your own understanding of the topic and offer insight into the various aspects of the chosen topic within a particular geographic region, city, or culture.

While the exchange reveals nuanced views of the mutual topic, as seen from each teammate's specific cultural perspective, it simultaneously allows for the communication of another, deeper, layer of cultural information. Thus, your view of your topic and each other will broaden. Photographic exchanges stimulate fruitful dialogue about the topic at hand—and a whole new round of cultural questions. Not only will you grow your interest in your topic by examining it through your remote teammate's eyes, but you will also build trust, curiosity, and interest in each other.

Visualizing multiple perspectives on the shared topic

If your entire workplace or classroom group (split up into smaller teams) is focusing on a similar topic, such as water sustainability, this method can provide very enlightening results for all of you. For example, when we sent teammates located in New York and Qatar to document "a day in the life" in terms of their own personal water usage and interactions with water, their findings provided the entire group with a wealth of visual information about the shared topic of water sustainability. Individuals shared their photos with their teammates, but also with the larger group of participants in New York and Qatar, and because everyone was focused on some aspect of water sustainability, the photos were of interest to everyone. Exploring everyone's contributions kicked off a variety of questions, comments, and ideas; led some teams to shift their focus; and pushed others toward different types of solutions than they might otherwise have uncovered.

The hard work of intercultural collaboration does not end once you and your team find your rallying point. Throughout your work together, remember to constantly check in with your own assumptions and biases—not only the ones you have about your teammate's culture but also the ones you have about your topic. It is also beneficial to reflect frequently on the unique learning aspects of your collaborative experience so as to remind yourself and your teammates of the value of the collaboration, even when it is hard. Frequent self- and team-reflection will help you remember why you are engaging in intercultural co-working in the first place.

Benefits & outcomes

- Exchange visuals to broaden cultural learning and views of your team's common topic
- Learn socio-cultural insights from teammates' daily lives and communities
- Consider a topic from local and global perspectives
- Discover interesting topics by discussing both the beautiful and the mundane

---

a. Activity

Cultural & Geographic Perspective Exchange

The Cultural & Geographic Perspective Exchange promotes cultural learning through exploring and sharing the environmental similarities and differences of your local community with your teammates. Guided by two oppositional concepts (word-pairings such as *natural/man-made*), you and your teammates will take photographs and swap them for discussion, comparison, and analysis. The purpose of the word-pairing is to help you focus on illustrating two contrasting concepts in your local community. Because all teammates will take photographs based on the same word-pairings, the words create a common reference point to compare how these terms manifest within each community. The goal is to explore multiple facets of your physical location, from beautiful green spaces to dilapidated signage. In the process of this activity, you will gain an appreciation for the unique features of your local surroundings, and experience a different landscape through visual exchange and dialogue with your remote teammates. This multimedia exchange of imagery and written elements can serve as a starting point for further exploration—see the Photo Juxtaposition option.

→ **People:** Local colleagues/remote teammates/individual
→ **Duration:** Half-day to capture images; 3–5 days to complete the exchange
→ **Technology:** Digital camera or camera-equipped mobile device, shared document or folder, messaging or email
→ **Other resources:** Notebook or paper/pen

Tips

- **Beauty in the mundane:** Go out into your community and try to see it with fresh eyes. Do not shy away from things that you see on an everyday basis or feel typical to you. In fact, it can actually be useful to focus in on these mundane features of your daily life. Believe it or not, these things are especially interesting to remote teammates because they provide insight into a unique aspect of your town, city, or culture that might not be seen otherwise.
- **Variety:** Throughout your journey, try to apply an investigative strategy to the way you capture imagery. Shoot from a variety of angles, making sure to showcase the unique features of the place, object, or elements you want to share with others. Zoom in closely to examine the fine details and texture. Step back and examine the surrounding area to showcase additional characteristics.
- **Analog before digital:** You might find yourself ready to jump onto the computer and create digital juxtapositions immediately after you receive your teammate's photography. Try to hold off on this phase of the project and engage with the image juxtapositions by hand at first. This will engage your sensorimotor processing, amplifying the meaning of your interactions with the content you and your teammates have collected.
- **Photography:** To engage with this activity, you are not expected to be a professional photographer by any means! However, it is still important to keep in mind the clarity and readability of your images. Utilize the features of your camera or mobile phone and zoom in on an object. If you need to get closer to capture the details, go for it. The time of day is also important to the lighting of your images. If you think an image is blurry or too dark, take another one!

Plan

Phase 1: Working individually

1. **Plan Ahead:** Depending on where you're located and your access to transportation, you'll need at least half a day to complete this activity. After taking photographs, be sure to set aside adequate time to gather your images and notes so that you use your time efficiently and are ready to exchange with your teammate on schedule.

Phase 2: With remote teammates

2. **Select:** Use one of the word-pairings from the following list to begin this activity. Coordinate with your remote team to ensure you make a selection that affords many different interpretations.
   - Natural/Man-made
   - Small/Large
   - Hard/Soft
   - Quiet/Loud
   - Dangerous/Safe
   - Historic/Modern
   - Open/Closed
   - Liberal/Conservative
   - Formal/Casual
   - Native/Foreign
   - Professional/Playful
   - Convenient/Inconvenient
   - Orderly/Disorderly

3. **Discuss:** With your remote team, talk about possible interpretations for you selected word-pair. Critically examine the influences of economy, commercialization, history, and culture on your city or town. Try to go beyond your initial interpretation of the terms and challenge each other to think of new or expanded meanings.

   Example:

   Open/Closed: This could refer not only to doors or restaurants but also to minds, people, and societies. How would you reflect the latter in a photographic image?

Exploration

Phase 3: Working individually

4. **Photograph:** Using a phone or digital camera, go out into your community and try to see it with fresh eyes. With your assigned word-pair in mind, take at least 20 photographs that could represent each of your two words (at least 40 total images). Think about capturing a variety of images, from landscapes, like a skyline or beach (macro), to minute details of daily life,

like lettering on a storm drain or something for sale at a local market (micro). Shoot from a variety of angles, keeping in mind focus, lighting, depth of field, and time of day.

5. **Take Notes:** During your photographic exploration, use the following questions to take notes. These will help you remember details to later share with your remote teammates:
   a. How do you feel about the images?
   b. How do they connect to your assigned word-pair?
   c. Why did you choose the particular subject matter?
   d. Any other cultural details you might want to mention to your teammate when exchanging images.

Analysis

Phase 4: With remote teammates

6. **Discuss:** Exchange collections of images and notes via email, shared folder, or Fourth Space. Include some of your notes and insights about your location. If possible, meet via videoconference or use asynchronous media to compare and contrast your geographic locations verbally and visually, working to understand the cultural influences that appear in the photography. Use the following guide for discussion.

DISCUSSION GUIDE

- Which keywords describe your location? Your teammate's location?
- What would you tell a friend about your country/city if they had never visited?
- What do you love about your country/city? What do you find annoying?
- What might be hard for a visitor to understand?
- Is your own experience of living in your country/city different than the way a tourist would experience your country/city? Why?
- What questions do you have for your teammates about their country or city?

b. Activity

Topical Perspective Exchange

Visual ethnography is the study of a culture from the perspective of someone living in that culture represented in images, such as photography or film. This Topical Perspective Exchange is conducted as an ethnographic photo-swap of a "day in the life" of each teammate. In contrast to the first variation, this option focuses specifically on a particular topic or idea through a photographic journey from your particular cultural perspective. For example, if you are focusing on a specific topic, such as water sustainability, you would photograph all of your daily interactions with water, noting your water usage over a 24-hour period (including eating, drinking, kitchen use, and bathroom use). The resulting images, and discussion that follows, will engage remote teammates in talking about the findings and provide a snapshot into one another's personal lives.

→ **People:** Remote teammates/individual
→ **Duration:** Half-day to capture images; 1–2 days to complete the exchange
→ **Technology:** Digital camera or camera-equipped mobile device, shared document or folder, messaging or email
→ **Other resources:** Notebook or paper/pen; black & white/color printer; scissors; tape; large sheet of paper or wall for viewing image combinations

Plan

Phase 1: Working individually

1. **Narrow:** As a starting point, think about a specific question or sub-topic related to the larger topic or rallying point your team established in the Focus Quest, for example, "daily water usage." Be sure to stay within the bounds of your team's topic when you choose a sub-topic to explore photographically (e.g., if your shared topic is water sustainability, choose a sub-topic related to water, not something related to the community more broadly).

Phase 2: With remote teammates

2. **Discuss:** Talk with your remote teammates about the various ways your sub-topic can be interpreted. During the discussion, critically examine the influences of economy, commercialization, history, and culture on your city. Try to go beyond your initial interpretation of the sub-topic, challenging each other to think of new or expanded perspectives. A journey into "daily water usage" might require you to photograph your personal consumption habits related to kitchens and bathrooms, but also to take into account less obvious consumption embedded in your food or clothing. The contrasts in teammates' images can reveal interesting and surprising differences, which can lead to engaging discussions.

Exploration

Phase 3: Working individually

3. **Photograph:** Using a phone or digital camera, go out into your community and try to see it with fresh eyes. Take at least 20 photographs that are in some way representative of your sub-topic. Do not shy away from things that seem mundane to you; these are often interesting to remote teammates as a point

of reference or comparison. Remember to shoot your photos from a variety of angles, keeping in mind focus, lighting, and time of day.

4. **Take Notes:** During your photographic exploration, use the following questions to take notes. These will help you remember details to later share with your remote teammates:
    *   How you feel about the images
    *   How they connect to your assigned word-pair
    *   Why you chose the particular subject matter
    *   Any other cultural details you might want to mention to your teammate when exchanging images

5. **Discuss:** Share your collection of images and notes with your teammates, along with any insights you had about the topic and your physical location. Compare and contrast your two experiences verbally and visually, working to understand the implications of the photography collection.

Analysis

Phase 4: With remote teammates

6. **Discuss:** Use the following guide to discuss what you have learned together through this process.

DISCUSSION GUIDE

*   What did you learn about your shared topic through this activity?
*   What did you find most interesting about your teammate's photos?
*   What did you learn from comparing all of the collected photos?
*   What facts, assumptions, and opinions could be related to your images?

c. Activity

Photo Juxtaposition Perspective Exchange

For the final phase of this photographic journey, there is an opportunity to gain additional socio-cultural insight about your intercultural collaboration by juxtaposing the images gathered during either of the prior variations. *Image juxtaposition,* a tactic often used in art and design, makes a visual argument by placing two seemingly similar or outwardly dissimilar subjects side-by-side. Sometimes they are two complete images placed next to each other (e.g., a photo of tall skyscrapers and a photo of tall trees); sometimes the images are placed next to each other so that they appear to become one new image (e.g., skyscrapers that merge with treetops). This side-by-side placement enables the viewer to compare and contrast the images—which can be very effective in making a serious point or in revealing humorous elements. There are a number of ways to complete this creative activity, and your choice will depend on variables such as resources and skill levels. You could choose just one option, or work through all three in a sequence. The process transforms your individual photographs—Thought Objects—into provocative conversation-starters—Dialogue Objects.

→ **People:** Individual/remote teammates
→ **Duration:** 1–3 hours, depending on the option
→ **Technology:** Black & white, or color, printer, digital camera or camera-equipped mobile device, shared document or folder, messaging or email, image-editing software

Option 1: Print & shuffle

Phase 1: Working individually

1. **Choose:** Of the images collected by you and your teammates doing the photo exchange, select some specific images. What catches your eye? What is interesting or unique?
2. **Print:** Print your favorite images, either in color or in black and white. Try to print at least five images per teammate. Depending on how many teammates you have, you may end up with a wide range of options.
3. **Pair:** Shuffle the images, then place different photos side-by-side. As you choose pairs, see if you can highlight a similarity, show contrast, or examine another interesting aspect of juxtaposition. How many different pairings can you create? What different meanings emerge from different juxtapositions? What similarities or contrasts between the two photographic journeys do you notice? What have you learned about your teammate, their city, or the shared sub-topic that you didn't expect?
4. **Document:** Take photos of your favorite juxtapositions.
5. **Stick them together:** If desired, affix your image juxtapositions to another sheet of paper and hang them on the wall of your workspace.

Phase 2: With remote teammates

6. **Send:** Share your documentation with your teammates via email, videoconference, or Fourth Space. Include a brief written explanation of why you think each pair is interesting.
7. **Discuss:** Connect with your teammates synchronously to discuss your juxtapositions using the discussion guide at the end of this activity.

Option 2: Simple digital compositions

Phase 1: Working individually

1. **Choose:** Pool together the photos gathered by your team. Depending on how many teammates you have, you may end up with a large collection of images. What catches your eye? What is interesting or unique?

2.   **Pair:** Import all of these images into a shared document. If needed, scale the images down so you can fit two images side-by-side. Move the images around to juxtapose the different photos. See how many different pairings you can create. When you have arrived at a set of pairings that you'd like to share with your teammates, move it to its own separate page of the document. What similarities or contrasts do you notice?

3.   **Describe:** For each image juxtaposition you create, write a brief description explaining why you think that particular juxtaposition is interesting.

Phase 2: With remote teammates

4.   **Connect:** Contact your teammates to let them know you have completed this activity so they can review your image juxtapositions and vice versa.

5.   **Discuss:** Meet with your teammates synchronously to discuss your juxtapositions using the discussion guide at the end of this activity.

Option 3: Complex digital compositions

Phase 1: Working individually

After you have completed one of the earlier image juxtaposition options and reviewed your teammates' work, begin to think about how you can create more sophisticated compositions based on your initial pairings.

1.   **Research:** Brainstorm about what you've learned subjectively from both sets of images, making notes on your ideas, opinions, and impressions of the photographic findings. After this preliminary brainstorming period, conduct objective online research about the city, culture, and/or sub-topic. Use your research to revise your initial opinions and impressions and to develop questions to submit to your remote teammates. Seek information relevant to your mutual interests as well as information that will help you to get to know your teammates' culture(s).

2.   **Summarize:** Write a few paragraphs explaining what you have learned.

Phase 2: With remote teammates

3.   **Exchange:** Share your research summary with your remote teammates as inspiration for the next phase of the project.

4.   **Design:** You and your teammates will develop a series of posters about your collective research and photographic findings. Your posters will be a visual response to the research and should utilize at least one of your image juxtapositions. As you create the posters, incorporate some of your writing about the juxtapositions. Include words, phrases, or thoughts from your teammates that shed light on their cultural perspective related to the shared

topic. Check out the Creative Remix activity (6.2b) for inspiration and ideas for managing a collaborative design process.

5. **Communicate:** Maintain an open dialogue with your teammates throughout the process, asking additional questions as needed and exchanging visuals for feedback. (Select an intercultural critique activity from Chapter 5.)

Analysis

Phase 3: With remote teammates

6. **Discuss:** Use the following guide to discuss what you have learned together through this process.

DISCUSSION GUIDE

• How did the process of juxtaposition add value to your project or exchange?
• What unexpected findings emerged from this process of creating image juxtapositions to highlight similarities, differences, or other insights?
• What else would you like to share with your teammate about the topic that wasn't captured in your photographs, juxtapositions, or posters?
• How can you use objective and subjective information to challenge your teammates to think about the topic in a new way?

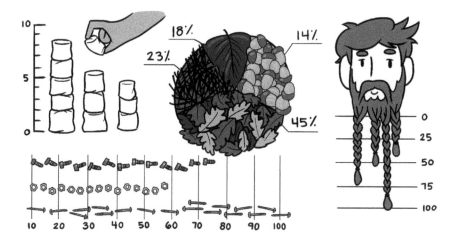

4.4

Datastorming:
Bringing information to life

Datastorming is essentially brainstorming with *quantitative* or *qualitative* data. Quantitative data is measurable, or numbers-based, which can be appealing to the objective fact-finders on your team. Qualitative data is generally observational, and not numbers-based, which may interest teammates who lean toward more subjective information. This distributed research approach asks each teammate to individually look at an issue through the lens of various secondary sources. Engaging in a *Datastorm* can add value to a team project in many ways, from both topical and collaborative perspectives. This shared approach to learning new information can pinpoint important details related to a team's rallying point topic. Based on their data discoveries, teammates then create an *information visualization* that they can easily share with and use to explain to the rest of the team.

Information visualization is the visual depiction of quantitative or qualitative information that is communicated visually in order to reveal patterns, describe high-level analysis, or showcase particular insights. Information that would otherwise only appear as words or numbers is instead given a graphical or visual representation (Tufte 2001). This treatment should make the key points of the collected information more accessible and easier to understand, without requiring the viewer to read the original numbers or words from which the visualization was derived. The products of a *Datastorm*, however, need not always represent quantitative data.

In context: Datastorming as creative research

In one of our studies, a team was interested in the social role of libraries. The team considered ways to change or update the way libraries function. After independently researching this topic from various perspectives, one teammate found an article that described the various ways people in her local community use their library. While the article included specific data (e.g., 23% of respondents use the library to conduct internet searches), that data was scattered throughout the text and not pulled together in a readily accessible manner. The teammate transcribed all the data from the article and created a bar chart that quickly and easily conveyed to viewers the library usage data they had discovered. This began a dialogue about ideas and next steps, as well as some interesting comparisons with information that some other teammates had found during their research.

Another team was focused more specifically on cultural learning, rather than a topic outside of their intercultural collaboration. This team found resources that talked in a more in-depth way about how different cultures perceive each other. While researching, one teammate, based in the United States, found a map of the Gulf Region depicting the percentages of US college students who could correctly identify four of the countries depicted on the map. The percentages of correct guesses were sadly low. This data gave everyone on the team a clearer picture of the gap in cultural and geographic understanding between the United States and Gulf Region.

Accessible methods

As these examples show, you do not need design expertise to participate in *Datastorming*. While there is an entire subset of the communication design discipline devoted to information visualization, there are also many approaches to make this process accessible to all teammates. You have probably seen some of these methods, such as bar graphs or pie charts, in news programs, magazine articles, or academic literature. The *self-quantification movement*, which encourages people to track data about themselves (e.g., through wearable devices that record daily physical activity), has made data visualization familiar to many people who might not otherwise see it on a regular basis. See the definitive *Feltron* annual reports created by designer Nicholas Felton for humorous and extreme examples of self-quantification (Felton 2015).

Beware of data bias

It is important to keep in mind that data is not neutral. It is collected, interpreted, and shared by people, which makes it vulnerable to our human imperfections. *Data bias* is a term for describing the ways data can intentionally or unintentionally reinforce positive or negative biases. This type of bias can be the outcome, for example, of survey questions that result in skewed responses because they are written with a particular political slant or are influenced by the survey creator's own implicit biases.

Redlining maps exemplify data bias

In the creation of information visualizations, data bias can impact the way people regard each other. It can influence behavior and perpetuate long-standing inequities and misinformation tied to nationality, gender, and race. One famous example of data bias is the redlining maps of many US cities. Created during the New Deal era (1930s–1940s) by the Home Owners' Loan Corporation, the maps were intended to provide information for mortgage companies about residents' potential credit risk versus their "credit worthiness" when trying to purchase a home. Far beyond this explicit purpose, however, these maps have reinforced centuries of racial, social, and economic inequality in the United States by painting a vivid picture of privileged and underserved neighborhoods (University of Richmond Digital Scholarship Lab, n.d.).

Thinking critically about forms of data bias

As concerns about fake news and the realities of data bias continue to impact people's views of local and global information, there is an increased responsibility to bring an independent and critical awareness to our understanding of how information is communicated and disseminated. Critical thinking, as it relates specifically to data awareness, is an essential skill for navigating the complexities of our information-saturated world. Data-driven bias can occur in places where you would least expect it, such as in research studies circulated by the media, and in academic or professional research projects, from the planning and collection phases to the analysis and publication of findings.

By examining how data is represented, we have an opportunity to mitigate the significant risks associated with viral misinformation and distorted perceptions of what constitutes truth and reality. Verifying sources, cross-referencing findings, considering who benefits from a study, and looking for gaps in who is (or is not) represented are all critical to that process. Understanding one's own values and biases also helps to decrease biased interpretation of visualized data from the viewer's perspective.

Benefits & outcomes

- Practice crucial information skills in collecting, interpreting, and communicating data
- Exploring various visual forms for showing the information
- Share creative research with your team through information visualizations
- Think critically about data bias and other media issues

Activity

Datastorming

It is critical to examine how data is presented in the world and its effect on people, behaviors, and public sentiment. Data visualizations can appear within academic studies, scientific literature, the popular press, and other sources. It is important to keep in mind that these images can have a significant impact on the viewer and are often used to support the agendas of individuals, organizations, and governmental entities. While this sounds serious—and while data bias can have grave implications—Datastorming is intended to be a hands-on method for engaging teams with new information relevant to their rallying point topic. This activity encourages you to explore secondary sources on your team's shared topic and offers you a way to present your findings to teammates in the form of visual data or information.

→ **People:** Remote teammates/individual
→ **Duration:** 3–4 days, depending on time differences. Real-time interactions are recommended, but the results are similar even if some time elapses between the two teams completing the Datastorming activity.
→ **Technology:** Camera, videoconferencing software
→ **Other resources:** Paper, markers, and whatever other materials are useful for creating your visualization (string, yarn, glue, paper cups, blocks, pipe cleaners, popsicle sticks, scissors, tape, colored paper, etc.)

Tips

- **Distributed research:** This activity is a *distributed* research approach, meaning that each member of the team does some work individually and then teammates pool their results to create a collective resource, thereby helping the larger group. Creating information visualizations to support this process encourages individuals to do some synthesis and analysis of their findings, even before those findings are shared with the larger group.
- **Expand your search:** If you are someone who typically gravitates toward your favorite search engine for answers, this approach can provide you with perspectives that are not readily apparent in your usual search results. Also, keep in mind that online search results are often skewed based on geographic location, search engine algorithms, and, for better or worse, the unconscious bias inherent in the keywords you typically choose.

- **Go analog!** Experiment with a range of media, tools, and materials. You'll get much more out of this activity if you are physically handling materials or objects and thinking about how to use them to represent your data rather than tinkering with the colors in a digital bar chart. What if you used pieces of pasta to show quantities of people engaged in a particular activity? Or marshmallows and toothpicks to construct a three-dimensional bar chart of quantitative survey data?
- **Online tools:** If you do not have any background in visual communication and/or any access to design tools, there are some online tools and other resources that can teach you or assist you in creating a data visualization. To the previous point, we encourage teammates to create physical (rather than digital) representations of data first, in order to make this activity engaging across multiple sensorimotor channels.

Formulate

Phase 1: With remote teammates

1. **Discuss:** Engage in a discussion with your remote teammates about how you would like to use data to learn more about your topic. What types of data are most relevant to your team's chosen rallying point? These might range from quantitative statistical or population data to qualitative expressions or phrases that appear within an interview or news article. For instance, if a team is looking at the topic of global migration, they may decide to explore how many times the word "migrant" or "immigrant" appears in the local newspapers of major cities (quantitative), or collect a range of quotes capturing different people's feelings on the topic (qualitative).

Phase 2: Working individually

2. **Research:** Each member of your team will conduct individual research on the topic you are exploring together. Use your own resources, such as typical news sources, databases, journal articles, and other sources of quantitative and qualitative data. When exploring resources, look for things that help to help you better understand your rallying point topic in relation to your specific discipline(s).
3. **Visualize:** Create a data visualization to represent your findings. You may use a digital or analog approach to create your visualization, but we encourage you to explore materials such as pipe cleaners, strings, blocks, or photographs of physical objects (arranged aesthetically). For example, one teammate might build a stack of Legos and use the stack to represent data from a bar chart; another may take a more digital approach and use spreadsheet tools. Yet another teammate might create a word cloud using string.

4. **Share:** Photograph your data visualization and share with your remote team via videoconference, email, a shared document, or the Fourth Space. Be sure to include original sources and any high-level takeaways for reference. The goals are to share your own visualization, and use it to convey some of the research others have done on this topic.

Phase 3: With remote teammates

5. **Explore:** Browse the other teams' visualizations and ask questions. Talk with your remote teammates about what you learned from this activity.
6. **Write:** Work together to write a succinct overview statement based on your collective findings. Based on what you've discovered, what is the nature of the data surrounding your topic? Compare and contrast your findings with your remote teammates' findings to better understand how your shared topic is perceived in a different part of the world. What kinds of insights or opportunities do these findings suggest? Where are there gaps in research or news coverage? Discuss possibilities for further work with your teammate. What can you learn from this?

Analysis

Phase 4: With remote teammates

7. **Discuss:** Use the following guide to discuss what you have learned together through this process.

DISCUSSION GUIDE

- What was your initial response to your teammates' visualizations?
- Were you reacting to the information that was represented, the way it was represented, or both?
- Is there a significant difference in the way people share or discover information in your culture compared to your teammates' culture(s)?
- How do concepts such as data bias play a role in your cumulative findings?
- What can your findings tell you about media freedom or constraints in each culture?

4.5

Fictional Character Exchange: Explaining cultural nuances

Starting with our initial research study, we have incorporated Fictional Character Exchanges into most of our subsequent studies in intercultural collaboration. We find that creating and sharing fictional characters can be an accessible way for your remote team to have conversations about cultural questions or nuances you might not otherwise think to ask or might feel too self-conscious to discuss. It can be easier for teammates to engage in cultural discussion and share opinions in the third person through their fictionalized characters.

Not your typical persona

This activity has some roots in a design research tool called a *persona*. Those familiar with physical and digital product design may already be acquainted with the concept of personas; these visual layouts provide a "snapshot" of a product's typical users by combining *psychographic* information and *demographic* information (Cooper 2004; Laubheimer 2017). Psychographic information is qualitative, pertaining to one's behaviors, motivations, interests, personality traits, and values, whereas demographic information is socio-economic in nature, describing one's physical location, race, marital status, age, level of education, income, and so on.

Research-based personas have long been an important and ubiquitous tool for quickly characterizing and representing different clusters of potential users or audiences, typically derived from quantitative survey and qualitative interview or observation data. Personas are valuable to user experience (UX) and product design teams because they help designers maintain an empathetic connection to potential users. They also encourage designers to stay focused on the development of their products as they pertain directly to consumer behaviors, goals, and needs.

Fictional characters

Unlike traditional personas, fictional characters do not necessarily rely upon the layers of quantitative and qualitative research, synthesis, and analysis that drive typical persona creation. We have learned that the process of creating and exchanging characters is an effective cultural learning tool even outside of the context of a specific design project. For the purposes of cultural learning, fictional characters don't necessarily need to be based on research. Because the purpose is to share some of your embodied cultural knowledge, these characters can be developed from your own cultural experiences, awareness, and expertise.

In context: Learning cultural nuances through fictional characters

One of the fictional characters that a US teammate created was a representation of a middle-aged, divorced, spandex-clad, male cyclist living in Northern California. The cyclist gave rise to questions and conversation about commuting, exercise and fitness; marriage, dating and relationships. Another teammate, meanwhile, read a *New York Times* article about an Emirati man who had earned some fame as a chef in New York City. The chef raised questions of social acceptability; caste systems; the role and prevalence of domestic laborers; lifestyle choices; and social expectations, for example "Who does the cooking at your house?" and "Who does the cooking at your favorite restaurant?"

The role of readings

To jumpstart the Fictional Character Exchange, be sure to seek out local news sources as well as national and international coverage of events and stories related to your community. As you read, make notes to yourself about what kind of fictional character you might create. Your readings might bring to mind specific types of people who might be impacted by the events or issues described in the texts. Another approach might be to think about who specifically (in your culture) might be reading and reacting to the same piece of writing. Readings might also center around local news; unique characteristics of the particular countries or cultures involved in the collaboration; and cultural questions raised by teammates in either culture.

Benefits & outcomes

- Develop and exchange characters based on your own cultural knowledge
- Highlight and discuss various cultural nuances in your distinct geographic locations
- Consider potential project audiences, both local and global
- Discuss how insights from the fictional characters are applicable to your rallying point

---

Activity

Fictional Character Exchange

Fictional Character Exchange is an opportunity to engage in third-person cultural discourse and share culture-specific insights. To ensure a wide range of perspectives, teams begin by reading a set of texts (such as news articles, essays, book excerpts, or other prose) to highlight various cultural nuances and developments in their distinct geographic locations. In addition to drawing inspiration from your readings, you can create a fictional character based on a wide range of options, including your own social, family, or cultural knowledge, awareness, and expertise. Simply creating and exchanging the fictional characters is not enough; the real cultural learning comes via the discussion that follows the exchange. Discussing each other's fictional characters helps remote teammates educate each other on cultural intricacies, providing windows into their different backgrounds.

➜ **People:** Individual/remote teammates
➜ **Duration:** 1 day for reading; 2 hours for the character creation activity and discussion; 1–3 days to exchange and discuss characters with remote teammates
➜ **Technology:** Email, cloud-based file sharing, online community, videoconferencing
➜ **Low-bandwidth version:** Sketch and photograph responses
➜ **Other resources:** Paper, markers, pens/pencils, photos or illustrations of people, pushpins, tape, sticky notes

---

Tips

- **Inspiration:** You can learn a lot from looking at external sources. Begin by drawing inspiration from the readings, along with observing and thinking about real people you know. Gathering a range of perspectives will help create a well-balanced view of any content; in the case of creating a fictional character, it can help you identify both unique and representational aspects of your culture.
- **Dynamic characters:** In your written character description, focus on local cultural nuances that may not be widely known outside of your geographic area. Think about your outrageous best friend, or that person you always want to strike up a conversation with at your local coffee shop. The intention with this activity is not to create stereotypical interpretations of a culture, but to aggregate interesting characteristics from real people in order to share aspects of your culture with teammates.
- **A dash of humor:** The characters also provide great opportunities for self-reflection and humor, including the internal humor in realizing just how weird things about your own culture might be when you take a step back and consider them from an outsider's perspective.
- **Embed in your next project:** In addition to intercultural learning opportunities, fictional characters represent an important moment of potential growth when used in project-based teamwork. The exchange allows you to consider potential project audiences in a different way, both locally and around the world, helping you better understand whether ideas are appropriate, communicative, and relevant to another culture.

Research

Phase 1: Working individually

1. **Read:** Read three to five news articles about cultural events in your community and consider the leading characters driving those events. Review local news sources as well as national and international coverage of events and stories in your community. As you read, begin thinking about what kind of fictional character, or persona, you'll create, based on the characters you've encountered in your reading.
   - Swap at least one article with your remote teammate (you may agree to exchange more than one).
   - If the article is not available in your teammate's native language, check to make sure it can easily be translated easily online. If not, choose another option.

- Highlight or make notes of interesting passages or phrases as you go. What might entice, stimulate, or provoke readers?
2. **Choose an Audience:** Now that you have some possible fictional characters in mind, work independently to select an audience demographic for your fictional character. Examples could include:
   - Child of reading age, tweens, or high-schoolers
   - 20-something university student
   - Married or single 40-something
   - Grandparent
3. **Write It Down:** Using the provided worksheet or a blank sheet of paper, write down your character's name, age, and occupation. These details should be based on what you've determined is realistic given your cultural perspective and interests.
4. **Narrate:** Write a paragraph or two that tells a story about your character's life: their interests, opinions, hobbies, motivations, goals, and troubles. What do you think this person's life is like? Describe it in approximately 200 words. Keep in mind that your character should be fictional and not a description someone you know. However, you can think about friends, relatives, or one of the real-life characters from the news sources to help jumpstart your ideas.
5. **Sketch:** Sketch, draw, or find a photograph to represent your character. Keep in mind the cultural relevance of the following and whether you want to include it: jewelry, hair styles or coverings, clothing, and other types of body adornments.

Share

Phase 2: With remote teammates

6. **Send:** Send your character to your remote teammates.
7. **Print:** When you receive your teammates' fictional characters, print them out and read them.
8. **Read & Highlight:** Use a marker or pen when reading to highlight points of interest or elements that you would like to learn more about later from your remote teammates.
9. **Reflect & Discuss:** Recall the fourth dimension, Assess Information (*our individual and culturally informed patterns affect the ways we gather, understand, and verify what we know*). With remote teammates, take some time to ask questions based on the points of interest you highlighted on each other's fictional characters. Discuss what you have learned from this exchange, and how the experience of creating and reading fictional characters connects to your preferences for objective and/or subjective information-seeking. Use the following guide.

DISCUSSION GUIDE

- What aspects of your teammates' fictional characters are you most excited to learn more about?
- What information source(s) did you use to create your fictional character? How was this similar or different to your teammates' approaches?
- What cultural information did you learn about through the exchange of fictional characters? How is this different than what you may have learned online?
- In what ways has this activity changed how you assess information?

References

Brown, Tim, and Barry Katz. 2009. *Change by Design: How Design Thinking Transforms Organizations and Inspires Innovation.* 1st ed. New York: Harper Business.

Cooper, Alan. 2004. *The Inmates Are Running the Asylum.* Indianapolis: Sams.

Design Council. 2015a. "The Design Process: What Is the Double Diamond?" Design Council. March 17, 2015. www.designcouncil.org.uk/news-opinion/design-process-what-double-diamond.

———. 2015b. "Design Methods Step 1: Discover." Design Council. March 18, 2015. www.designcouncil.org.uk/news-opinion/design-methods-step-1-discover.

Felton, Nicholas. 2015. "2014 Feltron Annual Report." Feltron.Com. 2015. http://feltron.com/FAR14.html.

Laubheimer, Page. 2017. "Personas vs. Jobs-to-Be-Done." Nielsen Norman Group. August 6, 2017. www.nngroup.com/articles/personas-jobs-be-done/.

Mayer, Richard E. 2002. "Multimedia Learning." In *Psychology of Learning and Motivation*, 41:85–139. Academic Press. doi:10.1016/S0079-7421(02)80005-6.

Tufte, Edward R. 2001. *The Visual Display of Quantitative Information.* Vol. 2. Cheshire, CT: Graphics Press.

University of Richmond Digital Scholarship Lab. n.d. "Mapping Inequality." University of Richmond. Accessed July 28, 2019. https://dsl.richmond.edu/panorama/redlining/.

Willis, Judith. 2006. *Research-Based Strategies to Ignite Student Learning: Insights from a Neurologist and Classroom Teacher.* Alexandria, VA : Association for Supervision and Curriculum Development.

5

DECODE COMMUNICATION STYLES

Exchanging constructive feedback
through critique

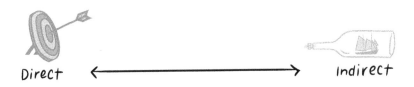

Direct ⟵⟶ Indirect

DIMENSION 5: Decode Communication Styles

We use language in different ways to relate to and communicate with other people.
   **These critique approaches can be useful as discussion tools for
activities your team has already completed. It is helpful to first
engage in the Practice Critique (5.2) with local colleagues. Then,
with your remote teammates, choose from the remaining activities.**

   Chapter 5 explores giving and receiving constructive feedback, or critique, as a communication tool that can be useful throughout a collaboration
to refine and finalize ideas. For some teams, different communication styles
can impact the process of providing feedback. In terms of inter-team dynamics, learning how to critique offers an opportunity to preserve relationships
and find the courage to share opinions while boosting individuals' cognitive
flexibility.

| **DIRECT:** I speak my mind and share my true intentions without sugar-coating things because I want people to know exactly what I think. While this straightforward approach may run the risk of offending some people, my clear communication style means that others are less likely to misunderstand me. | **INDIRECT:** I often use metaphors or sugar-coat my opinions in order to avoid tension because I don't want to hurt people's feelings. While my implicit approach may be less likely to offend other people, it brings greater risk of misunderstanding or misinterpretation. |

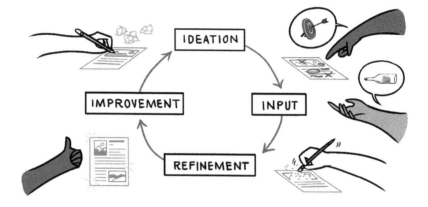

5.1

Exchanging constructive feedback through critique

The process of giving and receiving constructive feedback, or *critique*, is all about communication: thinking, offering ideas, listening, and asking questions. Coincidentally, these are also the key ingredients in a successful intercultural collaboration. When performed effectively, a critique can stimulate important dialogue and promote the exchange and application of ideas in new ways. In addition to the context of remote teamwork, becoming proficient in feedback exchanges can benefit your work in future personal or professional projects. Critique can even benefit your relationships by helping you become more receptive and open to opportunities for growth and by cultivating your ability to see the potential in those around you.

Feedback improves ideas

It is hard to expand your thinking, evolve new ideas, and ensure the originality of your concept without critique. As a form of exchange, critique is certainly not easy, but it can be a wonderfully fruitful way to spur creative innovation by pushing your work further. Consider the alternative: Your team receives no constructive feedback or analytical perspective and ends up pursuing just one idea that came to mind early in the process. You run with it as is, without altering the direction or considering alternatives. But, later in the process, the team realizes that it isn't a new idea after all.

Considerations for critiques across cultures

During an intercultural collaborative project, there will likely come a point where you need feedback in order to move the project further along and better understand how your ideas communicate to others. However, intercultural critique comes with its own special set of challenges. Due to its western origins, certain aspects of critique may challenge cultural values in some contexts.

Moreover, learning to give and receive feedback while maintaining positive interactions is the age-old predicament of critique. Overcoming these hurdles can become even more amplified in an intercultural exchange. If your team can overcome them, though, your project will likely benefit from multiple perspectives. Well-structured critique can greatly enhance the outcomes of collaboration because it offers teammates a way to discuss work more deeply. Because the critique formats in this chapter encourage contributions from all teammates, if well managed, they can promote a sense of equity and inclusion that brings teams together.

An additional consideration is that intercultural collaborations almost always involves language differences, which means that audio is not always the optimal channel for delivering, receiving, and processing constructive feedback. To compensate for this, most of the activities in this chapter offer an opportunity to organize thoughts by creating words and images, which we find can increase buy-in between teammates who don't speak the same native language.

A productive exchange of ideas

Constructive feedback is an important tool that is at the heart of innovation. This is an opportunity to understand if your work is communicating in a way that fits within one or more of the following four fields: commercial, responsible, experimental, or discursive in nature (Tharp and Tharp 2018) (for more discussion of the four-fields framework in action, see 6.2).

In some fields, critique has cousins that go by other names, such as *feedback* and *peer review*. While we may use these terms as synonyms, critique in design disciplines is viewed as a productive exchange of ideas. For the purposes of this book, it is important to know that critique is used by creative professionals, such as designers, writers, artists, and actors as both a noun and a verb.

Critique is a noun and a verb

Critique, noun: The exchange of feedback on a project or idea. ("We're going to have a critique in five minutes, pin up your best ideas so far!") *Critique, verb:* The act of providing constructive input during the process of designing something. ("Let's critique the use of color in these five illustration ideas.") Whether the setting is a professional or academic environment, critique is an integral part of the creative process. And learning to give and receive feedback is paramount to the collaborative process.

Critique is not criticism

Mentally separating the idea of *critique* from the negative and one-sided connotations of *criticism* can soften the blow for the person whose work is being evaluated. The recipient of the feedback hears positive comments on either side of the constructive ones. And even negative comments can be framed constructively so that they come across as suggestions rather than judgment. When giving and receiving feedback, it is important for both the critic and the presenter to remember that this is an evaluation of the work, not the person who made the work. Judy Reeves (2002) expands upon this notion in her book *Writing Alone, Writing Together*, in which she describes criticism as "passing judgment" while critique "poses questions."

Critique structure

In the professional sector, a constructive critique can significantly improve outcomes and products. Design disciplines typically conduct critique in team settings. The process generally involves one person presenting work at a time, while others listen, view, consider, and then respond by verbally offering their input. The process is most effective for all parties when presenters note upfront the specific aspects of their work that they would like reviewers to evaluate or ignore. Reviewers then offer positive feedback on these aspects as well as suggestions for improvement. AIGA, the US-based professional association for design, describes the structuring of a critique as a "love sandwich": The things you love about the work are the bread, and areas that need improvement are sandwiched between the things you love. Improvements are articulated as suggestions instead of as failures or negative attributes (Lawless and Crabill 2015).

Engaging the visual through feedback sessions

The subject of a critique may seem obvious; in design practice, constructive feedback is usually directed at 2D or 3D visualizations or prototypes. While other forms of ideas can also be evaluated through critique, creating images can help to convey ideas across language barriers, and also to make ideas more concrete by giving visual form to feelings and concepts when words alone do not suffice. Whether through informal sketching, capturing photographs or screenshots, or engaging in diagrammatic approaches such as mapping, images offer a great deal of information. For example, visual mapping can provide clarity about the distinct phases of a project or help define what is needed to complete a shared task. In other instances, the visual representation of teammate engagement in providing analysis can strengthen team cohesion.

Tangible and sensorimotor forms of reflection

Because of its deeply communicative properties, creating imagery is a productive form of reflection and pairs well with writing. Combining these two complementary approaches can lead to new insights and dialogue. These strategies help organize one's thoughts in new and different ways, creating new opportunities to engage in intercultural learning as each person unpacks the shared information. Combined with traditional approaches such as speaking about your project, writing, sketching, and other forms of visualization—as tangible and sensorimotor activities—might even engage different parts of your brain in the development of your collaborative work.

Critique in intercultural collaborations

The critique process may conflict with cultural values around team cohesion in some contexts. In these cases, combined verbal and visual approaches help reframe feedback exchange so that it does not feel as confrontational or personal as a traditional face-to-face oral critique. According to science and technology scholars Joyce Thomas and Deana McDonagh (2013), visual and verbal variations of intercultural communication helps teams successfully develop a "shared language" for critique that comprises mutual respect, keeps in mind their shared intentions or project goals, promotes patience, and works toward compromise. Similarly, related studies confirm that providing a range of options for expression and interaction creates more inclusive opportunities to give and to receive feedback.

Impacts of social structure

For example, due in part to the tight-knit personal relationships and social harmony of *collectivist* cultures, some teammates can be averse to participating in traditional forms of critique. A collectivist teammate would prioritize the team's harmony and needs over those of individuals. Because the project or idea is understood as belonging to the individual or team who created it, the act of providing constructive criticism can be seen as infringing upon the creator's authority over their own ideas. This infringement could disrupt the social fabric of the community. While giving and receiving feedback can also be uncomfortable for *individualistic* teammates (who prioritize individuals), these teammates may have an easier time separating the evaluation of the work from the people who created the work.

Cognitive flexibility and ambiguity tolerance

Ambiguity tolerance—the ability to manage uncertain or potentially uncomfortable situations promotes *cognitive flexibility*. Communication scholars Matthew M. Martin and Carolyn M. Anderson (1998) describe cognitive flexibility as a type of intellectual openness and adaptability combined with awareness. Cognitive flexibility can help us in many ways, such as adjusting to new or unfamiliar circumstances, or even in selecting different approaches to communication. Their research indicates that humans rely on cognitive flexibility in order to cope with life's various challenges (Martin and Rubin 1995; Martin and Anderson 1998). Critique is an exercise in ambiguity tolerance. In addition, it can make your team more cognitively flexible. Over time, this "tell me more" mentality can shift your thinking and improve your ability to give and to receive feedback.

Examples of cognitive flexibility in daily life might look like

- Trying to improve on a recipe by including a secret ingredient
- Working through a challenging discussion with a close friend
- Adjusting to a new home or city
- Welcoming a new human or furry member of the family

Cognitive flexibility among your team might look like

- Listening to an idea you disagree with, identifying positive points
- Rewording something or offering an explanation to help a teammate understand something
- Considering how to combine seemingly disparate ideas into a topic or problem statement that everyone feels excited to work on together

Formats for critique

Along with the other media theories discussed in Chapter 3, *synchronous* and *asynchronous* forms of communication are once again relevant to consider when engaging in long-distance critique. As a reminder, *synchronous* communication occurs when two or more parties communicate simultaneously in real time; *asynchronous* communication is not simultaneous.

Asynchronous critique considerations

Asynchronous critique is an untraditional format in the design disciplines that is becoming a necessity as more people work remotely together. Asynchronous critiques utilize lean, low social presence media in an exchange that is not simultaneous. Instead, it depends on the back-and-forth relay of information via virtual tools such as email, shared documents, blogs, and comments. The delays inherent to asynchronous conversation can lengthen the feedback process, but this also enables more time to think about and answer questions, thereby helping people to formulate more composed communication.

Asynchronous critique, in particular, aims to make constructive feedback exchanges possible under certain circumstances, such as extreme time differences or technical challenges. It provides space and time for teammates to reflect on and formulate responses, helping to close communication gaps in situations in which teammates must communicate with each other in languages other than their mother tongue. Success in this kind of exchange requires agreement among teammates with regard to building a social presence around the exchange and to ensuring timely response expectations.

Synchronous critique considerations

It is important to keep in mind, however, the impact of synchronous critique for second-language speakers, who may feel more pressure to respond quickly or feel more self-conscious about their language abilities when providing or receiving feedback in synchronous formats. Regardless of language proficiency, teammates should set aside adequate time to prepare in advance of synchronous critique in order to support a calm, considered, and developed discussion. In other words, just because the exchange happens simultaneously, it still requires significant preparation before it even begins.

Mix-and-match many variations of critique

Critique skills are learned and refined with time, regardless of one's cultural background. We are excited to share what we have learned about how to make intercultural critique more effective and less offensive. This chapter includes many different options for critique. These include a Practice Critique with local colleagues; asynchronous and synchronous virtual critiques; and written reflection. The chapter concludes with a conflict-resolution activity that enables you to reflect upon and provide constructive feedback to improve team dynamics. Each option could be used on its own or combined to create sequences of ongoing feedback. Experiment to discover what works best for your team.

General communication guidelines for critique

- **Plan ahead:** The critique format you choose impacts the efficacy and outcomes of the feedback exchange. Knowing that teammates have agreed to a specific structure, timeline, and format for exchanging feedback can alleviate stress and concern. Planning for the critique beforehand improves its efficacy and ensures that feedback is beneficial and well-received.
- **Check in:** While the critique guide introduced in the following section will be the primary focus of your discussion, remember first to check in with each other on a personal level. Whether critiquing via video chat or an asynchronous tool, a simple and sincere "How are you doing?"— and taking the time to listen to the response—goes a long way toward building trust and a good relationship. These moments also give you the opportunity to learn about your teammate outside the context of your work together, which can provide meaningful insights into your lives, culture, and how you relate to each other.
- **Listen:** In the reviewing role, your job is to actively listen. Focus your full attention on the presenter. Taking notes on paper can help with active listening by simultaneously activating your visual learning channel. When presenting, pausing is important because it creates opportunities for your listeners (reviewers) to think and respond.
- **Summarize:** Translate your handwritten notes into a shared document online that everyone on the team can access. This post-critique summary is particularly useful for helping everyone to parse the feedback and to have additional in-depth sidebar conversations within the team about the communication nuances and implications that are a part of this feedback exchange.

(Continued)

- **Discrepancies:** Are there any major discrepancies when you read your shared post-critique summary? If so, discuss them with your teammate. This discussion is important for avoiding misinterpretations of the feedback and discussion. You can have this conversation in a non-confrontational way by taking responsibility for what you don't understand: I think I may have misheard you when we talked. I thought you meant X, but I see in our notes you wrote Y. Can you please help me understand? I want to make sure we are on the same page!
- **Talk about it!** Do you need further clarification on certain words, idioms, or phrases that were given during the feedback that may have muddied the clarity of statements? If so, ask! If you feel like the quality of your feedback or your teammate's feedback could be improved, have a conversation. Ask for more depth, more clarity, and even more opportunities to discuss. In addition, it is important to follow up with your teammates with at least one question about the presentation or the feedback you have received.
- **Go deep:** It is important to provide people with meaningful and rich feedback when engaging in the critique process. Make sure to do your own research on the topic and avoid giving feedback that may come across as generic
- **It is not personal:** Try not to be self-conscious. The feedback is about the work product(s) of the collaboration, not the teammates. Hurt feelings are always an obstacle in critique. Even if there are not actual hurt feelings, the possibility and concern that you might hurt someone's feelings is ever-present.
- **Role assignment:** If delivering direct feedback is overwhelmingly uncomfortable for you, consider a different role. For example, you could be a dedicated note-taker or facilitator for the team's critique who records comments and feedback. (Obviously, this tactic only works in a team-based approach, not in a dyad. If self-consciousness continues to overwhelm someone in a dyad, please see Section 5.3 on possible asynchronous critique methods.)

5.2

Practice Critique:
Honing feedback skills as a first step

Because delivering and receiving critique effectively is a learned skill, this section walks you through a low-stakes Practice Critique with your local colleagues. This experience asks you to take turns presenting and reviewing each other's work, with the aim of helping you to feel more prepared and comfortable when you embark later on either asynchronous or synchronous critiques with your remote team. With time and practice, all teammates can begin to acclimatize and, in a way, to desensitize themselves to the potential emotional and mental challenges embedded in the process.

The Practice Critique invites local colleagues to generate a team list of adjectives that stimulate thinking about how to frame feedback, with the aim of choosing new adjectives to empower individuals with greater control over the critique process. Because this is often the first time people may be engaging in a critique, the activity prompts the creation of a long list of sketches and written adjectives as a guide. Coming up with adjectives, such as "inventive," "witty," or "risky," serve as parameters for the tone of the feedback. The reviewer, meanwhile, is challenged to think of creative ways to employ the adjectives meaningfully, perhaps in terms of describing the work's underlying strategy, how it communicates, or its overall impact.

Examining how you communicate

Think about how your background may influence the way you participate in or respond to critique. For many people, an intercultural collaborative project may present the first-ever opportunity to learn this method. Depending on the educational model in which you were taught, you may or may not have had an opportunity to speak up or to question ideas of other students in class or the teacher. Top-down, lecture-driven approaches to education can make it hard for people to feel confident in a critique space.

Unpack your critique baggage

Though someone may be comfortable sharing an opinion in some socially acceptable settings (e.g., commenting on news articles posted on social media), that does not mean that same person will be good at delivering an effective critique. Some people may be at a disadvantage because they have been encouraged to believe that their opinion is "the only one that matters," even when their comments are completely unfounded. (*"I just like it."* Okay, but *why*?) Some teammates with that particular type of experience may resort to delivering one-liners or have difficulty backing up their ideas with facts, examples, or further discussion.

Even for those who frequently Practice Critique, offering articulate suggestions and opinions based on facts, observations, and an analytical perspective can still be an uncomfortable experience. For newcomers, there is a tendency to frame comments with a sense of protective diplomacy, but it is important not to let your fear of rocking the boat prevent you from sharing your feedback. At the same time, there is no one-size-fits-all approach to critique. Regardless of your background, do not let this new experience of critique stop you in your tracks! There is much to gain from learning to give and receive productive feedback.

Benefits & outcomes

- Understand a structure for constructive feedback
- Practice giving feedback both visually and verbally
- Practice receiving feedback and responding with effective questions
- Recognize the power of language and respectful word choices

---

Activity

Practice Critique

This activity is an important precursor to the other intercultural critique methods that follows because feedback is a necessary ingredient for stimulating crucial dialogue and promoting the exchange of new ideas. Learning the language of constructive criticism is not only necessary for creating a positive shared environment for co-creation but is also a twenty-first-century professional skill. Critiques can be conducted in a range of settings and generally involves one person at a time presenting their work while others view, consider, and offer input. The activity draws attention to the power of language, visual metaphors, and respectful word choices, as a way to grapple with writing meaningful feedback. Because both reviewer and presenter have a stake in contributing to and selecting from the collection of adjectives, incorporating these words will help you frame your observations, opinions, and ideas in a more relatable form for each other.

➜ **People:** Local colleagues
➜ **Duration:** 1 hour
➜ **Resources:** Paper, pen/pencil

Tips

- **Revisit:** Refer to the General Communication Guidelines for Critique in 5.1
- **Speak up:** Notice who leads discussions during synchronous conversations and discuss how to share power within the team in other mediums. This will help better prepare for asynchronous dialogue and potential misunderstanding with future remote teammates
- **Provide substantial feedback:** During this kind of activity, it is especially important to encourage substantial feedback versus feedback along the lines of "you spelled this word wrong." This activity will enable you to practice these skills with your local colleagues first, before using them with your remote teammates.
- **Push past initial discomforts:** The aim is for all teammates to see the constructive aspects of critique and come to appreciate various aspects of the process and its outcomes. The process essentially induces temporary discomforts for the benefit of the project, thereby ultimately improving the work.

Framing feedback

Phase 1: With local colleagues

1. **Brainstorm:** With your local colleagues, generate a collection of sketches and written adjectives. In subsequent stages of this activity, both you as the presenter and your reviewer will use these adjectives to describe the work offered for critique. Each person should contribute at least four words and four sketches to the team collection. As your team generates their list of adjectives, anything goes—but keep in mind that everyone will be working

with an item from this list to engage creatively in this practice session and in future critique sessions.

Example:

> Adjectives such as *inventive, rational, goofy, genuine, witty, hilarious, safe, risky,* and *unassuming* are examples of words that can be used to describe the intentions, visuals, audiences, or communication strategies employed in someone's work.

Phase 2: Working individually

2. **Document:** Make sure to photograph and write down the complete list of adjectives and sketches generated by your local colleagues.
3. **Choose four:** From the list on the board, make four selections that you would like your reviewer to use to critique your work. Choose one sketch, one word that feels practical or related, one word that feels like a challenge or aspiration, and one that seems completely random.

Assess

Phase 3: With one local colleague

4. **Pair Up:** Among your local colleagues, find someone to exchange pieces of work that need feedback. You will take turns as *presenter* (sharing your work) and *reviewer* (evaluating and sharing feedback on the work).
5. **Review:** Take a moment to review the idea you have received. The work could be in a variety of forms. For example, you might read a written piece, flip through a multi-page presentation draft, or view documentation of a 2D or 3D prototype.
6. **Reflect:** How would you describe this work? What are you seeing? What is the presenter's intention? What is the presenter saying with this work? What makes it interesting, useful, and/or relevant? Would you describe the idea as primarily commercial, responsible, experimental, discursive, cultural, or some combination of these?
7. **Make three lists:** In considering your presenter's contribution, write three lists of:
   a. As many positive attributes as possible.
   b. Things that could be improved.
   c. Questions you have about the work.
8. **Revisit Teamthink Constellation:** Reflecting on your selections for the fifth dimension, Decode Communication Styles, keep in mind potential communication differences in terms of how you might deliver feedback and how your local colleague might interpret it. This is a helpful practice for intercultural critiques where communication differences may be more pronounced.

9. **Write:** Working with your lists and the presenter's selected adjectives, use the following formula to write and/or sketch some feedback on their work:

   a. One sentence based on your reflection: How would you describe this work? What did you first notice about it? Incorporate at least one of the presenter's selections into this sentence.

      Example:

      > *"What first caught my eye was the color scheme; on closer examination, I realized that the **witty** use of color extends visual puns to a new level in that they…"*

   b. Two to three positive attributes: Choose a few of the top items from your list and write about these in more detail. Avoid adjectives like "nice" and "good." Try to give more specific reasons for why you liked something, why it provoked your interest, and so on. Write at least one sentence that includes one of the selected words or sketches.

      > *"The imagery is a **risky** choice but is still impactful because…."*

   c. Three to five ideas for improvement: Instead of just making a list of what is wrong with the contribution, frame these observations as suggestions for improving the work. Write at least one sentence that includes one of the selected words or sketches.

      > *"Including more **goofy** language in this piece might excite your intended audience because…"*

   d. Two to three questions: Include a few thought-provoking questions for your teammate to consider. Bonus points if you can include a selected adjective into one of your questions!

      > *"Could your piece feel more genuine if you included a wider range of people's faces?"*

   e. One more positive attribute: Close the evaluation on a positive note.

Exchange feedback

Phase 4: With local colleague

10. **Share:** Exchange written critique with one of your local colleagues in a manner that feels comfortable for both people. Based on your learning style and personality, different locations or physical positions might impact how you feel about or engage in the critique, or how you relate to the work you are evaluating. You might consider finding space away from the larger group to sit down and engage in a deep discussion. Perhaps you would prefer to stand and walk around the presenter's work and use sticky-notes to point directly to discrete areas of a physical object or visual piece. Maybe you want to express all of your thoughts about your teammate's work first, before your teammate shares their perspective. Alternatively, you could take turns sharing bits of feedback in a back-and-forth conversation about both of your works.

11. **Respond:** Think about your reviewer(s)' feedback, then pause to consider it before responding. Because critique can provoke emotional responses, it is important to remind yourself that the feedback is directed at improving your work and is not a personal evaluation. Consider your teammate's suggestions: What sounds interesting to you? What is feasible? Do you have answers to your teammate's questions or new questions? Be thoughtful in your response, and thank your teammates for their time and insights.

Analysis

Phase 5: With local colleague

12. **Reflect and Follow Up:** Use the following discussion guide to reflect on the process and help you continue to improve your constructive criticism skills.

DISCUSSION GUIDE

As the recipient:
• Did you understand the feedback your critique partner gave you? What kind of follow-up questions could you ask in order for your reviewer to offer clearer explanations?
• Was the critique you received useful and relevant to you? Why or why not? What could you have done differently to draw out more feedback or delve deeper into your reviewer's viewpoint?
• How did you personally feel when reading the feedback from your reviewer? Was there anything that made you feel especially excited about the way you might proceed?
• How did you respond to feedback that you did not expect or agree with? Did you choose your responses carefully? Did you take it personally? Did you take notes for later review and consideration?
• How did receiving feedback in different formats (spoken, written, or visual) impact you?

As the critic:
• How did you feel while offering a critique?
• How did you prepare beforehand?
• Could you have improved your delivery? How?
• How was your feedback received? How could you have made yourself more clear?
• What similarities or differences did you observe regarding the ways different people presented work and delivered feedback?

Preparing for intercultural critique:

- How do you think exchanging critique with your remote teammates will be similar to or different from exchanging critique with a local colleague?
- What communication styles will you use with your remote teammates?
- What will you do differently the next time you engage in this process?
- What feedback from the Practice Critique can you use as a conversation-starter when beginning a critique with your remote teammates?
- Are there particular questions related to your teammate's values that come to mind?

5.3

Asynchronous Feedback:
Lean media and sequenced approaches

Aimed at improving your team's ideas through a collective exchange, a*synchronous critiques* are feedback sessions that do not happen simultaneously and often use tools such as email or online communities as a means of exchanging input on ideas. However, the process is not as simple as emailing feedback to your teammates about their ideas. As with real-time approaches to feedback, *asynchronous critiques* require careful planning and preparation for them to be effective.

The primary objective of Asynchronous Feedback is to enable you to exchange critique in a productive way that yields substantial feedback and actionable suggestions. As in the previous Practice Critique, local colleagues will continue working with their previously generated lists of sketches and adjectives as a lens for developing feedback. This time, however, swapping these lists with remote teammates, and selecting adjectives and images from the teammate's list, provides an opportunity for interesting cultural insights into visual metaphors, use of language, and the respective use of words from the other culture.

Asynchronous critique

In many cases, asynchronous critique is the only option for remote teammates if a collaboration involves a significant time difference. This approach fits easily into widely divergent schedules because presentations and feedback responses do not need to be scheduled at a specific time. Either party can respond when it is convenient for them, although it is helpful if you follow a prearranged deadline and/or set of guidelines for accountability purposes.

There are three specific ways to engage with an asynchronous critique that can be used separately or in combination with each other.

1. Email exchange (low-bandwidth)
2. Discussions via a private online community (medium-bandwidth)
3. Sending commentary via pre-recorded videos (high-bandwidth)

All of these activities create their own record of the information that has been exchanged; teammates can always return to re-read an email or a post in an online forum, or to replay a video. In fact, this built-in documentation factor is one advantage of asynchronous methods over their synchronous cousins. Synchronous approaches require either efficient, real-time note-taking that is later checked for cultural bias and/or separate written accounts from all teammates so that it is possible literally to "compare notes" on the exchange.

Email: Think before hitting "send"

A critique that takes place solely via email can be challenging. While succinctness can be a benefit in some situations—for example, it can lend the feedback clarity or make it easier to understand—brevity in critique most often means that a teammate is not fully engaging or providing meaningful, constructive feedback. We have found that critiques via email often produce very brief, superficial responses. For example, responses such as "We like your idea, it's nice!" do not provide any substantive information or ideas, nor do they raise any provocative questions or seek to engage the recipient. This virtual pat on the back may feel warm and fuzzy at first, but in the long run, it does not do the team any good because there is no investment in improving the collaborative work and outcomes.

Asynchronous methods can sometimes feel one-sided in dyads where one teammate initiates and the other does not reciprocate. Because real-time methods are not always possible, it is important to remember that accountability to your teammates is of utmost importance. Sure, emails can sometimes fall through the cracks or get nabbed by spam filters, but we have found that, most often, a lack of response means that a teammate is feeling confused, shy, self-conscious, scared, or otherwise stuck because of the urge not to rock the boat and risk upsetting their teammate. The email approach is the most problematic in this regard, as it does not easily lend any kind of formal accountability or oversight with the team.

Community space: The power of the panopticon

Creating a shared online community space for collaborations and critique can be a game changer. These community forums are only accessible to teammates. By incorporating critique into this "closed"-community environment, it prompts more frequent and in-depth feedback exchanges than our previous email-based critiques. In these spaces, teammates can talk to each other and participate in constructive dialogues about shared topics or interests, which have an additional positive impact on team morale and bonding.

Additionally, the critique process feels more real to teammates because they are posting in a visually oriented online community accessible to all teammates. Commenting directly on the in-progress work posted by teammates and others in a group builds accountability and a visual history of the feedback. Establishing this exchange in a visible back-and-forth contributes to an increased sense of emotional and time investment from peers on the team's project. Other benefits include improved team cohesion, frequency of feedback, and self-initiated dialogues.

Share critique via video exchange

While community forums can encourage more organic participation and dialogue, as well as contributions from non-teammates, such as facilitators, it can be similarly difficult to establish procedures for formal accountability or oversight, because tracking individual contributions and progress can be difficult and time-consuming. In this context, video exchanges tie in well with the online communities—sharing presentation and feedback videos in a forum that is public to the entire team helps improve accountability on all fronts.

Remember you are not alone

Although participation in online communities can help reinforce camaraderie among teammates, one potential downside is that you may initially feel like you're working alone due to the lack of spontaneous discussion. You will put something out there and then await a response. We make this point so that you know to be prepared for the time-consuming nature of this process. During asynchronous critiques, remember that you are "in it" with your teammates—and the goal of this critique activity is to improve your team's ideas and output collectively as you work together.

Video: Put feedback in motion

Bandwidth and socio-cultural conventions permitting, video exchanges are another effective way to bring teams together asynchronously. This format presents some logistical challenges because it can take more time and preparation to create, share, view, and respond to videos. However, video bridges some of the issues raised by the asynchronous approaches to critique previously discussed because, as a high-resolution format, video captures more nuance and detail than words alone can convey (Robert and Dennis 2005).

Whenever possible, we encourage your enthusiastic participation in video exchanges because they can add a great deal of personality, detail, and cultural information to your intercultural work, particularly in situations when synchronous communication is not possible. Nonverbal information, such as tone of voice, facial expressions, and physical location or context, can have a great deal of impact on how the viewer interprets and responds to ideas presented in the video.

Activity

Asynchronous Feedback

The point of Asynchronous Feedback is to propel your project forward, learn to provide and receive critical analysis, increase written communication skills, and sharpen your methods of evaluation. The team-building and cultural understanding exercises outlined in earlier chapters will help you to build relationships so that you can take risks in contexts such as critique. The first risk is engaging in the critique itself; the second risk is following up with a question(s); the third risk is asking for more clarification or asking more questions. Remember that the process is not personal; feedback should be aimed at improving the product(s) of the collaboration, not at the collaborators as people. Emotional support is an essential ingredient for a successful critique, and workshopping questions and responses beforehand can be a useful intermediary step.

➡ **People:** Remote teammates/individual
➡ **Duration:** 1–2 days, based on the time difference and meeting schedules.
➡ **Technology:** Online community, SMS/instant messaging applications, email
➡ **Other resources:** Paper, sticky notes, markers

Tips

- **Revisit:** Refer to the General Communication Guidelines for Critique in 5.1
- **Questions:** Incorporate different types of questions into email exchanges to elicit lengthier responses involving cultural concepts or topics that require further explanation. This helps teammates feel acknowledged and prevents the lonely feeling that their contributions have been sent into a void with no response.
- **Interactions:** Agree upon a minimum number of interactions, and regularly check in with members of your remote team during the process in order to encourage follow-up.

(Continued)

> • **Community spaces:** We have tendencies in today's various online spaces to communicate in short phrases, emojis, and one-liners. These expressions are largely phatic and not necessarily conducive to extended conversation or dialogue. Partners engaging in critique through online community spaces should, therefore, encourage each other to always contribute more than one phrase or sentence and to thoroughly explain their ideas.

Coordinate

Phase 1: With remote teammates

1. **Reflect:** Remember your experience from the Practice Critique (5.2). What did you learn that can benefit your experience? Given what you learned from your critique, what particular aspects will you keep in mind to inform this critique?
2. **Plan:** Together with your remote teammates, agree on a strategy for exchanging critique. Establish a timeframe that takes into account the time difference and any technological constraints so that nobody becomes frustrated by delays. Identify a partner if your team is larger than two people. What other parameters might you need to establish together to guide the critique so that the experience is both fruitful and rewarding for all teammates?
3. **Exchange:** Once you have established the critique parameters, all teammates will exchange lists of adjectives from the Practice Critique (5.2) and your work/concept/idea via email or in your online community space. As an icebreaker, share an interesting outcome about using the adjectives in your Practice Critique.
4. **Choose four:** Make four adjective selections from your partner's list that you would like for them to use in evaluating your work. Choose one sketch, one word that feels practical or related, one word that feels like a challenge or aspiration, and one that seems completely random.

Assess

Phase 2: Working individually

5. **Review:** Take a moment to review the idea you have received. These could be in a variety of forms. For example, you might read a written piece, flip through a multi-page presentation draft, or view documentation of a 2D or 3D prototype.
6. **Reflect:** How would you describe this work? What are you seeing? What is your teammate's contribution trying to accomplish or communicate? What is your teammate saying with this work? What makes it interesting, useful, and/or relevant?
7. **Make three lists:** In considering your teammate's contribution, write three lists of:
   a. As many positive attributes as possible
   b. Things that could be improved
   c. Questions you have about the work

8. **Write:** Working with your lists and your teammate's selected adjectives, use the following formula to write and/or sketch some feedback for your teammate. Refer back to 5.2 to see examples of adjectives in use. Keep in mind potential communication differences in terms of how you might deliver feedback and how your remote teammate might interpret it.

   a. **One sentence based on your reflection:** How would you describe this work? What did you first notice about it? Incorporate at least one of your teammate's selections into this sentence.

   b. **Two to three positive attributes:** Choose a few of the top items from your list and write about these in more detail. Avoid adjectives like "nice" and "good." Try to give more specific reasons for why you liked something, why it provoked your interest, and so on. Write at least one sentence that includes a selected word or sketch.

   c. **Three to five ideas for improvement:** List your observations as suggestions for improving the work, not a list of what you found wrong with the work. Write at least one sentence here which includes a selected word or sketch.

   d. **Two to three questions:** Include a few thought-provoking questions for your teammate to consider. Bonus points if you can include a selected adjective into one of your questions!

   e. **One more positive attribute:** Close the evaluation on a positive note.

9. **Preview** (Optional): Ask a local colleague to read your critique before you post and give you feedback on your language choices, clarity, and so on.

10. **Post:** Share your critique in the agreed-upon venue or format.

Reflect

Phase 3: Working individually

11. **Read & Respond:** Read your teammates' feedback. Then, pause to consider it before responding. Because critique can provoke emotional responses, it is important to take a moment to remind yourself that their feedback is directed at improving your work and is not a personal evaluation. Consider their suggestions—what sounds interesting to you? What is feasible? Do you have answers to your teammates' questions or new questions for them? Be thoughtful in your response and convey your thanks.

12. **Reflect:** Use the following guide for personal reflection.

DISCUSSION GUIDE

- How did you feel about writing constructive feedback for your teammate?
- How did you feel about receiving feedback on your own work?
- Were there aspects of your teammate's feedback that were unclear to you?
- What questions could you ask in order to gain the clarity you need to move forward?
- What are some specific elements of the work that you could ask your teammate to review?

5.4

Synchronous Feedback:
Real-time approaches with rich media

Synchronous critiques are feedback sessions that happen simultaneously with re-mote teammates in real time and often use tools such as videoconferencing, personal conferencing, and texting. When a remote team has the opportunity to exchange feedback in real time, it can make for a valuable learning experi-ence and allow more intimate discussions. While this format offers teammates opportunities for conversational and immediate feedback, ensuring success with synchronous approaches requires careful consideration of your audience and the flow of output and feedback.

We have experimented with various critique formats, structures, and ap-proaches. We find that one-to-one (one person presenting to another person) or one-to-team (one person presenting to a small team) are the most effective strat-egies for synchronous critique. In contrast, a many-to-many approach, in which large teams give feedback to each other, is difficult to manage on many levels and tends not to be specific enough for the feedback to be effective.

In context: Chat-based approaches to feedback

Text-based chat

Rita, located in the United States, agrees to meet Rashid, her teammate in Qatar, at an appointed time to exchange feedback via an instant messaging application. When their meeting starts, they log into the designated chat program, and, because they have been working in the cloud, they already have access to the latest version of each other's files. They start with Rita's work: She types in a brief explanation and then waits while Rashid looks through the applicable files and writes his response. They have the opportunity to ask each other questions and ask for clarification—and then repeat this entire process so that Rita can review Rashid's work. Even though they do not see each other's faces, this chat-based approach still feels immediate and intimate because they know that the other person is online and reviewing work at the same time, and so there is no lag time in response.

Videoconference

A small team decides to connect with each other via videoconferencing to engage in a mid-project critique. They connect at the designated time, and after briefly greeting each other, they decide which teammates will share their work first. While that first team shares their screen and quickly walks the team through their in-progress ideas, everyone else listens intently, and takes notes. When it comes time to share input, those presenting listen and take their own notes. To make sure that everyone has a chance to ask questions, pursue suggestions, or seek additional clarity, a brief discussion period follows each set of presentations.

Post-critique summary

After either of these types of exchanges, all teammates write a post-critique summary. Ideally, this summary is created in a shared document so that everyone in the team has access. This step helps prevent confusion and misunderstandings and helps to reduce the number of "lost in translation" moments that can occur during feedback exchanges.

One-to-one and one-to-team approaches

When working together in real time, you will find that one-on-one dialogue and one-to-many formats (such as presentations and round-robin critique sessions) are more successful. From a logistical standpoint, one-to-many (one person presenting to a larger group) and many-to-many (e.g., one small team presenting to an entire group) both present a number of challenges. While synchronous large-group introductions can be an exciting way to kick off a collaboration, large-group feedback sessions via videoconference are more difficult to manage than these more intimate approaches. In smaller feedback settings (one-to-one and one-to-team), where coordinating the back-and-forth is less cumbersome, teammates can focus on active listening and the quality of the feedback they are delivering to teammates. In either case, this sort of experience might take place via videoconference, audio conversation, or some kind of instant messaging system that both parties are using simultaneously.

Benefits & outcomes

- Practice active listening
- Exchange ideas and feedback in real time
- Offer observations and suggestions in a conversational format
- Understand how your "diplomacy filter" can prevent effective critique

---

Activity

Synchronous Feedback

Remote teams can generate substantial feedback and discussion with real-time critiques. Part of the goal is to avoid the "diplomacy filter" or self-censorship that can happen when more time elapses between the presentation of the work and the giving of feedback, as in the asynchronous approach (5.3). Teams should follow the format of presentation, input, and follow-up questions. All synchronous critique sessions should be followed by a post-critique summary, ideally shared in a format or location that is accessible to all participants. The broader process of intercultural exchange is embedded in these smaller-scale interchanges of ideas. Partners have the added value of seeing and interpreting each other's facial and body gestures as well as emotional tone while interacting in this format.

- ➔ **People:** Remote teammates/individual
- ➔ **Duration:** 20 to 30 minutes per person/team, plus 1 day of preparation time
- ➔ **Technology:** Shared file folder(s) and document(s), videoconferencing software and hardware
- ➔ **Other resources:** Critique guide, black and white printer

- ➔ *Throughout the process, refer to the discussion guide at the end of this activity.*
- ➔ *SMS or other instant messaging tools can be used for this activity if videoconferencing tools are unavailable.*

Tips

- **Revisit:** Refer to the General Communication Guidelines for Critique in 5.1
- **Eliminate distractions:** In either role, be sure to eliminate distractions prior to connecting with each other. This shows respect for your teammates and the project, and helps you to make the most of the critique.
- **Take turns:** Make sure that everyone gets a turn to speak. Keep in mind time differences and the challenges of videoconferencing.
- **Audio:** In a videoconferencing environment, audio often lags, creating confusing and frustrating delays, particularly in the noisier environment of a large-group chat. These types of delays are especially problematic when multiple people in the room are trying to speak at the same time, as often occurs during the spontaneous discussion portion of a critique.

Plan

Phase 1: With remote teammates

1. **Plan:** Meet with your remote teammate in a shared document, or work back-and-forth via email, to set goals for the kind of feedback you want to receive in relation to the project you are working on together. How do you want your work to be evaluated? What kind of feedback do you want to receive? What kind of feedback do you feel most prepared to give? Develop these initial questions and integrate them into a critique guide. Identify a partner if your team is larger than two people. During your live discussion, take turns as *presenter* (sharing your work) and *reviewer* (evaluating and sharing feedback on the work).
2. **Choose Tools:** Review the devices and viewing environment you'll be using, and discuss the ways in which these tools may impact how you relate to each other via videoconferencing. Dual screens, small screens, mobile devices/phones, and so on can all impact the communicative space.
3. **Send, share, & notify:** Post your work in the Fourth Space, in a shared folder, or send via email. Notify your teammates when you have shared it.

Assess

Phase 2: Working individually

4. **Reflect:** How would you describe this work? What is the presenter's contribution trying to accomplish or communicate? What is the presenter saying with this work? What makes it interesting, useful, and/or relevant?

5. **Make three lists:** In considering your teammate's contribution, write three lists on a piece of paper or in your project notebook. These should include:

    a. As many positive attributes as possible

    b. Things that could be improved

    c. Questions you have about the work

6. **Make one more list!** Think of a particular person you know or think back to your Fictional Character Exchange (4.5). How would that person respond to your teammate's work? Write a list of their responses ranging from predictable to ridiculous. Because this is a third-person opinion and not necessarily your personal opinion, you can feel free to say almost anything with this list of statements. Here are some examples to get you started:

    "My grandma would say…"

    "Here is a picture of my fictional character reacting to/interacting with this thing…"

7. **Write:** Working with your lists, use the following structure to write and/or sketch some feedback of the presenter's work. Keep in mind potential communication differences in terms of how you might deliver feedback and how your remote teammate might interpret it.

    a. At least one sentence responding to the work from the perspective of your selected individual or fictional character (from Step 4, Reflect)—this will help break the ice!

    b. **One sentence based on your reflection:** How would you describe this work? What did you first notice about it?

    c. **Two to three positive attributes:** Choose a few of the top items from your list and write about these in more detail. Avoid adjectives like "nice" and "good." Try to give more specific reasons for why you liked something, why it provoked your interest, and so on.

    d. **Three to five ideas for improvement:** Instead of just making a list of what is wrong with the contribution, frame these observations as suggestions for improving the work.

    e. **Two to three questions:** Include a few thought-provoking questions for your teammate to consider.

    f. **One more positive attribute:** Close the evaluation on a positive note.

Exchange feedback

Phase 3: With remote teammates

8. **Meet:** Connect with your team via videoconference.

9. **Order:** Decide whether you want to share feedback with one person at a time or would prefer to go back and forth as you walk through your notes. Everyone on the team should have a chance to participate.

10. **Choose Your Words:** As you transition to discuss your notes, remember to keep your language neutral: it's about the work, not the person as an individual. Avoid the use of "you," and instead, use specific descriptions of the individual work/teamwork (i.e., use phrases like "the written piece" or "the prototype"). Be aware of your tone of voice, facial expressions, and body language.

11. **Acknowledge:** While your written lists and sentences will be the primary focus of your discussion, remember first to check in with each other on a personal level. Reference your notes, but try to give attention (and screen space) to your teammate.

12. **Listen:** It is important to listen actively, to take handwritten notes, and to reflect on new ideas throughout the conversation. Ask questions throughout the process. If your teammate's input is unclear or not thorough enough, it is your responsibility to ask them for more details.

Phase 4: Working individually

13. **Summarize:** Following the critique, each team should work to translate handwritten notes and create a shared online written summary. This document improves team communication and morale by helping to clarify the discussion outcomes. It is also an opportunity to ensure that all members of the team are on the same page with regard to next steps in the project, what was said during the discussion, and how the conversation was interpreted. Use the following guide for discussion.

DISCUSSION GUIDE

- What was the first thing that popped into your head when you saw your teammate's work?
- Did you share this first impression with your teammate? Why/why not?
- What did the statements from the perspective of a fictional character or third-person "opinion" contribute to the feedback session?
- How do you think your team could work with each other's communication preferences to make your feedback sessions more effective?
- How did you feel about verbally delivering your feedback to your teammate? Is there another delivery method you would prefer?

5.5

Outside Input:
Learning from relevant external perspectives

Seeking various forms of input from outside sources can be beneficial for improving new ideas, works in progress, rough drafts, or more refined prototypes. The Outside Input critique format offers teammates real-time feedback from a different set of perspectives. As outlined in the following section, this approach involves looking outside of your team to invite people with a variety of backgrounds to share their responses and thoughts about your work or ideas. Working with local community members and stakeholders helps teams determine next steps for a project and ensures their work is culturally sensitive, appropriate, and communicative.

Outside Input can vary in style, taking the form of focus groups, co-design sessions, formal critiques or presentations, usability testing, product demonstrations, crowdsourcing, exhibitions, and even hackathons, to name a few. Asking for input from people outside of an intercultural collaboration creates opportunities to discuss how the cultural perspectives inherent to a team are being represented in the work.

Identify stakeholders

Incorporating input from outside the team is not a new idea in business or design. Stakeholder theory states that *stakeholders*—individuals who have a vested interest in a product, service, organization, and so on—should be involved in contributing ideas and feedback to its evolution, and that the involvement of stakeholders creates greater value (Freeman et al. 2010). In business, everyone who interacts with the company in some way shares equal status as a stakeholder—from employees to janitorial staff to customers—and can contribute to the way the company operates (Parmar et al. 2010). In a different way, stakeholders are also considered essential constituents in product development and user experience design. For example, creators can improve work based on input from the people who will use, experience, or come in contact with their product or service. Your team can involve external stakeholders at any stage of a project, during various intervals of ideation, development, and refinement. One common characteristic across most of these approaches is that input sessions with stakeholders are aimed at capturing qualitative information (and sometimes also quantitative data) for later synthesis and analysis.

In context: Sharing stories of water sustainability

Two remote teammates, Sara and Shahad, were working together on the topic of water sustainability based on a shared passion for the environment. Together, they engaged in a series of visual thinking activities to get to know each other, research the topic, and work collaboratively on a project related to their shared interest. An exhibition opportunity enabled both Sara and Shahad to invite local community members to review their work in Qatar and the United States.

During Shahad's opportunity for Outside Input, she was asked by one exhibition visitor to describe why Americans were so concerned about bottled water. The visitor did not realize that in many cities in the United States, tap water is a good source of clean water. In Shahad's local context, most people heavily consume bottled water for their daily water needs due to desalination and lack of access to drinking water.

For Shahad, who had been engaged in many deep conversations with Sara about the environmental impacts of bottled water, this was a meaningful opportunity to share what Sara had learned from the dialogue and offer new perspectives about how water usage might be addressed in the Gulf Region.

Meanwhile, at the Outside Input session in the United States, Sara had a chance to talk to the Director of Sustainability Initiatives at a local university, who was well-versed in the topic of water sustainability within the region. The director provided feedback on how to make the topic more appealing to people in the local community through messaging and visual communication styles, and gave the teammates a list of resources to provide more background on the topic based on their specific location.

New perspectives: Going outside of the team for input

Such opportunities for sharing beyond the bounds of the collaboration help to spread the benefits of intercultural learning to a much wider community and, in turn, help teammates to appreciate the uniqueness of the work they are doing together. Along these lines, there may also be ideas that do not translate across cultures. Outside Input is a great way to register not only the appropriateness of an idea for a particular audience but also to fuel discussion among remote teammates about why and how an idea could be improved.

Depending upon the team dynamic, seeking external feedback may be more effective than some of the other critique options because it shifts the responsibility of providing feedback to visitors from outside the team. Therefore, this feedback may feel less personal, yet it is still beneficial to a team's progress. This approach offers an alternative way to obtain and share constructive feedback on project ideas by going outside of the remote collaborative team. For works-in-progress, this is a great tool for moving ideas forward, jump-starting stalled teams, or cutting through the overwhelming sense of diplomacy that may be thwarting the effectiveness of a critique.

Collecting and sharing feedback from others outside of the collaborative team can also alleviate some stress for teammates who feel stuck in terms of their ability to exchange feedback effectively. Introducing the opportunity to obtain feedback from a third party relieves the pressure that teammates may feel to perform for each other and can bring teammates together as they analyze and try to make sense of the input they glean from people outside of their team or larger group. In some cases, outside views can also serve as tie-breakers that help teams resolve conflicts or clarify priorities.

Benefits & outcomes

- Gather feedback from stakeholders to improve your ideas
- Engage your local community in the ideas of your remote team
- Practice guidelines for generating and responding to critique
- Use various forms of documentation to share input with teammates

---

Activity

Outside Input

Outside Input can be beneficial for improving new ideas in their early stages, works-in-progress such as rough drafts, or even refined prototypes. This is an exciting opportunity to gain valuable feedback from local stakeholders or community members, which may shape the next stages of your project. Looking outside of your team for input is valuable because it brings fresh perspectives to the project and may help you understand specific cultural perspectives on your team's topic or project idea. Some people find clarity in analyzing this feedback to share with their remote teammates, which can lead to interesting new insights.

→ **People:** Local colleagues/remote teammates/local stakeholders and community members

→ **Duration:** Variable, this can be done quickly and spontaneously during a regularly scheduled meeting or planned in advance with a longer duration. Alternatively, teams can invite guests for multiple or recurring scheduled feedback sessions.

→ **Technology:** Video recorder, audio recorder, camera, or phone capable of making recordings and taking photographs; online or paper survey tools, videoconferencing software

→ **Other resources:** Digital or analog means of taking notes; survey tools, worksheets or culture probes; communication tools to send invitations and/ or engage people outside of the collaboration (email, text, video chat, audio message, shared documents, Fourth Space, etc.)

Tips

- **Revisit:** Refer to the General Communication Guidelines for Critique in 5.1
- **Identify:** Discuss and decide the appropriate audiences to participate in Outside Input. It is important to understand whose input will be sought and what outcome you hope to achieve with this process. Ask yourself: *Who are the right people to approach for feedback?*
- **Coordinate**: After setting a time, date, and location for the Outside Input, provide local guests with advance notice to ensure most people can attend. Ideally, your team should make an effort to conduct the feedback session in each cultural context around the same time.
- **Research:** Look for inspiration from user experience design, product development, and stakeholder theory to determine appropriate formats to document the feedback from your guests for later synthesis and analysis. These areas utilize a variety of input sessions such as focus groups, co-design sessions, formal critiques or presentations, usability testing, product demonstrations, crowdsourcing, exhibitions, and even hackathons, to name a few. Outcomes might take the form of qualitative information or quantitative data using surveys, think-aloud protocols, observation, or a worksheet the team creates.
- **Document:** Create a detailed plan for documenting the feedback. How will each teammate share local guests' feedback with the rest of the team?

Coordinate

Phase 1: With local colleagues

- **Identify:** Who is the appropriate audience for this activity? Think about inviting people whose experience and insight can add value to the next stage of your project, such as relevant members of the community and project stakeholders.
- **Locate:** Work together to choose a potential venue for sharing the in-progress work with relevant community members (e.g., on campus, in the workplace, at other locations in the community). What are the requirements for sharing the work? Are electrical outlets or internet connections required? Do you plan to bring your remote teammate into the experience in some way? Plan ahead to ensure your venue supports your team's goals for this feedback session.
- **Coordinate:** Set a time, date, and location. Organize an event around the feedback session and invite local stakeholders and community members to attend.

Plan

Phase 2: With remote teammates

- **Presentation Options:** With your remote teammates, discuss the options for sharing the work-in-progress with the audience. What potential communication differences or special requirements do need to address in order to get feedback?
- **Documentation Options:** Decide how you will document the session to share with remote teammates: take notes, take pictures of the critique session, or record brief videos to be uploaded. How will you arrange the information you receive into a format that can be shared? (For more ideas on arranging or visualizing data, see Datastorming, 4.4.)

Engage

Phase 3: With local stakeholders and community members

- **Document:** Ask your guests for permission to document the feedback session. Use the documentation options you decided on with your remote team.
- **Gain insights:** Invite your guests to share their responses and thoughts about your work or ideas. Engage audience members with questions to understand the aspects of the project you would most appreciate feedback on. You may decide to prepare questions in advance for your visitors.
- **Share:** Share the feedback you receive and any other findings with your remote teammates. You will need to think about how you want to capture and relay it. You may do this during a scheduled videoconference

(if available), through your shared online space, over email, or via another method. Keep in mind potential communication differences in terms of how you might deliver feedback and how your remote teammates might interpret it.

Analysis

Phase 4: With remote teammates

- **Discuss:** Using the following guide, discuss with your remote teammates the feedback you received during the Outside Input session.

DISCUSSION GUIDE

- What did the invited guests suggest in terms of updates to your project or idea?
- Was there any universal feedback you received that points to new directions or confirms the current approach?
- What insights from your session are you most excited to share with your teammates?
- What feedback will your team use to continue to improve the work together?
- Was there any feedback that seemed unrelated or irrelevant? If so, why do you think audience members may have misunderstood the project, idea, or work?

5.6

Mindful Reflection:
Writing and sketching for thoughtful individual analysis

Whether you are reflecting upon your overall learning experience, participation on the team, the function (or dysfunction!) of your collaboration, and/or project outcomes, Mindful Reflection provides a new way to think about your work and/or your collaboration. If you have been working through some of the previous activities within this book, you will realize that you have been doing this kind of reflection all along, in various forms. However, unlike making lists, quickly sketching, scribbling rapid-fire ideas, or composing a few sentences of constructive feedback for your teammates, Mindful Reflection invites you to pause and consider your experience in depth.

Some might wonder why Mindful Reflection appears within this larger chapter about giving and receiving feedback. Quite simply, this form of reflection, when executed with thoughtfulness and attention to detail, is a way to provide constructive feedback to yourself. Like other forms of feedback, reflective writing and sketching can be an opportunity for a thoughtful pause in your process. However, unlike other forms of feedback, this activity is not limited to discussions of the work. Thinking about your role, performance, behavior, and attitude is encouraged, as a way to gain insights that will lead to personal growth and refinement of your interpersonal communication and collaboration skills. So, while it's introduced here in Chapter 5, you might find it useful to try variations of Mindful Reflection at different points throughout your experience. For example, you could do a brief written reflection after each activity or at the conclusion of each chapter within this book.

Benefits & outcomes

- Take a temporary break from the intensity of collaboration to reflect alone
- Reflect on your experience through words and images
- Recognize growth and learning from intercultural collaboration
- Generate thoughtful team statements or material to use in later projects

---

Activity

Mindful Reflection

The activity asks you to look back on your intercultural exchange, reflect on the experience, and share your thoughts in writing. In some cases, if the collaboration has led to a tangible outcome, this activity can help your teammates articulate their thoughts about the project and even craft a team statement, which can be a helpful addition when publicly sharing project outcomes (see 5.5, 6.6). Another aspect of Mindful Reflection is that you can do it at different times over the course of the entire collaboration process. Like other forms of constructive feedback, Mindful Reflection can ramp up in terms of length, rigor, or intensity, or be toned down to feel less intense. It can be executed privately, for your eyes alone, or shared with your local colleagues, remote teammates, or the public.

→ **People:** Individual/remote teammates (optional)
→ **Duration:** 15 minutes to 1–2 hours. If all teammates are writing reflections, agree on a duration.
→ **Technology:** Word processing software, videoconferencing software
→ **Other resources:** Paper, pen/pencil

Tips

- **Success Sketch:** Before you get started on this reflective activity, it can be useful to understand your personal goals and aspirations for the project and collaboration. One way to do this is by engaging with the Success Sketch (1.3) to map your pathways to success and better reflect on your progress. Through this introductory opportunity for reflection, you can begin to stimulate your thinking about the writing process and how it can contribute to your work and learning.
- **Multiplicity:** Try to reflect on your progress and learning at different points throughout the duration of your collaboration. You could do a brief written reflection after each activity or at the end of each chapter in this book.

(Continued)

- **Generate:** Try writing your own questions and/or writing questions to swap with your teammate. Your questions should be written with the aim of understanding different aspects of your work together and how you might increase understanding and communication.
- **Keeping it real:** You can use reflective writing in a variety of ways and for a variety of reasons. These reasons could be personal, a way to manage some of the natural stresses that come with any collaboration. Writing could also serve as a strategy for better understanding how to share intercultural learning with a wider audience. In considering the range of opportunities for using reflective writing, think about how your reflection might change if you were to share it with a remote teammate versus keeping it private. For example, a private version can be used to develop your own thinking, whereas the public version could go on your team's project blog.

Reflect

Phase 1: Working individually

1. **Reflect:** Looking back at your experience and journey together, what have you learned? Take some time to reflect on your experience using one (or all) of the following prompts. If you completed the earlier Success Sketch (1.3), review it to stimulate your thinking about how you envisioned the process before starting compared to how it turned out in the end. Make some loose notes based on your thoughts and reflections and draw a sketch to represent your response to each question
   - **Impact:** What core ingredients of the intercultural experience impacted you the most? What stood out to you in terms of learning about each other's geographic locations, project exploration, or something else?
   - **Significance:** Describe and analyze one significant decision your team has made together in the evolution of your project. Why did you make that decision? How does the team rationalize the design choices you have made in order to communicate and reinforce your message? Provide specific examples, such as a communication moment or collaborative moment with your remote teammates.
   - **Culture:** How do you think your team would have approached the project differently if you had been creating for your cultural context only? Or for your teammate's cultural context only?
   - **Memory:** Share a detailed description of one lasting thought, idea, or impression from the work you've done with your teammate on this project. (You could imagine it this way, but in your own words: "One thing I'll carry with me from working with my teammate is….")

2. **Write:** Write for the allotted time or meet any minimum/maximum re-quirements. (If crafting a team statement, come to a consensus with your teammates about word count.)

3. **Review:** Take time to read over what you have written and review your sketch(es), thinking about whether there's anything you want to add or change. Make changes or updates, as needed.

4. **Reflect:** Use the following prompts to guide your personal reflection.
   • How has the collaboration shaped the direction of your project and/or influenced the final outcomes?
   • Thinking back to your introductory activities, which were most mean-ingful for you in terms of personal growth, intercultural learning, and project development?
   • How did your collaborative experience impact your relationship with your team?

Team statement (optional)

Phase 2: With remote teammates

5. **Swap:** Share your written piece and sketches with your teammates in an edita-ble document; review their submissions when you receive them. Make notes by commenting on things you find interesting and ask questions where applicable.

6. **Merge:** Work together to edit the submissions into one team statement. As part of this process, consider whether you'd like that statement to be one cohesive submission with a uniform voice throughout, or whether you might want to reflect everyone's individual contributions in a more obvious way, such as with a question/answer "interview" format, as one might see in a magazine (in this case, the questions would be part of the document, together with some of the individual responses).

Analysis

Phase 3: With remote teammates

7. **Discuss:** Take some time to discuss what you have learned together through this process. Use the following guide for discussion.

DISCUSSION GUIDE

• How did you work with different communication styles in the process of crafting your team statement?
• How do you think other people will respond to your team statement?
• If you have come to the conclusion of your work together, can you envision using your teammate's perspective and expertise in future projects?
• Have you thought about ways to continue the relationship beyond this inter-cultural learning opportunity?

5.7

Circles of Understanding

→ *Flip to this section as needed throughout your collaboration. Much like critique, conflict resolution should happen regularly to keep communications running smoothly, maintain team morale, and channel conflicting views productively into your work together.*

This activity guides teams through a constructive feedback session that focuses on improving aspects of the team. This is an important tool because any creative collaboration comes with some turbulence. We offer several approaches for dealing with miscommunication or misunderstandings. Regardless of the approaches you use, the most important takeaway is moving past disagreement to focus on positive solutions that prevent the same conflict from recurring.

Choose cooperative conflict management

Even in the same cultural context, it is unlikely that two people will ever have identical goals, expectations, or values. Researchers Kenneth Thomas and Ralph Kilmann acknowledge conflict as a natural part of interpersonal interactions. They identify five strategies for managing and resolving conflict: Avoidance, defeat, compromise, accommodation, and collaboration. Avoidance may seem easiest, particularly in online collaborations, but this strategy does not help individuals or teams advance. As with other aspects of collaborative teamwork, choosing to cooperate is a productive approach to conflict resolution. Fortunately, there are a variety of cooperative options from various cultural traditions.

Focus on positive solutions

There are many reasons that teams can get off-track. Some common problems include:

- Miscommunication, mistranslation, or misunderstanding
- Need for more background information or cultural context
- Catching someone off-guard (with language choices, opinions, etc.)
- Fundamental differences in understanding problems, gathering information, or developing solutions—often based on personal and cultural values

  - **Individuals** can pause, reflect, and think through things prior to beginning conflict-resolution conversations with teammates. Cultivate mindfulness before broaching subjects of concern. The Mindful Written Reflection (5.6) can help you formulate thoughts.
  - **Teams** can discuss what approaches best address their concerns and use the Circles of Understanding activity to create a Thought Object to communicate an idea to oneself or from an individual to the team.

As an individual: Preparing for resolution

Shift your mindset with movement

Many cultures recognize the interconnection of mind, body, and spirit. With an emphasis on balance and harmony, that interconnectedness is an essential tenet of many traditional forms of healing, from indigenous North American (Cohen 2006) to Chinese medicine (Cohen and Doner 2006). In many cultures, these healing practices include movements to stimulate the connections among mind, body, and soul. For example, *Qi Gong, Tai Chi,* and *Yoga* are fluid physical movements that stimulate mental and spiritual well-being (Patanjali 1990; Cohen and Doner 2006).

Studies show that people who engage in physical movements that are *fluid*—smooth, flowing, graceful—subsequently showed enhanced creativity and cognitive flexibility (Slepian and Ambady 2012). Take a break and try fluid movements if you feel stuck while working on team communication, relationships, or tasks. You may find that you return feeling refreshed and more open to hearing your teammates' perspectives. You may also get some new ideas. You could:

- Take a walk
- Dance to soothing music
- Move your body in a focused, smooth, and flowing way
- Try Qi Gong, Tai Chi, or Yoga (look for videos online)
- Ask your teammates for movement suggestions
- Talk to teammates *while moving,* if it is possible to have an audio conversation

Save face

When managing team rapport and disagreements, people from different cultures can be concerned with avoiding embarrassment and protecting their own (and their teammates') self-image. Mutual self-preservation is described in English as *saving face*, which stems from a social concept of "face" across Asian cultures (Stover and Stover 1976). When conflict threatens our self-image, we tend to save or restore our "face." By the same token, if we respond to teammates without thinking, particularly out of shock or misunderstanding, we may accidentally embarrass them, causing them to "lose face." Thus, the opportunity for face-saving is important during conflict resolution, enabling each person to preserve dignity and self-respect.

Communicate clearly, but be sensitive

Not everyone on your team will be a direct communicator, but straightforward communication is important in conflict resolution. That may seem at odds with saving face, but clear communication in conflict resolution is critical to solving your problem and preventing further misunderstanding. Directness does not mean accusation or confrontation, but clarity; clarify teammates' ideas about how best to move forward together. Indirect communicators—who tend to offer ideas with roundabout language—may need to think about phrasing their thoughts more precisely and directly to help make the team's process most effective.

As a team: Finding resolution

Choose one or more approaches

While the following strategies guide teams in managing some types of conflict, there are no universal solutions. There are numerous other equitable, culturally sensitive approaches; individual teammates can draw on local resources, cultural traditions, religious communities, and other philosophies to discover appropriate strategies for productive teamwork. Here, we take a broader look at some co-operative approaches that can be appropriate for remote teams. The Circles of Understanding activity combines ideas from these approaches to engage teams in productive discussion, reconfigure relationships, and resolve problems (Brigg 2014).

Working as a team

Task-centered approach

A *task-centered approach* to conflict management refocuses the team on their shared goals. Developed by social workers William Reid and Laura Epstein, a task-centered approach to conflict resolution is a progressive approach that concentrates on the present moment. The steps include enhancing commitment, planning task implementation, analyzing obstacles, modeling behavior, and summarizing the plan (Reid 1975). Participants engaging in this process are empowered to solve their own problems, develop knowledge, build confidence, and agree on achievable tasks.

Restorative practices

With roots in indigenous North American communities, traditional restorative practices emphasize healing and community (re)balance by restoring a sense of self-respect and-worth to victims and offenders alike (Mirsky 2004). Inclusive discourse maximizes healing and minimizes harm when individuals take responsibility for their actions. This approach stands in contrast to a punishment model, which often leads to ostracism and does little to help offenders learn from their mistakes. Recently, restorative practices have been embraced in other communities and countries, including South Africa, New Zealand, Canada, and the United States (Zehr 2014). While restorative practices may involve some facilitation, unlike conciliation, there is not usually a mediator because the emphasis is on team problem-solving.

Seek external support

Conciliation and mediation

When the conflict feels too challenging to solve internally, a third party can help the team resolve the issue. *Conciliation* and *mediation* are two similar approaches. Both involve a facilitator from outside of the team who helps the team identify strategies and solutions that seem fair to all members. The facilitator's goal is to acknowledge, recognize, and promote understanding of alternative perspectives. A helpful outcome of this process can be the collective generation of a Collaboration Agreement (1.5a), or updates to an existing agreement. It is not effective to have one member of the team surprise others by bringing a mediator to a meeting.

Professional consultations

It is important to recognize when a distressing situation is beyond the capability of team-based problem-solving. Task-centered and conciliatory approaches are not necessarily intended to solve more challenging emotional or psychological issues that can arise during a collaboration. Wider structural or cultural issues may require a strategy that lies beyond simply identifying specific tasks. Individuals and teams may even require in-depth professional consultations, psychological support, or the use of other cultural practices to resolve conflict.

Embrace a restart

If clashes between individual interests lead to a breakdown in team dynamics, one remedy is simply to start over together. That can be done with or without the assistance of a third-party facilitator. Agree to begin again from scratch, with introductions, ideation, and so on. It can be helpful to pinpoint ahead of time where things went wrong and place particular emphasis on addressing that differently the second time around. Starting over does not mean you have failed or that you will fall behind. It just means that you have learned from your experience and are willing to try again.

Benefits & outcomes

- Practice collaborative problem-solving for team dynamics
- Use physical activity to shift your mindset to be more open to resolution
- Come together as a team to voice concerns and move forward
- Identify which strategies will best help your team

Activity

Circles of Understanding

Circles of Understanding focuses discussion on the present and the future of a collaboration, not on the wrongs of the past. The circle is a significant metaphor for the team. It enables you to envision yourself alongside teammates in a harmonious, symmetrical shape. The circle is nonhierarchical, placing all teammates on an equal and continuous plane. In this way, it symbolizes the ideal unity of your team, even if it doesn't currently feel unified. In moving forward, it is what you do to repair your conflict that matters, not the disagreement itself. The circular depiction of your team as a community serves as a Progress Object to communicate within the team and guide discussions around what you feel strongly about, what you believe is currently wrong, and what you are hoping for in the collaborative experience.

→ **People:** Local colleagues/individual/remote team
→ **Duration:** Approximately 2 to 3 hours, depending on the time difference
→ **Technology:** Videoconference
→ **Other resources:** Paper & pencil

Tips

- **The past is in the past:** We tend to focus initial discussion on how we feel wronged, misunderstood, or other feelings of injustice. Instead, in coming to a shared resolution, this activity asks all teammates to shift their focus from yesterday to today and tomorrow.
- **Speak of yourself, not others:** Frame things in terms of yourself, as an individual, using "I" or "myself" statement—or "we" or "us in reference to the team." Avoid using "you" statements toward any particular teammate, unless asking a specific person for clarity. When more than two teammates are resolving a dispute, avoid the groupthink mentality that can occur when others share your point of view. Groupthink can

become a perilous aspect of team scenarios wherein other teammates feel ganged up on or attacked. By speaking only about your personal feelings ("I" or "myself") and not speaking for others, you can avoid this trap. Writing down your feelings first, and sitting with them, can help you better articulate your issues and relate them to your personal values.

- **Positive orientation:** Frame things positively: "I really want us to find ways we can work better together...." If something is unclear or upsetting to you, speak from your perspective by asking for an explanation, "I really want to understand what you mean—can you please explain this to me again in a different way?"
- **Facilitator:** If you are able to meet in a synchronous format, you may find it useful to invite an outside mediator to help guide this activity. A mediator can facilitate conversation that feels safe and respectful to all members of the team.

Thought Object

Phase 1: Working individually

1. **Cool off:** If needed, excuse yourself from the situation, take a break. Go for a walk or find another way to do some other fluid movement, such as loose sketching.
2. **Draw a circle:** On a piece of paper, draw a circle to represent your team. Write your name and the names of your teammates around the circle. For teams working remotely—who cannot physically sit in a circle together—this is your restorative circle. It is important to envision your team as a circular form, which is non-hierarchical. You all play a role in the success and health of the team.
3. **Come to an understanding:** Working within the circle, write, draw, or create something related to the following five talking points, based on the nature of the conflict, your story, your relationship, preserving dignity, and maintaining communication. As you think through your responses, keep in mind potential communication differences in terms of how you might deliver information or feedback and how your remote teammates might interpret it.
   a. **Your story:** Use a story from your past to describe your feelings about the conflict. Your story helps your teammate understand why you feel the way you do and why it is important to address this issue (DeTemple and Sarrouf 2017). The following prompts can help you capture your story.
      - *Have you had similar feelings on an unrelated occasion, before this experience with your team? Or have you had another personal experience that relates to the issues at hand?*

- *How does this experience relate to your personal values?*
- *What happened then, and what you did or did not do?*
- *Do you feel conflicted about this at all? Could you see another side to it?*
- *Based on that experience, what do you want to do now?*

b. **Nature of the conflict:** Describe what is at the heart of this issue and what you want from this process. This is not a time to be vague or avoid the problem. Give yourself the opportunity to express your needs and pay attention to any strong emotions. Acknowledge and respect those feelings. Next, try to crystallize the issue by thinking through the following prompts, which are rooted restorative dialogues:

- *What happened and what were you thinking at the time of the incident?*
- *What have you thought about since?*
- *Who has been affected by what happened and how?*
- *What about this has been hardest for you?*
- *What do you think needs to be done to make things as right as possible?*

c. **Our relationship:** In an effort to preserve your collaborative relationship for future work, describe what you respect about your teammates. It can be useful to reflect on your Success Sketch (1.3) to remember your enthusiasm and positive outlook for the team.

- *What does your team offer in terms of collaborative power for a project?*
- *How has your team's perspective positively impacted your own thinking?*
  1. *What unique perspectives do they offer?*
  2. *What skills and assets do they bring to the table?*
  3. *What can you do to promote change together?*

d. **Preserving dignity:** While negotiating differences is challenging, respecting one another's opinions and feelings is also critical for coming to an understanding. Remember, this process is not about the person—it is about the problem. Ask yourself: *How can all members of the team preserve their dignity throughout the reconciliation process and save face?* Start by remaining flexible to teammates' ideas and keeping things positive.

- Describe what you believe are your teammate's good intentions.
- What you are hoping for in moving forward together?
- What does an ideal scenario look like to you?
- What is currently working in the collaboration?
- What could change and what might stay the same?

e. **Maintaining Communication:** To continue the dialogue and avoid potential miscommunication in the future, describe what communication strategies and styles work best for the team: Synchronous or asynchronous? Direct or indirect? Some combination of these?

- *What formats, forms, and frequency of communication will keep teammates receptive to ongoing dialogue?*

- *Which communication approaches feel most comfortable for sharing your thoughts and feelings?*
- *Which are best for team decision-making?*
- *Which are best for delegating tasks?*
- *Which can enable the team to more effectively gather their ideas, information, and thinking in one place?*
- *Which will allow time for more discussion?*

Resolution

Phase 2: With local colleagues/remote teammates

4. **Communicate sensitively, but directly:** Use your Thought Object to help you discuss each of these five aspects with your team. Referencing your circle helps you think before you communicate. If you are stuck at one level of conflict, move to another level, but make sure to eventually cover all five areas.
5. **Practice active listening:** As your teammates talk, add to your own circle. These additional notes and sketches represent their contributions to your idea of the team and its dynamics.
6. **Resolve to continue the dialogue:** Work as a team to brainstorm ideas about how to keep the dialogue going and what is needed to move forward. Coming to a team consensus may take some time, but the main purpose of this activity is building community. You may not resolve everything, but ongoing honest, authentic dialogue is important for acknowledging and responding to the teams shared needs. Use the following guide for discussion.
7. **Update Collaboration Agreement:** Putting solutions in writing helps rebuild trust and renegotiate accountability. If you do not already have a Collaboration Agreement to govern the way your team functions, this is a good time to create one (see 1.5a). If you have an existing Collaboration Agreement, update it to reflect ideas and resolutions from this meeting.

DISCUSSION GUIDE

- In your cultural context, how is conflict typically discussed or managed? How does this relate to your personal communication preferences (direct/indirect)?
- How do these factors impact your approach to solving team-based conflicts?
- What is your preferred method for approaching conflict?
- What can you do differently, in this case, to help your teammates feel understood and valued?

References

Brigg, Morgan. 2014. "Culture, 'Relationality', and Global Cooperation." Global Cooperation Research Papers 6. doi:10.14282/2198-0411-gcrp-6.

Cohen, Kenneth S. 2006. *Honoring the Medicine: An essential guide to Native American healing*. New York: Ballantine Books.

Cohen, Misha, and Kalia Doner. 2006. *The Chinese Way to Healing: Many Paths to Wholeness*. Lincoln, NE: iUniverse.

DeTemple, Jill, and John Sarrouf. 2017. "Disruption, Dialogue, and Swerve: Reflective Structured Dialogue in Religious Studies Classrooms." *Teaching Theology & Religion* 20 (3): 283–92. doi:10.1111/teth.12398.

Freeman, R. Edward, Jeffrey S. Harrison, Andrew C. Wicks, Bidhan L. Parmar, and Simone De Colle. 2010. *Stakeholder Theory: The State of the Art*. Cambridge, MA: Cambridge University Press.

Lawless, Kate and Shannon Crabill. 2015. "How to Give and Receive a Good Design Critique." March 27, 2015. AIGA Baltimore. baltimore.aiga.org/how-to-give-and-receive-a-good-design-critique/

Martin, Matthew M., and Carolyn M. Anderson. 1998. "The Cognitive Flexibility Scale: Three Validity Studies." *Communication Reports* 11 (1): 1–9. doi:10.1080/08934219809367680.

Martin, Matthew M., and Rebecca B. Rubin. 1995. "A New Measure of Cognitive Flexibility." *Psychological Reports* 76 (2): 623–26. doi:10.2466/pr0.1995.76.2.623.

McDonagh-Philp, Deana, and Howard Denton. 1999. "Using Focus Groups to Support the Designer in the Evaluation of Existing Products: A Case Study." *The Design Journal* 2 (2): 20–31. doi:10.2752/146069299790303570.

Mirsky, Laura. 2004. "Restorative Justice Practices of Native American, First Nation and Other Indigenous People of North America: Part One." www.iirp.edu/news/restorative-justice-practices-of-native-american-first-nation-and-other-indigenous-people-of-north-america-part-one.

Parmar, Bidhan L., R. Edward Freeman, Jeffrey S. Harrison, Andrew C. Wicks, Lauren Purnell, and Simone de Colle. 2010. "Stakeholder Theory: The State of the Art." *The Academy of Management Annals* 4 (1): 403–45. doi:10.1080/19416520.2010.495581.

Patanjali. 1990. *The Yoga Sutras of Patanjali*. Translated by Sri Swami Satchidananda. Buckingham, VA: Start Publishing LLC. www.overdrive.com/search?q=773A8A3A-4DD7-4A69-8CB4-4B10E324D9C3.

Reeves, Judy. 2002. *Writing Alone, Writing Together: A Guide for Writers and Writing Groups*. Novato, CA: New World Library.

Reid, William J. 1975. "A Test of a Task-Centered Approach." *Social Work* 20 (1): 3–9. doi:10.1093/sw/20.1.3.

Robert, Lionel P., and Alan R. Dennis. 2005. "Paradox of Richness: A Cognitive Model of Media Choice." *IEEE Transactions on Professional Communication* 48 (1): 10–21. doi:10.1109/TPC.2004.843292.

Slepian, Michael L., and Nalini Ambady. 2012. "Fluid Movement and Creativity." *Journal of Experimental Psychology. General* 141 (4): 625–29. doi:10.1037/a0027395.

Stover, Leon E., and Takeko Kawai Stover. 1976. *China: An Anthropological Perspective*. Goodyear Regional Anthropology Series. Pacific Palisades, CA: Goodyear Publishing.

Tharp, Bruce M., and Stephanie M. Tharp. 2018. *Discursive Design: Critical, Speculative, and Alternative Things*. Design Thinking, Design Theory. Cambridge, MA: MIT Press.

Thomas, Joyce, and Deana McDonagh. 2013. "Shared Language: Towards More Effective Communication." *The Australasian Medical Journal* 6 (1): 46–54. doi:10.4066/AMJ.2013.1596.

Zehr, Howard. 2014. *The Little Book of Restorative Justice: A Bestselling Book by One of the Founders of the Movement*. http://public.ebookcentral.proquest.com/choice/publicfullrecord.aspx?p=1922319.

6

DESIGN SHARED GOALS

Innovating together through creative projects

Attainable ⟵——————————⟶ Challenging

DIMENSION 6: Design Shared Goals

We use and develop our skills in different ways to create a shared sense of purpose in our work.

These activities will help your remote team specify both attainable and challenging goals for creating something together.

Chapter 6 focuses on goal-setting and coping with creative abrasion, two key competencies necessary for successful intercultural collaboration and for grasping the importance of global challenges. Goal-setting means establishing both attainable and challenging goals for yourself and your team. Depending on individual preferences and the stage of your project, your goals can range from open-ended to well-defined. Communication and teamwork are necessary for achieving conversational depth; effectively brainstorming ideas; exchanging substantive feedback; and working together toward possible solutions. The first half of the chapter offers preparatory activities for the projects in the second half of the chapter. Projects are more complex and intense than the activities offered in previous chapters. Chapter 6 builds upon the book's preceding activities and should be used only after your team has had an opportunity to practice coordinating communication and creation across time differences while cultivating trust and communication skills.

| **ATTAINABLE:** I set goals that are easy for me to accomplish and within my skill set and comfort zone. Getting things done makes me feel like I am making a positive contribution to a project and/or team. | **CHALLENGING:** I set goals that are a reach for myself, which may be outside of my current skill set or comfort zone. Trying and learning new things during the process helps me grow and also brings more interesting insights to a project and/or team. |

ANTICIPATORY

ENHANCEMENT-ORIENTED

MISSION-ORIENTED

ADAPTIVE

6.1

Innovating together through creative projects

Through the activities in this chapter, diverse teams transition from co-learning to co-creation. Understanding the relevant logistics will help you value your teammates' perspectives and see potential misalignments as a creative advantage, called *creative abrasion*. In this chapter, teams work together to understand their goal-setting tendencies and comfort zones. In any project, there are moments for big thinking and imaginative fun, but there inevitably comes a time for accomplishing key tasks and completing their work. You may find that your personal preferences determine which parts of this process you most enjoy.

Bonding through shared goals

In our research, we have seen particular success with teams who choose to pursue global challenges in their projects. We urge your team to keep this in mind. In addition to providing the unique opportunity to address pervasive problems from multiple perspectives, these types of collaborations also positively influence cultural sustainability. The United Nations itself is an example of a collaboration-based endeavor, albeit a very complex one. At its core, the organization is a group of people coming together from a variety of different countries, cultures, and backgrounds to brainstorm about issues that impact humankind. Together with their guidelines for intercultural competencies, the

United Nations Educational, Scientific and Cultural Organization's (UNESCO) seventeen strategic sustainable development goals (2003; 2010) address an array of social and environmental sustainability issues.

What we propose is not new; the UN has essentially modeled it for years. However, the internet-connected world makes it possible for anyone to try intercultural collaboration, from students to professionals. Based on our experiences as scholars and facilitators of intercultural learning about global sustainability challenges, we believe the ability to communicate and collaborate alongside international teammates will play a pivotal role in future global sustainability efforts and their outcomes. Our own shared goal to address important global and social issues through collaboration, in our view, is the most important reason for pursuing tricky topics and producing creative abrasion.

Many ways forward

A community that enables both collegial support and productive clashes is essential for intercultural collaboration. Part of that community-building includes ensuring that participants feel bound together by shared goals and agree on modes for engagement. This task involves a range of steps designed to bring teams together and cultivate shared values. You have encountered many of these ideas throughout the book, and we welcome you to explore them further as you work with teammates toward a shared goal.

1. **Create tangible objects.** As discussed in the introduction, tangible objects help teams build relationships, trust, and ideas. Thought Objects help you communicate an idea that you have, either to clarify it for yourself or to communicate it to the team. Progress Objects encourage communication within the team. Dialogue Objects communicate to people outside of the team.
2. **Recognize potential stressors.** Stress takes both positive and negative forms and can impact our motivation, focus, and well-being. Teammates must be aware that negotiating multiple identities and communication across cultures are two potential positive and negative stressors.
3. **Increase ambiguity tolerance.** You can give your brain a boost in terms of how it handles ambiguity. One approach is through deliberate exercises in lateral thinking (examples are prevalent throughout this book). Generative lateral thinking activities enable teammates to learn about each other and bond. Research suggests that multisensory experiences, specifically movement, can improve creativity and fluidity in social-cognitive processing.
4. **Bridge communication gaps.** Sometimes, stress arises because of different communication styles and/or linguistic proficiencies. As emphasized throughout this book, individuals have different preferences about communicating their thoughts, discussing projects, and coming to agreement. These

differences encourage creative innovation; however, negotiating difference also takes patience and time, as teammates with different communication and language preferences learn to adjust.

5. **Prevent and resolve conflicts.** Teammates can proactively agree to prevent and resolve conflicts. A good place to start is agreeing to steer clear of language that can be misinterpreted as personal critique. Task-centered and conciliatory approaches empower teams to solve problems collaboratively.

6. **Set goals.** Focusing on shared values and outcomes helps keep interactions positive and productive, ensuring that everyone plays a role in the process and feels invested in the project. Specifying a range of attainable and challenging goals motivates teammates and promotes creative abrasion.

Recognize potential areas of stress

No matter what, there will be bumps and snags in the collaborative process. Ideas clash, which can be positive and productive. In fact, participating in a collaboration that confronts you with possibilities for creative abrasion actually might make you more creative, even if the process feels difficult. However, interpersonal clashes are unproductive and can induce different kinds of stress. Effective communication throughout the collaboration can reduce negative stressors. Refer to 1.5 and 5.1 to remind yourself and your teammates about how to frame your communications positively.

Positive stress

While most people interpret the word "stress" as negative, it is important to discern helpful stressors from harmful ones. Eustress is helpful stress and is ultimately positive. Teams encounter eustress in creative abrasion, or when working toward a deadline, negotiating an idea, or receiving feedback. Eustress is shorter in duration and can promote motivation and excitement and increase focus and performance (Selye 1976; Mills, Reiss, and Dombeck 2008).

Negative stress

Distress, on the other hand, is negative stress; it is the feeling of being overwhelmed and anxious. Distress is associated with physical and mental side effects, including lowered focus and performance. Miscommunications among teammates can induce distress, as can personal conflicts between teammates. When individuals are in distress, motivation and focus suffer. Thus, your team must swiftly address distressing situations (Selye 1976; Mills, Reiss, and Dombeck 2008). Teammates may hesitate to discuss problems with each other for fear of causing or increasing conflict; in our experience, however, it is worse to leave these issues unattended. Circles of Understanding, 5.7, offers strategies in conflict management.

Multiple identities and stress

Research indicates that individuals juggling multiple identities—whether cultural, racial, or social—may experience stress while navigating certain social situations. A similar kind of stress can occur for those working alongside a range of diverse collaborators for the first time. Figuring out where and how you fit into the greater whole can feel overwhelming.

But these stresses have positive side effects. In consistently living and working with multiple backgrounds, perspectives, or identities, people often show greater resiliency, are able to interpret adversity in positive ways, and also score higher on creativity measures (Gaither et al. 2015; Wei et al. 2019).

Interestingly, one study demonstrates a positive correlation between immersing oneself in a diverse community and cognitive flexibility. In the study, white students from mainland United States tested higher in terms of cognitive flexibility after being immersed in a multiracial academic institution in Hawaii and forming relationships with non-white students (Pauker et al. 2018), suggesting that exposure to diversity can shift mindsets.

"Glocal" stressors can impact the team

Teams must also recognize that members may be experiencing distress due to *glocal* challenges, which have global impact but are felt locally. It may not seem as though current events impact the team's inner workings, but addressing teammates' mental well-being can bring the team together in a different way and can even alleviate stress for the concerned teammate. Such discussions also put global issues on the radar of those who might not otherwise be aware of them, and acknowledging individual teammates' concerns can foster overall team solidarity.

For example, the 2018 U.S. travel ban was enacted during a collaboration, causing distress for teammates in the Middle East and in North America. The travel ban prevented citizens from several primarily majority-Muslim countries from entering the United States; when teammates in the Middle East discussed their distress, their concerns were validated by their teammates in North America who were also upset about the ban. Despite their different contexts, the participants had shared concerns. Hearing about the other's distress made both parties feel embraced and understood.

In section 5.7, the discussion of restorative practices and the Circle of Understanding activity offer a useful approach for bringing such pressing topics to the table. Although presented as a strategy to resolve internal team conflicts, with its emphasis on addressing concerns through mutual sharing, acknowledgement, and understanding, the activity can also be useful for addressing glocal stressors.

Cognitive diversity brings positive challenges

For all of its potential benefits, engaging in creative abrasion can be a mentally taxing process. Conflict is necessary to produce abrasion, and it can leave some feeling downtrodden. Creative abrasion is a way to understand and utilize the outcomes of cognitive diversity. Originally coined by Gerald Hirshberg, then director of Nissan Design International, creative abrasion frames the challenges of cognitive diversity in a positive light, asserting that potential conflicts between teammates with differing views (abrasion) can be used to achieve new ideas (creativity). In this way, cognitive diversity, even with its likely discomforts and disagreements, becomes an important ingredient for innovation because it sets the stage for very different ideas to bump up against each other (Leonard-Barton 1995; Hill et al. 2014).

Diverse teams and innovation

As challenging as creative abrasion may be, abundant research supports that teams which are intentionally diverse across many dimensions have positive outcomes and create better ideas. Research suggests that teams comprised of varied skills and intelligence increase creativity and are able to solve multifaceted challenges when members reach peak levels of creativity together (Sawyer 2008). In addition to demographic dimensions, diversity in teams should ideally encompass disciplinary backgrounds, communication styles, and approaches to thinking and problem-solving (Hill et al. 2014; Sawyer 2017; Gratton and Erickson 2007).

Disrupting routine processes

Business strategist Dorothy Leonard-Barton discusses how most people rely upon specific ways of solving problems based on their particular types of in-depth knowledge, ways of thinking, go-to processes, and inclination toward certain tools (1995). Due to the relationship between these characteristics and individuals' workplace identities, Leonard-Barton describes these as "signature skills." In this case, the natural tendency is to view problems from a particular perspective and, similarly, rely upon the same discovery process time after time. There is a natural human tendency to become set in our ways as patterns of learning and working become more rigid over time (De Bono 2010). Usually, people feel more secure when they can rely on their previous knowledge, experiences, skills, and proficiencies.

Signature skills

Working alone or in a homogeneous team, however, people can become trapped within their signature skills. But when teammates with a diverse range of signature skills can establish trust and a protocol for discussing differences as a route to improving ideas, their differences can positively influence each other and result in highly creative outcomes (Leonard-Barton 1995). When members can openly and safely disagree with each other's ideas and listen to each other's responses, innovation arises from the space where different sets of signature skills, or ways of thinking, bump up against each other. Openness to learning new things is valued across many different cultures. As an example, this is exemplified in the "beginner's mind" discussed in Zen philosophy. The idea that "in the beginner's mind there are many possibilities, but in the expert's there are few" (Suzuki 2010) eloquently expresses the limitations of confining ourselves to our signature skills.

Opportunities for creative abrasion through signature skills

- **Experience and knowledge:** Abrasion is channeled creatively when specialists learn how to explain their ideas or expertise to teammates with different specializations or interests. Think about a balance between contributing knowledge you already possess and gaining new knowledge through the process.
- **Information gathering and verification:** Promote creative abrasion by working through some of the Chapter 4 activities, which expose teammates to different preferences for gathering, understanding, and verifying what we know. This point merits particular focus, since Leonard-Barton argues that "cognitive style preferences" are the characteristic most likely to push people apart.
- **Tools for problem-solving:** Knowledge, experience, and information processing overlap during problem-solving. Creative abrasion occurs when teammates recognize and try to learn from each other's preferences for particular problem-solving processes and tools.

With these numerous benefits in mind, please do not go into this chapter without working through prior chapters! The preceding activities build relationships and trust through the creation, sharing, and discussion of tangible objects—that foundation is essential for project work with your diverse team. The multisensory learning opportunities in this chapter, and their resulting objects, enhance the team's commitment level and offer the collaborations a sense of realness.

In context: Realizing shared goals

Project outcomes can be improved through shared goals, ambiguity tolerance, and flexibility around signature skills. After completing the Project Generator (6.2a), one team realized that their North Star objective (6.2a) was to encourage religious tolerance as a form of cultural sustainability. The Creative Remix (6.2b) got them excited about bringing together people in one of Doha's public spaces to discuss similarities among religions.

(Continued)

However, implementing their ideas in a physical space was outside the scope of the collaboration's timeline and technical abilities. Nevertheless, the team persevered, discovering that Collaborative Storyboard & Video Sketch (6.5) could be a useful route toward envisioning and refining their concept for inclusive social spaces and ultimately sharing the concept with a wider audience.

The team planned their video using the Goal & Role Tracker (6.3). Defining their roles enabled the team to finalize the idea. However, ultimately it was their flexibility in working together and drawing on each other's ideas that led to the successful, dynamic communication of their concept through video. Teammates combined skills in typography, set design, video editing, recruiting actors, and finding props. Their process was full of creative abrasions that led to beautiful ideas and collective creativity.

Their video sketch depicts digital projections of verses from the Holy Quran and the Bible on a wall in a courtyard space. The selected verses have similar messages. Visitors to the space sit in a *majlis*—a traditional seating cluster. There is a table laid out for coffee, with cups bearing questions to spark curiosity about various religions. Objects characteristic of Gulf hospitality—the *dallah* (Arabic coffee pot) and *mabkharah* (incense burner)—welcome people into the space.

The team presented their final vision for the space in a Public Display (6.6). Along with its embedded questions and messages, the video inspired interest in religions and promoted inclusive conversation among invited guests.

Is your team ready for a project?

This concluding chapter provides activities that engage intercultural teams in goal-directed projects. To achieve positive project outcomes, your team must first be prepared. This work takes teams out of their comfort zones to do something totally new. There is no secret sauce, no fool-proof route to innovation, but intercultural teamwork has incredible value for cultivating new problem-solving skills.

The checklists in this section help your team determine if you are ready to move into the more complex projects offered in Chapter 6. Because the success of collaborative initiatives relies on interpersonal competencies, the previous chapters focused on building your skills in communication and collaboration, along with trust in your team. Communication and teamwork are necessary for achieving conversational depth; effectively brainstorming ideas; exchanging substantive feedback; and working together toward possible solutions. As they begin a project together, teams rely on these skills and simultaneously hone them. These competencies are necessary for successful intercultural collaboration and for grasping the importance of global challenges.

What kind of project?

The activities and project plans in Chapter 6 can support a range of project opportunities, such as:

- Working together as a team to define a project
- Approaching workplace assignments from supervisors, clients, or other stakeholders
- Fulfilling an academic assignment or project brief

Before moving ahead, determine whether your team is ready to take this step.

How to use Chapter 6

Chapter 6 is organized differently from previous chapters. While earlier chapters support a pick-and-choose approach, Chapter 6 is divided into two parts: Part A: Project Planning, and Part B: Project Descriptions.

Prepare for project work

Because the prior activities in this book help teammates learn about each other and establish a community of trust, it is important to work through some of them together first. Projects are more complex and intense, and the preceding activities give you an opportunity to practice coordinating communication and creation across time differences while building trust and communication skills.

Read through the following lists to determine if your team is ready to undertake a project together.

Understand yourself and teammates

Read through the following questions by yourself. Respond to them in your head or in writing:

- *Who are you?*
- *What are your values?*
- *Who are your teammates?*
- *How do each of you prefer to work?*
- *In what ways do you communicate as a team?*
- *What are your interests?*
- *What are your team's interests?*

If you cannot answer most of these questions, your team should work through some of the prior activities. If you can answer some questions, but your team has not yet found a rallying point, we recommend returning to Chapter 4 and completing some of those exploratory activities. Finding common interests, causes, and passions is a useful starting point for this and other Chapter 6 activities and will prevent future frustration. The Focus Quest (4.2) is designed to help your teammates find commonality regarding potential topics and problem spaces before addressing those interests.

If you can answer most of these questions, please continue reading.

Understand what comes next

Once you've established your rallying point, the preparatory activities and project ideas in this chapter will help you do something innovative, regardless of whether the outcomes are utilitarian or discursive. The following questions represent challenges your team will encounter while working toward your shared goal. This chapter will help prepare you to address this list. As you read, consider other ambiguities that might arise during a collaborative project:

* *What is the problem you're going to address?*
* *What are the best ways to address the problem?*
* *Who is going to do what?*
* *What critique protocols will the team use to make ideas better?*
* *How will external community partners or stakeholders to react/relate to what you've contributed?*
* *What will our outcomes be?*
* *How will it all work out in the end?*

If your team finds these questions exciting, you're ready to tackle a project!

Part A: Project planning

After reading 6.1, the team should complete all of the planning activities in Part A before moving on to one of the detailed projects in Part B. Take a look at the project ideas in Part B to get a sense of what your team might want to do, or come up with your own outcomes using the Project Generator and Creative Remix. Then, return to the Part A activities to organize and plan your project.

* 6.1 Design Shared Goals
* 6.2 Project Generator & Creative Remix
* 6.3 Goal & Role Tracker

Refer to the following examples as your team works through Part A: Relationship between objectives, goals, tasks, roles, and actions

---

6.2 Project Generator & Creative Remix: Objectives & larger goals

* **North Star objectives** are big-picture goals that inspire further collaboration and co-creation and are driven by the team's ideals, research, and problem statements.
  * ○ Example: Improve awareness of water sustainability.
* **Goals** lead to outcomes developed according to North Star objectives.
  * ○ The team might look at individual behaviors or smaller aspects of larger systemic problems to make a topic such as water sustainability feel more manageable.

6.3a Goal & Role Tracker, Part 1: Smaller goals & tasks

- **Goals**, whether attainable or challenging, inspire the specific tasks, or "to-do lists," necessary for achieving them. Goals can be directly related to the team's intended outcomes or can be personal ambitions that are met along the way as the team reaches its intended outcome.
- **Tasks** can be broken down into one or more actions necessary for task completion.

6.3b Goal & Role Tracker, Part 2: Roles & actions

- **Roles** match people to tasks based upon individual skill sets, interests, and learning goals. Roles describe the types of tasks (and related actions) a particular teammate will complete.
- **Actions** are short-term steps individuals can fulfill to complete particular tasks. Most tasks can be broken down into multiple actions.

Examples of project-specific objectives, goals, tasks, roles, and actions

6.2 Project Generator: Objectives & larger goals

- North Star objective: *Improve awareness of water sustainability*.
- Project Generator prompt: Create an **adaptive**, **responsible**, and **discursive** solution for the following idea: A video that introduces a new **reusable water bottle** for **mothers of small children** who frequently visit the **local mall** and are concerned about the **social perceptions and health risks of consuming desalinated water.**

6.3 Goal & task spreadsheet: Smaller goals & tasks

- The example in 6.3 defines goals in terms of various desired team outcomes and personal ambitions; one of these was to **produce a short video**. A task that contributes to this goal is **creating a storyboard.**

6.4 Visual project timeline: Roles & actions

- The **task** of creating a **storyboard** (discussed in 6.3) can be broken into the following **actions**. The teammate filling this **role** could be described as the *Storyboarder*.
  1. Communicate with teammates to develop an understanding of the goal, audience, and narrative (in parallel, teammates in different roles will address those as part of their own tasks)
  2. Collaborate with the teammate serving in the script-writer role

3. List what needs to be shown to determine which scenes to depict in the video
4. Gather sketching materials
5. Sketch a first round of ideas, based on the selected scenes, using paper and pencil
6. Make notes to describe each sketch
7. Repeat this process several times in order to create options for team review
8. Meet with the teammate serving in the project manager role
9. Share with teammates for feedback
10. Revise and update sketches
11. Share with teammates for feedback
12. Finalize storyboards: Refine the drawing style and use ink (or digitize them)
13. Share final storyboards with team

6.2

Project Generator & Creative Remix:
Creating value through collective intercultural creativity

Your team may want to implement a marketable product, catalyze a conversation, or both. Perhaps you wish to deepen the intercultural learning you've already started together. Maybe you're feeling stuck trying to figure out how to start a project together. The Project Generator activity will get you thinking and talking about your larger motivations and objectives.

The Project Generator helps you understand your individual and team intentions and then have fun combining different possibilities to create a variety of possible starting points. Using a lateral thinking approach, these activities help you generate project prompts to stimulate thinking. From there, you will start translating your ideas into visual forms that you can share and improve upon with your team. This sets the stage for team engagement in the optional Creative Remix, which guides teammates as they combine their ideas in exciting new ways.

Frame larger innovation goals

Combine values to create value

In this chapter, your team will reflect on individual and cultural values (see Chapter 2) and discuss how those individual values inform your team's values.

In turn, your team's shared values drive the overarching objectives for your project. In other words, by addressing your team's values, you create value. Rosen offers several definitions for value creation: It can bring ideas to market more quickly, boost profits for businesses or shareholders, provide a useful product or service for customers, or rapidly solve a problem. In addition, it can also empower and enrich lives. Creative practitioners also create value in ways beyond typical capitalist interpretations. In this view, the design of systems, services, and artifacts is a form of value creation. Keeping this in mind, recall our discussion of stakeholders (5.2) and consider how involving stakeholders in your team's workflow might reveal additional possibilities for value creation.

North Star objectives

Incorporating your team's shared values into your mutual interest in a topic can be a powerful way to bring the team together (see Focus Quest 4.2). *North Star objectives* unite messy or challenging topics with ideas for how to address them. By helping teams to focus on what matters most, North Star objectives enable them to focus subsequent ideation efforts toward a range of practical, theoretical, or educational outcomes. These big-picture goals unify the team and keep the ship of collaboration on course, like sailors using the actual North Star for guidance. At the same time, these "constraints for creativity" (Stokes 2005) actually enable teammates to think more broadly and openly within this defined range.

Innovation as value creation

Innovation is a new or different way of approaching something—whether a tangible 2D or 3D object, interface, or physical location or an intangible method, strategy, process, or system. Although innovation takes many forms, it is ultimately a form of value creation.

The Observatory of Public Sector Innovation (OPSI) is a great resource for learning more about innovation from an international perspective. OPSI (2018) developed a schema that describes four categories of innovation: anticipatory, enhancement-oriented, mission-oriented, and adaptive. It is important for teams to consider these different modes of innovation as they begin a project because innovation styles offer additional insights into teammates' interests and larger goals.

Not to worry: Previous experience in innovation is not required for this last phase of your journey. Regardless of your differences, it is possible for your team to work together creatively once you've established shared goals.

Five fields for intent and interpretation

Stephanie and Bruce Tharp's Four-Field Framework is a helpful resource for describing design intent and interpretation according to four different capacities: commercial, responsible, experimental, and discursive (Tharp and Tharp 2018). The framework also suggests ways for the team to create value, which may help you envision how to transform your rallying point into a concept or project outcome. Like the different facets of innovation, this framework also allows for overlaps. For example, a project that is primarily responsible could also be commercial or experimental, thus creating business value while simultaneously empowering and enriching lives. To the Tharps' four fields, we add "cultural" as a fifth option. Consider these **five fields** as your team brainstorms ways to create value from your collaboration.

Shuffle and share

Once your team has determined North Star objectives and populated the spreadsheet, you will mix and match your objectives and spreadsheet content to create project prompts. This process stimulates lateral thinking and encourages you to think of a variety of ideas beyond those that first occur to you. This is a helpful approach when you are feeling stuck because it encourages you to think about—and work with—ideas that you might not otherwise have. This approach also promotes collective creativity (Hill et al. 2014) by providing a straightforward way for you to see and interact with teammates' ideas.

Remixing ideas across the team

After generating your project prompts, the Creative Remix is an opportunity to take your team's ideas in new directions by exchanging and working with each other's Progress Objects. You may be familiar with the idea of "remixing" in musical terms: Combining existing songs in different ways to develop a new auditory composition. The beauty of the Creative Remix is that teams similarly create something completely new from preexisting elements. As with a musical remix, your Creative Remix should not detract from the original, but offer a fresh experience.

Convergent divergence

Recall the divergent and convergent double diamond model of design innovation (see 4.1 for more details). During the Creative Remix, ideas stemming from different perspectives (divergence) are brought together to form new ideas (convergence). The generation of remixed ideas gives teams a broader set of options to consider (divergence) as they converge toward the development of their primary concept. Thus, by the end of the process, they have converged toward a single concept, project, or product that nevertheless represents many different ideas, perspectives, and observations.

Managing stress

Sharing ideas, files, timelines, and other components while working on a project is critical to cooperative work in the digital age. However, it can also be scary to consider sending a beloved brainchild into the hands of a distant collaborator—in some cases, a stranger—in a faraway land. Much like other aspects of team-based work, the success of this process hinges on a certain degree of mental flexibility.

In recent years, a number of accessible collaborative tools have emerged to help make the task of sharing work components easier. Cloud-based documents, online spreadsheets, and file-sharing systems all promise seamless sharing, but, of course, teams must be willing to share in the first place. Additionally, teammates must condition themselves to regularly use these shared repositories for saving and cataloging all of their work; otherwise, the system will not serve its intended purpose.

Share folders and make digital copies

One way to combat natural feelings of ownership—and forestall a negative reaction to people changing your ideas—is to back up files. Another approach is to keep your own individual process logs in a single shared folder and then create a separate folder for saved copies of items that are specifically designated as available for remixing, editing, reuse, or other adaptations. Or teammates could agree that items in any of the individual folders can be used by anyone on the team at any time, as long as the unedited, original version is preserved in the original author's folder. Logging separate copies of individual contributions to the team's components can also help individuals maintain a sense of ownership and place within the process.

When there are multiple copies, teammates know that the version they release to the team for evaluation and use is not the only version that exists. Creators can always return to their original versions for reference, discussion, and process evaluation. Knowing that you can still do future work with the originals—and that your teammates are working with copies—can reduce stress related to feelings of attachment. The released copy then becomes less precious, which feels less risky when others critique, utilize, remix, or turn it into something else through revisions and editing. An overall sense of security about how your work will be used fosters successful exchange and collaboration.

Benefits & outcomes

- Unify teammates around big-picture goals, or North Star objectives
- Develop project prompts to stimulate thinking
- Practice "value creation" to transform your rallying point into project ideas
- Mix and match teammate ideas, creating new Progress Objects to advance your project

a. Activity

Project Generator

The Project Generator prompts teammates to discuss their interests according to different modes of innovation and concept creation relative to the rallying point. Understanding teammates' interests and inclinations can focus your team's overarching North Star objectives. Once larger aims are defined, teams can subsequently develop ideas to be executed through smaller, actionable tasks. The facets of innovation and the five fields for intent and interpretation are also good lenses for analyzing and discussing each other's early prototypes. When you understand a teammate's intention, you can assess whether their prototype clearly communicates it.

→ **People:** Individual/remote teammates
→ **Duration:** Allow a minimum of 2–3 days based on time difference
→ **Technology:** Shared spreadsheet, instant messaging software, videoconferencing software
→ **Other resources:** Physical prototyping materials such as paper, pencils/pens, tape, scissors, glue, cardboard, string; digital drawing or image editing tools (optional)

→ *Throughout the process, refer to the discussion guide at the end of this activity.*

Tips

- **Feeling Stuck?** Deciding which project to work on together can be challenging when you have so many big ideas! If you feel stuck, consider returning to Chapter 4 to see where your interests align. Perhaps you can think of a social or political issue that is relevant for all teammates. You might also consider what changes you would you like to see in your neighborhood, local community, or city. What can you do to promote that change?
- **Creative abrasion:** Be mindful of the differences between productive conflict and destructive conflict. Focus conversations on the aspects of the collaboration that excite you. If conflicts arise, find ways to work through these challenges constructively (5.7).
- **Embrace new ideas:** Part of the beauty of your intercultural collaboration are the new approaches and viewpoints your teammates bring to the table. Do not dismiss them because they feel unfamiliar! This is a wonderful and tricky part of working with people who are different from you. By embracing various approaches, your team will be able to create new and unexpected, ideas, initiatives, and value.
- **Cross-pollination:** This activity helps cultivate a shared sense of ownership. While you may encounter some creative abrasion, it is important to get on the same page about your shared goals and to read

from the same script. Uncovering shared interests, goals, and engagement styles will go a long way toward helping the team develop something that is exciting and satisfying for every teammate.

Identify North Star objectives

Phase 1: Working individually

1. **Identify possible topics:** Reflecting on your remote team's prior research
   and interests or rallying point, make a brief list of topics of interest. It can be
   helpful to explicitly define the problem first in order to focus on solutions
   later in this process. Writing problem statements or open "how might we"
   questions are two helpful starting points.
   Example of problem statement: The government should aim to increase public
      awareness about the importance of water consciousness so that commu-
      nity members' wasteful practices do not continue.
   Example of an open question: How might we address the negative social per-
      ception and health risks of consuming desalinated water?
2. **Assess:** Working independently with the self-assessment worksheets included
   at the end of this activity (pages 244–245), figure out which of the five fields
   and innovation factors most appeal to you. Do you want to get people talking
   about your idea to create buzz? Conduct an experiment? Bring a product to
   market? Address a deep social need? How might you go about doing it?

Value discovery

Phase 2: With remote teammates

3. Team project values: Discuss your individual topic ideas and self-assessment
   responses. What do you see as the larger social value of your teamwork?
4. Map: As a team, create a shared spreadsheet or document with six columns
   (in physical or digital format) with the following headers: innovation factors,
   five fields, themes, artifacts, audience, and location.

Think laterally

Phase 3: Working individually

5. Populate: Working individually in the team's shared document, fill in the
   information according to these guidelines:
   a. Innovation factors: Write down the innovation factor(s) you were most
      drawn to in the self-analysis.
      Examples:
      • *Adaptive innovation*
      • *Mission-driven innovation*
   b. Five fields: Write down one or more of the five fields you were most
      drawn to in the self-analysis

Examples:
- *Responsible*
- *Commercial*
- *Cultural*

c. Themes: Break down your team's umbrella topic or North Star objective into more accessible themes by writing three to five things about the topic/objective that most excites or interests you.

While the broader objective might seem challenging, there are ways to make it feel more attainable. Your team's North Star objective may be "improving awareness of water sustainability through responsible concepts," but on its own, this is a difficult project topic. However, when you examine it at a local level, looking at individual behaviors or smaller aspects of the larger systemic problems, this bigger objective feels more manageable. The following are three related themes.
Examples:
- *Social perception and health risks of consuming desalinated water*
- *New possibilities for water bottle recycling*
- *Individual water use consciousness*

d. Artifacts: Write three to five different types of artifacts, media, or outcomes, physical or experiential (e.g., a bus stop, a group dining experience, a podcast, a garden). Include a range: Things that would be easy for you to show or create; things that would be difficult for you to create; things that you enjoy but would never create yourself.
Examples:
- *Interactive video piece*
- *Bus wrap*
- *Bedtime story*
- *Reusable water bottle*
- *Mobile tool*

e. Audience: Write three to five potential audiences for your project outcome; one should be a person who would be receptive, one should be someone who will need convincing, and there should be a couple other wild cards. (Keep in mind the Fictional Character Exchange (4.5) as a way to bring your audiences to life!)
Examples:
- *Mothers of small children*
- *College students who shower more than once daily*
- *Hydroponic gardeners*

f. Location: Where would the final outcome reside? List three to five potential digital or physical environments or specific contexts for the project.
Examples:
- *At the local mall*
- *On a dedicated website*
- *At the movie theatre*

Ideate!

Phase 4: With remote teammates

6. **Identify:** After everyone on the team has contributed to the spreadsheet, peruse the responses. Circle, star, or underline any combination of items in the spreadsheet. Be sure to choose some that are not your own.
7. **Combine and compose:** In a new column of the same spreadsheet, write out new combinations of project prompts based on your selections. For each combination, be sure to incorporate at least two selections that are not your own.

    Example combination and prompt:

    Create an adaptive, responsible, and commercial solution for the following idea. A reusable water bottle for mothers of small children who frequently visit the local mall and are concerned about the social perceptions and health risks of consuming desalinated water.
8. **Ideate:** Based on your selections, create prototypes, or Progress Objects. These might includeseries of sketches, mind maps, storyboards, physical models, writings, or other visual depictions of ideas or outcomes. It's okay if your own skills are not sufficient to fully execute these ideas—just think about ways to communicate them to your teammates.

Discuss

Phase 5: With remote teammates

9. **Share & Discuss:** Meet to share the project ideas generated from this activity and your sketches. As part of the discussion, review and apply the critique protocols and formats you practiced in Chapter 5.
10. **Define North Star objective:** After reviewing all of the ideas, what larger theme or goal emerges? Work as a team to put this into words—this is your North Star objective. Write it down in your Fourth Space, shared spreadsheet, and so on.
11. **Iterate:** Has your team landed on a project idea that excites you all? If so, congratulations—move on to the Creative Remix, 6.2b! If not, that's normal. You could do another round of this activity based on one specific area of interest, or proceed to the Creative Remix for a fun way to come up with a new idea by combining your ideas with your teammate's ideas.

DISCUSSION GUIDE

*   What forms of innovation excite you most? Why?
*   How can your "Project Generator" idea make use of what you have already learned throughout this book and from your teammates?
*   How might you align your team's different interests and intentions?
*   How might your values align with what you will create?

SELF-ASSESSMENT (PROJECT GENERATOR, STEP 2)

Rate your interest in the four facets of innovation (adapted from OPSI 2018)	Fill in the blocks to indicate your level of interest		
Anticipatory innovation invites teams to speculate and design for possible futures by exploring and predicting issues or problems that might surface down the road. Anticipatory innovation supports experimentation and "big ideas," which are easier to manipulate in preliminary phases before the anticipated problem is solidified. Ideas in this realm can go against the grain or intentionally disrupt the status quo.	low	med	high
Enhancement-oriented innovation is a more traditional approach to innovation often used by organizations or governments to improve upon existing systems, programs, or practices. The process often involves exploiting previous initiatives or programs, changing perspectives, and working with others to innovate.			
Mission-oriented innovation is a top-down approach to innovation that defines and articulates a larger aim. Developing this aim enables the necessary organization and direction for its achievement. In addition to "missions," we categorize strategic and systems innovation in this intangible, directed realm. This type of innovation pushes against or works within existing structures or archetypes.			
Adaptive innovation is driven by a bottom-up perspective in response to changes in environmental conditions, such as new discoveries, technical innovations, public policies, or business models. Ranging from radical to incremental in nature, this kind of innovation is typically driven by citizens, but the innovation may be embraced later in public policy or organizational practices.			

Rate your interest in the five fields (adapted from Tharp and Tharp 2018)	*Fill in the blocks to indicate your level of interest*		
Commercial concepts have value in the marketplace. These are ideas that can be transformed into products or services that can be produced or delivered, bought or sold. The primary focus is on delivering a marketable object, experience or idea.	low	med	high
Responsible concepts have value in society. These ideas attempt to address systemic issues and challenges through creative solutions that range from simple to complex. The primary focus is improving on a problem that impacts people or planet.			
Experimental concepts have value in testing and proving the efficacy of something. Though these ideas may also have a practical function, their primary goal is to understand, test, and push limits. Experimental ideas can play a role in producing new knowledge.			
Discursive concepts have value in disseminating ideas. These concepts aim to create discourse by inviting people to interpret them and speculate about their implications. The primary focus of discursive concepts is to stimulate critical thinking and dialogue and to envision possible futures.			
Cultural concepts have value in creating shared learning opportunities between teammates. The primary focus is for teams to further their cultural learning by creating *Dialogue Objects* as cultural mediators. As opposed to external drivers, teams could be prototyping for their own internal purposes and might not have an "end user."			

b. Activity

Creative Remix

Many people are familiar with musical *remixes*, which alter an original piece of music by combining it with other musical pieces, adding to it, or distorting it. The beauty of the Creative Remix is that it similarly creates something completely new from preexisting elements shared among teammates. Remixes are not limited to music and can apply to a wide range of media including writing, strategy development, coding, systems thinking, and creating new procedures. As with a musical piece, your remix should not detract from the original, but instead offer a fresh new approach to it.

→ **People:** Local and/or remote teammates
→ **Duration:** Allow a minimum of 4–5 days based on time difference. This varies depending on number of teammates, desired frequency, depth of topic, and the time difference. Remixes can be repeated several times in a row to help teams generate and evolve ideas and/or conducted over a longer period (e.g., one week) to produce more refined concepts.
→ **Technology:** Digital drawing or image editing tools, shared folder, instant messaging software, videoconferencing software
→ **Other resources:** Physical prototyping materials such as paper, pencils/pens, tape, scissors, glue, cardboard, string

Component exchange

Phase 1: With local team/remote teammates

1. Plan: When will you deliver your components? After completing the Project Generator (6.2a), use your Shared Calendar (1.4) to establish a timeline for exchanging your project components.
2. Establish a shared location: How will you deliver your components? Working together as a team, decide on the appropriate modes to exchange files: Cloud-based documents, online spreadsheets, file-sharing, or the Fourth Space (1.5b).
3. Decide quantity: How many components will each teammate or set of teammates plan to create in order to enable a rich exchange? Do you need to create more than you did during the Project Generator (6.2a)? Your components could include a range of materials generated by the team—visual files, written documents, code, sketches, video clips, and so on.
4. Follow up: Using your team's preferred mode(s) of communication, notify teammates whenever you add new components to your shared folder. Look at the contributions made by teammates and ask clarifying questions if needed.

Creative Remix

Remixing is accomplished by combining ideas, a process that might involve printing out items and collaging them together or merging images with visual editing software, if available. It can involve simple sketches and hand-generated items or more complex forms of visual communication. As your confidence with the process of remixing grows, you might scale up to more in-depth approaches, such as:

*   **Photo remixes:** Shuffle and recombine parts of a static image with digital or analog tools to convey a new idea
*   **Digital collages:** Recombine multiple digital images into a new composition
*   **Sketch/prototype mashup:** Physically deconstruct, then re-draw or digitally reconstruct each other's physical or digital process objects.

→ *Throughout the process, refer to the discussion guide at the end of this activity.*

Phase 1: With remote teammates

1. **Partner up:** After everyone contributes files to shared folders and/or Fourth Space, decide who will be remixing together. Suggestions:
    a. **Two teammates (duo):** You will each work with the full collection of the other person's contributions
    b. **Three teammates (trio):** Each teammate works with the other two teammates' full collection: Teammate A remixes teammate B's & C's contributions; Teammate B remixes teammate A's & C's contributions; Teammate C remixes teammate A's & B's contributions

    c. **Four or more teammates:** Form pairs or trios within the team until everyone has at least one other Remix exchange teammate, then follow the suggestions for two to three teammates. Pairs or trios should plan to go do at least two rounds of the Remix in order to give everyone an opportunity to shuffle and work with ideas from across the team.

2. Plan: Create a timeline or update the Shared Calendar (1.4) for the exchange to set expected deadlines for completing Remixes and sharing.

Phase 2: Working individually

3. **Remix:** Engage in either analog or digital remixing, depending on your situation and preferences. Every Remix is an opportunity to combine new and existing components. The process should involve one or more aspects from the following prompts:

    a. Add something new to one of your teammate's ideas.

    b. Combine one of their ideas and one of your ideas, using components that are obviously derived from both options.

    c. Evaluate one of your ideas and one of your teammate's ideas, and make something entirely new based on a mashup of different aspects of each.

4. **Describe:** Write a short description that explains your new ideas. Let your teammates know when you have added your drafts to your shared folder. Allow at least 1-2 days to turn around a Remix.

Phase 3: With remote teammates

5. **Discuss:** If possible, meet via a videoconference to discuss your ideas (this step is encouraged, but meeting in real time may not be necessary for those with significant time differences if you take the time to describe your ideas in writing). If needed, ask clarifying questions.

Phase 4: Working individually

6. **Repeat:** Don't worry if your first attempts feel clunky or rough; the purpose of this activity is to enable teams to start putting your ideas together. Making time to engage in a few rounds of Remixing will enable you to think more critically about your ideas and likely improve the execution and craft of your remixes.

7. **Refine:** After a few rounds of Remixes, each teammate can select one new idea to refine, edit, and improve. Upload these refined versions to shared folders or the Fourth Space.

Phase 5: With remote teammates

8. **Present:** Using the guidelines for critique detailed in Chapter 5, talk through your refined versions as a team. Perhaps there are possibilities for further remixing these refined ideas to converge them into one final idea, or perhaps you could implement more than one of them.

DISCUSSION GUIDE

• Have you previously worked on a collaborative project that required file exchange? If so, what was that like? How was this process different?
• What digital formats do you think are best for sharing files? Why?
• In what ways do the outcomes relate to your team's North Star objectives?
• In what ways did the ideas evolve through remixing?
• What will you do with the new ideas that came from this activity?

Have you found your North Star?

Before working through this section and activity, we recommend that your team complete the Project Generator (6.2) to help establish some of your broader North Star team goals. The Project Generator introduces you to the Four Facets of Innovation (OPSI 2018) and the Four-Field Framework (Tharp and Tharp 2018) to guide your pathway toward your topic of mutual interest or rallying point and get you started on some rough directions for more in-depth work.

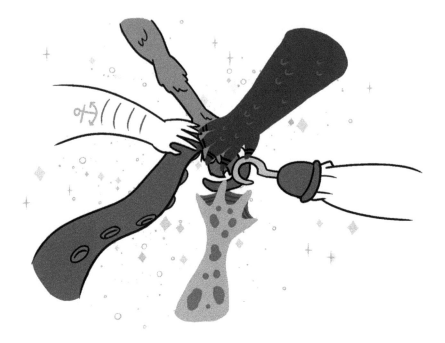

6.3

Goal & Role Tracker:
Envisioning attainable, challenging, and specific team intentions

➜ *Use the Shared Calendar (1.4) and Project Generator (6.2) to prepare for these activities.*

Goals and roles go hand-in-hand. This section invites you to define your goals as a team and take control of your project together from the beginning. Set you team on a path toward team-building by establishing shared goals, tasks, roles, actions, and a timeframe for completing the project.

As you begin, look back at the Six Dimensions of intercultural teamwork and your goal-setting preferences from the Teamthink Constellation activity (1.2). The sixth dimension, Design Shared Goals, discusses how to use and develop our skills in different ways to create a shared sense of purpose in collaborative work. Take the time to have a conversation about how individual preferences for attainable and challenging goals might impact your project and the roles you will each play. There is comfort in doing what we are good at, but there is also value in going outside your comfort zone. Assessing the skills and interests of each person, in alignment with your project goals, will allow the team to celebrate the strengths of its members and view collaboration as a boon to success. Opportunities for teams to work within, and outside, their established skill sets also promote creative abrasion.

Establishing a common set of goals also establishes your team's direction for your work together, and helps you break challenging projects into attainable tasks. Effective goals require a strong foundation—both understanding time differences and establishing lines of communication to create a shared vision and collective purpose. Teammates then feel more open to exchanging dialogue, constructive feedback, differing ideas, and contrasting viewpoints. While the latter may sound uncomfortable, the trust-building and sense of community established during team goal-setting can help overcome these hurdles (Hill et al. 2014).

Through the Goal & Role Tracker, your team learns to break larger project goals into smaller tasks. During this process, your team must discuss what is necessary for completing the project, while still allowing for spontaneity and discovery along the way. When combined with the Role Assignment activity in the next phase, the Goal & Role Tracker maps actionable tasks to individuals and helps teammates figure out how to use time differences to their advantage.

Connect objectives to goals, tasks, roles, actions

Before doing these activities, it is useful to understand the relationships among North Star Objectives, goals, tasks, roles, and actions. The North Star objective drives your team, your big-picture purpose, which should feel somewhat challenging. *Goals* help you reach this objective and are divided into *tasks*. In order to meet larger team objectives, individuals assume the *roles* that put them in charge of overseeing thematically grouped tasks.

In Adding Roles & Actions (6.3b) to your Goal & Role Tracker, you will identify your interest in fulfilling certain tasks. Your selections should take into account your existing skill level and the tasks that help you fulfill personal learning goals or hone new skills. Articulating your personal learning goals as you match your specific skills to the team's goal helps teams push against the confines of their signature skills. Individuals assume their roles and then choose the best actions to fulfill specific tasks, detailing them in the Tracker.

Blend attainable and challenging goals

Depending on the nature of your project, your team's array of attainable and challenging goals may be short or long term. You could have co-creation and interim progress goals, or milestones, to help the team work toward that end goal. Your team might also have goals for the kinds of changes your innovation will effect, the conversations it will start, the learning that can occur. Your own definition of the goal may even evolve or change over time as you learn more about the topic or problem.

Motivate action through goals

Setting goals makes individuals and teams feel more motivated, instilling a sense of responsibility to the team that drives effective teamwork. Collaborative teams can embrace idea-sharing early on by having teammates think about their individual approaches to goal-setting. Keep in mind that goals can be *intrinsic*—motivated from within—or *extrinsic*—motivated by factors outside of one's self (Locke and Latham 2002). In setting both individual and team goals, understanding which are intrinsically or extrinsically motivated helps all teammates remain accountable.

In addition to the project goals, think during the planning process about your personal project and collaboration goals. Your personal goals can make you feel inspired and motivated to work hard for your team. In discussing and combining individual goals, teams come to understand that they are working together toward collective goals, and each teammate feels a sense of investment in the process and outcomes. Completing a goal prompts individuals to set higher goals and increases their motivation to complete new goals (Locke and Latham 2002).

Divide goals into tasks

Once your team has determined its big-picture objectives and placed its larger project goal(s) on the Goal & Role Tracker, think about what tasks are needed to reach those intended goals. Project goals such as producing a video, bringing a new water bottle to market, or designing an allegorical children's book all have myriad embedded tasks. In addition to achieving larger team goals, teammates should identify some individual goals related to their own skills or learning that they can accomplish alongside the team goals.

Let's say your team is making a video (see 6.5). One teammate's **personal goal** may be to learn more about video editing so that they can contribute to that aspect of the project. They assign themselves three **tasks**: (1) Watch some video-editing tutorials online. (2) Take notes on the videos. (3) Download video-editing software to practice new skills. Breaking the first task into even smaller actions, they decide to watch and take notes on five tutorial videos. Watching each video is an **action** that contributes to the fulfillment of the task. They need to complete this task early in the project timeline in order to contribute to video editing later in the project. This person completes their tasks as their teammates work on storyboarding, script-writing, or finding voice actors. These individuals must also determine which actions are necessary to complete those tasks.

Using the Goal & Role Tracker, the team agrees on a date for completing these preliminary tasks. On that date, they will check on each other's progress at convenient, previously agreed-upon time. This example shows how the larger team goal of creating a video can be broken down into smaller goals, tasks, and actions, negotiated, communicated, and shared through the creation and updating of the Goal & Role Tracker.

Assume roles, take action

Actors play roles, portraying specific interactions and feelings. Similarly, teammates play roles in the "theater" of the collaborative project. Once the team has discussed and outlined goals and tasks, individuals can begin to think about the roles they will play to fulfill the team's goals. Roles are descriptive designations, a sort of shorthand, that help teammates remember which tasks and actions each person will complete. Teammates often take on multiple roles and can also share or switch roles. Each role assumes responsibility for one or more tasks and their attendant action(s). You'll choose the best approaches to your specific tasks by determining the necessary actions. Your team will determine individual roles and detail related actions in activity 6.3b.

Beware your signature skills

This is the point where you start figuring out how to work within and beyond the signature skills described in 6.1. These are your go-to skills—your knowledge and the areas where you excel your typical Work Style, and tools you like. These skill sets instill confidence—but can be problematic when everyone wants to do things their "signature" way. When teammates' signature skills collide, friction can occur, but being open to collision promotes creative abrasion, which can blossom into productive new thinking.

Benefits & outcomes

- Define common team goals and develop actionable tasks to achieve them
- Assess teammate skills and interests to assign roles and actions equitably
- Take advantage of time differences in planning work assignments
- Anticipate potential obstacles to curtail conflict and make room for creative abrasion
- Cultivate investment among teammates and promote accountability

---

a. Activity

Goal & Role Tracker, Part 1

This activity invites you to establish goals as a team and take control of your project. The path toward team-building begins with establishing shared goals, tasks, actions, and a timeframe for completing the project. Refer to the Six Dimensions of intercultural teamwork and your goal-setting preferences from the Teamthink Constellation (1.2). Individual preferences for attainable and challenging goals will have an impact on your project and the individual roles teammates will assume. Remember that the sixth dimension, Design Shared Goals, is about using and developing your skills to create a shared sense of purpose in your teamwork.

Key time-related actions for teams

As you plan, think about how your team will:

- Develop and agree upon overarching and detailed work plans for the project
- Determine checkpoints for assessing progress or delivering work (including deadlines)
- Decide to structure work based on individual and collective working preferences (See 6.3b to assign roles)
- Communicate and check in with each other (modes and frequency)
- Adapt when the plan changes

Talking through each of these points and accounting for them in the creation of a shared Goal & Role Tracker helps teams get to know and understand each other better while setting expectations and promoting accountability. This process is useful when managing longer-term collaborations and projects, especially combined with a detailed Shared Calendar (1.4). Some teams also find this process comes in handy for coordinating with each other on shorter-term activities within this book.

→ **People:** Individually/remote teammates
→ **Duration:** 1–2 hours, if working synchronously; 1–2 days, if working asynchronously
→ **Technology:** Videoconferencing or messaging software, shared document
→ **Other resources:** Paper, pen

Tips

- **Completed Tasks:** Establish a way to show when a task has been completed. This will help the team see what tasks and actions remain, through strategies such as strikethrough text, color change, or addition (or removal) of an icon. Teams might also consider creating a separate document indicating completed tasks. Individuals might also add a note to the Fourth Space (1.5b) or send an email or message to let the team know when a task is complete.
- **Inevitable Challenges:** This activity encourages the team to identify collaborative hurdles early on. Likely challenges will include time differences and task distribution.
- **Be Reliable:** Your team needs to be able to count on you, so if you plan a meeting, show up. If your team asks you to deliver work by a certain time, do. Teamwork is at its best when everyone knows they can count

on each other to fulfill specific roles. You can discuss and shift roles as the project progresses, but always do so in discussion with your team. Don't make excuses; pull your weight. If everyone contributes, the collective efforts will be evident in the end results.

- **Take Notes:** There should always be a team note-taker who documents and shares the discussion on behalf of all members. It is important to recap developments and discussion so that everyone can stay up-to-date. Decide who will assume the note-taking role. Make a habit of regularly documenting and promptly sharing meeting notes and critiques in a designated location where the team knows to find them.

Goals, tasks, time

Phase 1: With local and/or remote teammates

1. **Discuss:** Talk about your team's goal-setting tendencies based on Teamthink Constellation. Now that your team has a project in mind, return to the results of your Teamthink Constellation (1.2) assessments to discuss your individual tendencies around creating goals.
2. **Read:** Visit Section 1.4 and complete the Shared Calendar activity if your team has not done so already.
3. **Review:** As a team, look at the Shared Calendar and consider a feasible and realistic project deadline. After agreeing upon deadlines, work backward from these dates to develop a project timeline.
4. **Create:** Create a shared document using a digital tool accessible and editable by all teammates (such shared scheduling or calendar applications, spreadsheet, or document). Title the document with the team's North Star objective.
5. **Columns:** Insert three columns with the following headings: goals, tasks, and time.
6. **Populate:** Working together, populate the goals and tasks column of the document in the following order. Think about what you need to accomplish in order to complete the project on time.
   a. **Goals:** Discuss and then populate the shared document with attainable and challenging goals related to the team's intended outcomes and individual ambitions.
      Example goals:
      - Inform people about different ways to reduce water consumption
      - Explain the benefits of water dispensers

- Explore how people in other communities use water
- Learn video production methods and mediums
- Produce a short video
- Participate in a film festival

b. **Tasks:** Write out the specific set of tasks needed to accomplish each goal. Think of ways to break down the challenging goals into smaller tasks to make them seem more attainable. Each goal in the first column, should have a number of "to-do" items listed in individual cells next to it. If the task seems too large, work together as a team to break them into smaller pieces.

Example tasks:
- Identify an audience
- Research the audience's patterns of behavior regarding water usage
- Interview audience members
- Define a medium for communicating with the audience
- Craft the message for the audience
- Storyboard
- Coordinate with actors in the film
- Source graphics

c. **Timeframe:** Now, turn your attention to the third column of the document. Consider and assign the time you expect is needed to complete each goal and task.

Example questions about time:
- What tasks are short-term?
- What tasks are long-term?
- Will certain tasks take one hour? One day? One week?
- Are there aspects of learning that you might need to account for? For instance, your team might be interested in building an app to track an individual's daily water usage but might not have the skills to accomplish the task on its own.

7. **Update and Post:** After completing your spreadsheet, we strongly recommend you move to 6.3b to complete the Adding Roles & Actions assignment together.

8. **Discuss:** Take some time to discuss your experience. Use the following guide for discussion.

DISCUSSION GUIDE

- Which of the team's goals feel more attainable or more challenging?
- What is your sense of commitment to personal versus team goals?
- Do see any opportunities to break larger goals into smaller, more manageable tasks?
- How can you add specificity to make the goals seem more accessible?
- How can the team divide tasks without stepping on each other's toes?

b. Activity

Goal & Role Tracker, Part 2

Assessing the team's skills and interests helps teammates learn about each other. When each teammate has the chance to bring their strengths to the project, everyone feels like a valuable contributor. Assessing roles and actions for each teammate in alignment with the project brief allows the team to celebrate its members' strengths and to view collaboration as a boon to the project success. At the same time, there is an opportunity to learn from each other and to teach new skills. Collaborative project outcomes can improve when teammates create an open environment for peer-to-peer teaching and learning, while also assuming some roles that pertain to their strengths. In-person teams may find value in doing this activity on a wall, with analog tools, before translating to digital calendaring applications and so on.

→ **People:** Local and/or remote teammates/individual
→ **Duration:** 1 hour, if working in real time; 1 day, if working asynchronously via email; and so on.
→ **Technology:** Videoconferencing or messaging software, shared document
→ **Other resources:** Paper, pen, camera/phone

→ *Throughout the process, refer to the discussion guide at the end of this activity.*

Determining roles

Phase 1: With local and/or remote teammates

1. **Revisit & Add:** Review Section 6.3 and complete the Goal & Role Tracker (6.3a) if your team has not done so already. As part of this process, you will add more details to the document as a team. Add two columns to the document with the following headings: roles and actions.

2. **Determine Roles:** Working in real time with your team, determine what roles are needed to accomplish your shared goals and tasks. Roles designate types of tasks (and related actions) an individual must complete. As a team, choose a descriptive word for each person's task or set of tasks—these are their **roles**. Some individuals may have more than one role. These might include any (or more) of the following:

   Example, Master list:
   - Project management
   - Interviewing
   - Writing
   - Storyboarding
   - Video editing
   - Presenting
   - Miscellaneous

3. **Rank Preference:** Each person should make a copy of the final master list of roles. Working individually, with 1 being the lowest and 5 the highest, mark each item on the list in your order of preference. These rankings are not necessarily related to your skill level in doing these things. Use a star, x, or another symbol to indicate skills you would like to learn or hone. You might add another symbol if you want to offer skill mentorship. NOTE: These examples show Role Assignment between teammates. If your team is larger, some tasks may be more distributed.

   Example, Teammate 1:
   - Project management 5★
   - Interviewing 4
   - Writing 3
   - Storyboarding 3
   - Video editing 4
   - Presenting 3
   - Miscellaneous 3

   Example, Teammate 2:
   - Project management 3
   - Interviewing 4
   - Writing 3
   - Storyboarding 1
   - Video editing 5★
   - Presenting 5
   - Miscellaneous 3

4. **Round-robin:** Each person takes turns sharing one of their top role preferences for the collaborative project. Teammate 1 will choose an item from the list, then Teammate 2 will choose an item, and so on, until all items have been selected. The round-robin model aims to reduce redundancies by addressing any gaps and overlaps in the list of skills. Be sure each person has claimed an area from the master list so that all aspects of the project are accounted for, even if that area is not someone's strong suit.

   Example, Combined list:
   - Project management: Teammate 1
   - Interviewing: Teammate 2
   - Writing: Teammate 1
   - Storyboarding: Teammate 1
   - Video editing: Teammate 2
   - Presenting: Teammate 2

5. **Share:** The team completes the round-robin by verbalizing their list of individual rankings in order to see opportunities for shared learning and

teamwork. During this time, the team should ensure all items on the master list have been delegated to at least one teammate and that all project needs are adequately addressed.

Example, Combined list:

- **Project management:** Teammate 1 *(Teammate 2 shares that this is a strength for them and agrees to provide guidance for Teammate 1 in this area.)*
- **Interviewing:** Teammate 2 *(Teammates 1 & 2 realize they had the same scores for Interviewing and Writing and agree to share these tasks)*
- **Writing:** Teammate 1
- **Storyboarding:** Teammate 1
- **Video editing:** Teammate 2 *(Teammate 1 shares that this is a strength for them and agrees to provide guidance for Teammate 2.)*
- **Presenting:** Teammate 2

6. **Roles:** Come to a consensus about what role(s) each person will need to take on in order to complete the project. Using the shared spreadsheet, populate the document with each person's roles for the project. This provides an opportunity to address any unexpected gaps or differences in understanding.

Tasks

Phase 2: Working individually

1. **Determine Actions:** Each person makes a list of actions to complete in order to accomplish each of their chosen tasks. Actions are short-term items that individuals can do to fulfill particular tasks. Working individually using a range of analog resources, such as sticky notes and markers, visualize the actions necessary for your completion of your designated tasks. Brainstorm each individual action or project phase on its own piece of paper.

   As an example, for a person in the role of storyboarder, the task of creating a storyboard (discussed in 6.3) might include the following actions:

   - **Communicate** with teammates to develop an understanding of the goal, audience, and narrative (these elements are being addressed in parallel tasks fulfilled by teammates in different roles)
   - **Collaborate** with the teammate serving as script writer
   - **Write** out lists of what needs to be shown to determine which scenes to depict
   - **Gather** materials for sketching
   - **Sketch** by hand a first round of ideas based on the selected scenes
   - **Make** notes to describe each sketch
   - **Repeat** this process several times to create options for the team to review
   - **Meet** with the teammate serving as project manager
   - **Share** with teammates for feedback
   - **Revise** and update sketches
   - **Share** with teammates for feedback
   - **Refine** and finalize storyboards
   - **Share** final storyboards with team

2. **Populate:** Using the shared spreadsheet, populate the document with the actions generated through the brainstorming activity.
3. **Time:** Adjust the time column to account for the increased detail of roles and actions.

    In addition:
    - Identify specific days and times during your project when you will meet for critique.
    - Designate time for teamwork, consensus-building, and collaboration to finalize the work together.
    - Think how your team might use time differences to your advantage (e.g., the "relay" model (1.4)).

Team agreement

Phase 3: With remote teammates

4. **Shared Calendar:** Update your team's Calendar (1.4) to reflect changes based on these activities. Do this together during a video meeting or take turns working in the calendar.
5. **Formalize:** After agreeing on collective goals and roles, develop a written Collaboration Agreement (1.5a) or update your existing agreement.

Project tracking

Phase 4: Working individually

6. **Print:** Print both the project timeline and updated Collaboration Agreement; sign and date it. Hang both visibly in your workspace. Remember that a physical reminder of your teamwork can help you feel more connected and accountable to the project.
7. **Add & Adjust:** As your team accomplishes different goals, mark these on your physical and digital project timelines. Adding sketches, printouts of screenshots, and images of your teammates will bring your printed timeline to life! Many people find it easier to log changes in hard copy, and we encourage this—just remember to reflect updates in the digital timeline.

DISCUSSION GUIDE

- Are there opportunities for teammates to learn or step into a role that will challenge them in some way?
- How will you ensure task distribution is equitable across the team?
- How can you distribute your tasks according to your time differences so you can best take advantage of the work relay?
- What skill gaps exist, and how will your team address these?

Part B: Project descriptions

After preparing for your collaborative project with the activities in Part A, choose one of the following Project Descriptions, or come up with your own using the Project Generator & Creative Remix (6.2)!

- 6.4 Fairy Tale Mashup
- 6.5 Collaborative Storyboard & Video Sketch
- 6.6 Public Display

→ If your team has a different project in mind, use the Goals & Roles Tracker (6.3) to help your team plan how to execute practical or theoretical outcomes.

6.4

Fairy Tale Mashup:
Local stories to celebrate cultures

The Fairy Tale Mashup encourages teams to celebrate community and culture. The activity gives teams who designate continued cultural learning as their North Star objective an opportunity to create something together. Teammates explore stories from both cultures and create a combined story with elements from multiple cultures. In the process, they learn to negotiate shared content ownership. Learning about each other's stories and sharing the new, combined story in the community promotes cultural sustainability.

Much like your experience in the Picture Story Shuffle (3.2), the Fairy Tale Mashup activity will challenge your team to consider story structure and cohesive narrative as you combine your story and your teammate's story. Working individually for the first phase of the activity, each teammate collects a number of locally based stories, fairy tales, and urban legends from community members, family, friends, and other sources. Explaining the story collections to teammates not only expands their readership but also exposes them to cultural foundations, mythology, and philosophy they might not otherwise experience.

Working together, teams select a single story from each of the collections and decide what parts to take apart and how to fit them back together. The goal is to consider the various ways in which the finished story can span cultural, linguistic, and ideological boundaries in a fun, engaging, and experiential manner. Much like crafting an experience, the team will need to consider whether the story will be told linearly or nonlinearly, or if it will be author- or reader-driven. Teams will also consider how to best depict and share their final stories.

Cultural sustainability and storytelling

Human civilization has long relied on oral storytelling to pass on knowledge, history, spiritual views, and lore. In our rapidly shrinking global society, there is increasing urgency to preserve languages and histories. Linguists are concerned about the rapid depletion of global languages, and the social structures supporting oral histories have begun to disintegrate, so important narratives are disappearing. As a cultural sustainability effort, storytelling and story-sharing can sustain heritage and traditions.

Because language is an essential human characteristic, we encourage teams to explore the role that multiple languages can play in their final outcome. Children who see a positive representation of their heritage and language in literature derive self-esteem and pride in the oral traditions of their homes (Ernst-Slavit and Mulhern 2002). However, many bilingual students are taught in systems that privilege one language over another, causing them to internalize the idea that writing itself is associated with that singular language (Pellicer 2004).

Benefits & outcomes

- Pay tribute to community and culture by sharing local stories and lore
- Gain exposure to cultural foundations and mythology
- Co-create new stories that span boundaries (cultural, linguistic, ideological, etc.)
- Engage an audience outside your collaboration with a Dialogue Object

---

Activity

Fairy Tale Mashup

All cultures have special fairy tales, urban legends, and fables. Idiomatic expressions and historical accounts also have stories behind them that can tell us a lot about their culture of origin. These narratives often promote moral values through entertaining, educational stories. In addition, sharing stories contributes to cultural sustainability by preserving cultural heritage. This activity asks teammates to share traditional stories with one another and then create a hybrid version, charting a new path toward learning, education, or entertainment.

→ **People:** Individual/local and/or remote teammates
→ **Duration:** 1 week minimum
→ **Technology:** Camera-enabled device (phone, video camera, computer, etc.)
→ **Other resources:** Note paper, pen/pencil

Tips

- **Share with kids you know**: If there are kids in your life, you could use this collaborative opportunity to create something for them that expands their curiosity and interest in cultural learning. Think about kids in your neighborhood, family, or extended family. Maybe there is a local library with children's storytime. This can be a fun way to engage others in cultural learning—particularly the younger generation.
- **Cultural learning opportunity**: Sharing and learning about culture through storytelling is a great way to engage people in your life, external to the collaboration, in the exciting work you are doing. While the team will work with only two selected stories, you have an opportunity to use the other stories in future projects or to share them with others in your local context. Consider ways to expand their readership in your own context, perhaps asking your local librarian to add a few to their next book order.

- **Mutual learning**: Teammates should encourage mutual cultural appreciation and value exploration in this activity. You can celebrate and learn more about another culture, while simultaneously acknowledging and cultivating respect for your own. It is not a "one is better than the other" mindset.
- **Roles & Actions**: Sometimes, a new role or action can arise while you are working on a project. Refer back to 6.3 when you have a question or feel like you might be treading into someone else's area of interest or expertise. Reminding yourself of who is doing what can help you efficiently direct your question or engage a teammate in your own work.

Story search

Phase 1: Working individually

1. **Brainstorm:** Research fairy tales, urban legends, fables, idioms, and historical accounts from your culture to share with your teammates. Is there a story that is especially unique to your area? Or one that is told within your family? What are the themes or moral components of that story? Keep in mind that the stories you brainstorm should not be commercially popular, as these stories have already been preserved and consumed by a wider audience.

2. **Select:** Find three compelling stories to share with your team that are manageable in length for reading and sharing with one another. You could even choose shortened versions of longer tales. Together, you'll select one to use for this activity. Start at home, with your personal collection of books and other reading materials, to find inspiration for particular types of stories or visual materials to share with your teammate. Expand your search by visiting the library and talking to your friends, family, and coworkers about what stories are meaningful to them.

Mashup

Phase 2: With local and/or remote teammate

3. **Share:** Each teammate will share their collection of three stories with each other. If possible, read the stories out loud to each other and explain any cultural nuances that might need clarification. Alternatively, share links to read online, or, if possible, upload them to a shared folder so that your teammates can read them. At this stage, you may need to provide simple translations of written versions in order for your teammate to read them. However, in the merged version, you are encouraged to combine different languages.

4. **Choose:** From the compilation of stories, work together to choose one from each teammate's collection to use in the Mashup. For example, individual teammates might each have a story about a warrior figure from their own cultures (e.g., Joan of Arc or Indrajit).

5. **Collect:** Pull together a collection of words, images, materials, colors, textures, and so on to help you explain the visual ambience of the selected story to your teammate. Your visual selections could be based on how the story is depicted in a book or on how you see it in your mind.

6. **Create:** Use your found images to create a *picture-board* (a collection of visual elements and representative images indicating a particular feeling) that exemplifies the range of ways the story is presented in your local context. Depending on the story, this might include photographs of storybooks from your at-home collection of books, along with other versions of the same story collected from friends, family members, or your local library.

7. **Exchange:** Share the picture-board with your team. Reread the story and examine the picture-board. Think about whether there are any comparable stories in your own culture. Ask your teammate to clarify any confusing elements. Perhaps the story includes a religious element or a local tradition, and you'd like to know more. If the story is a fairy tale or fable, for instance, discuss the moral components and what these represent for the culture.

8. **Merge**: One teammate should create a shared document where you will work together to write up the new story. Taking into account the two stories, begin to think about a new story that could be made by merging different aspects from both narratives. The hybrid, dual-story version might incorporate the characters of one story into the other, involve shifting the narrative arc, or adapt the moral of one story to the other. The choice is yours!

   - **Sequence:** Storytelling involves decisions about how the sequence of information is presented. Consider how you will order the new storyline.
   - **Clarity:** Think about what you need to add for the new story to make sense. Is the information structured in a way that the viewer must work to decode or interpret the message(s) to gain meaning from the work?
   - **Language:** If written words are used in the combined story, make a decision as a team about which language(s) you will use. If your team speaks several different languages, try combining them in the final version of your story. It is exciting to teach and learn from each other during the process.

9. **Visualize:** Working with your teammates and your picture-boards, combine existing images and add new ones to create a visual translation of your new tale. Then, work together to create a sequence of visuals that

more explicitly depict your new story, using techniques such as collage, photography, or illustration. Depending on the skill of the team, consider including graphics, where necessary, in order to communicate your new hybrid story. (You may also want to think about how these graphics might be superimposed or integrated into photographic images. See Collaborative Storyboard & Video Sketch for options on bringing stories to life through video.)

Share

Phase 3: With local community member

10. **Multisensory/kinesthetic:** Share the team's new story with an audience outside of your collaboration. This could be with a small community group, your family, a children's group at the library, or to a collection of peers. Act it out, read aloud, and share the visuals. How do they react? (See 6.6 for a discussion about disseminating products of collaboration.)

Analysis

Phase 4: With remote teammates

11. **Discuss:** Take some time to discuss the following ideas:

DISCUSSION GUIDE

- How do you personally define cultural sustainability?
- How has this definition expanded based on this activity?
- What did you learn about your teammates' culture from the stories they shared with you?
- What do you think is the best aspect of your newly created story?
- Will your new story be understandable to others who see your storyboards? Why, or why not?

6.5

Collaborative Storyboard & Video Sketch: Building shared narratives

Storyboards are sequential images that, when viewed together, tell a story. They can stand on their own as a way of communicating ideas, or they can assist with the process of creating a *video sketch*, which is a way to visualize a concept in video form by combining still images, moving images, text, voice-overs, and/or music.

Collaboratively envision ideas

Creating a Storyboard (6.5a) or Video Sketch (6.5b) enables remote teams to envision ideas collaboratively, while accounting for the team's multiple cultural perspectives and range of skills—and the logistics required to manage those issues across long distances. With both of these activities, consider the visual and textual elements of storytelling, so you will be working together to come up with the visual components of the narrative but also to write a script. Many video sketching goals can be achieved via storyboarding, the first phase of this activity. You can convey your concept by arranging the storyboard images into simple stop-motion sequences or by simply viewing and sharing them in static form. This activity can be adapted for other disciplines in academia and industry.

Learn together using basic tools

People with little (or no) expertise in visual design or video production can create storyboards and video sketches using basic tools. These can be used to convey valuable information about project concepts, immersive media, and spatial experiences to collaborators and audiences alike. Both formats help teams evolve and communicate ideas. As such, storyboards and video sketches can be used as a process—one that helps teams ideate a finished product or illustrate a concept for future production—or as a finished product.

You do not have to be a professional filmmaker to engage with these forms of strategic visual storytelling. In fact, you can use any number of digital tools to accomplish this task, ranging from the basic features afforded by mobile devices to more advanced video-editing software. Teams will work together to write a script and integrate that script with visuals in order to create a compelling video sketch about the project. If creating a video seems too intimidating, however, Storyboarding (6.5a) offers a more approachable route to visualizing your ideas in the form of a visual narrative.

Using video sketches to share big ideas

John Zimmerman, a faculty member in Human-Computer Interaction (HCI) and Design at Carnegie Mellon University, has developed a method for video sketching to demonstrate interaction design prototypes, which is significant for co-creation because it helps teams create a shared vision. We have adapted Zimmerman's method of video sketching for intercultural collaboration purposes with the goal of fostering a heightened exchange of ideas among teammates. The Collaborative Storyboard & Video Sketch activity engage teammates in written and visual storytelling methods to showcase an idea they are working on together (whether interaction design or otherwise).

Sharing mobile and web-based concepts

The beauty of a video sketch is that it allows teams to demonstrate their ideas, for both pervasive and immersive innovation, through an easily accessible format that does not require extensive technical knowledge. For example, say your team has an exciting idea that involves the creation of an application for mobile or web-based media to track community water usage. There are established protocols for showing prototypes on desktop, tablet, and mobile devices, but you do not have to be an interaction designer to bring this idea to life.

Pitch an idea before building it

Designing for immersive media, spatial experiences, and systemic changes can be time-consuming and costly. Prior to investing in a particular solution, creating a video sketch allows teams to propose, test, and refine ideas by illustrating how they might function. A team could use a video sketch to pitch their idea to a local organization or granting body who could provide resources to bring the idea to life. Also, as Dialogue Objects, video sketches can share ideas and encourage conversation with people outside of the team. Showing the video of the team's community water use tracker idea to friends, family, and other community members might encourage water conservation practices, for instance.

We encourage everyone to engage in the video production process—scripting, shooting still images, and compositing—with the aim of producing a short video sketch about a team's idea for a product, service, experience, or something else. The Collaborative Storyboard & Video Sketch enables teammates to use video for storytelling purposes, regardless of your topic or project. While this form of narrative can present huge logistical challenges, the payoff is worthwhile. Not only does the process help to increase communication between teammates; it also allows for the exchange of massive amounts of cultural information and nuance that may have gone unaddressed or undiscovered prior to the video creation process.

Benefits & outcomes

- Visualize a concept or ideate on a project
- Efficiently communicate large amounts of cultural content and nuance
- Incorporate multiple cultural perspectives into a single product
- Develop a Dialogue Object to encourage conversation with people outside of the team

---

Tips

- **Component exchange:** Making and sharing copies of visual Thought Objects is an essential step in the collaborative process. However, these components can feel precious to the creators, particularly if they have invested a great deal of time in them. Remember to back up files before sharing in order to maintain a sense of ownership and place within the process.
- **Big files, bigger opportunities:** Uploading video files and working with them will take longer than other digital formats. Make sure to keep teammates abreast of your process, and let them know when you upload your files to the shared digital space. Be patient and use the time difference between your locations to your advantage (Remember to use your Shared Calendar, 1.4).

- **Be Kind:** As you work through this activity, there will likely be moments of creative abrasion or bumps in the road. Choose your words carefully and be kind—speak from a place of supporting and improving the team's end goal. For example, instead of accusing a teammate of submitting work late, you could say, "It would be really helpful if we could all have the required materials in our shared folder the day before our meeting. That way, we will all have a chance to work with them before our next meeting."
- **Be Direct:** Directly confronting challenges with your teammates may feel scary at first, but is more effective in the long run than staying silent or relying on intermediaries. Team dynamics will benefit from open conversations and internal problem resolution. Your growth as an individual—and your ability to handle future workplace collaborations—will also increase if you tackle complexities head on. Grappling with a rocky experience now can lead to smooth sailing the second time around.

a. Activity

Collaborative Storyboard & Script

A *storyboard* is a design approach that involves sketching a time-based narrative frame-by-frame and describing the actions taking place. Depending on the team's goals, storyboarding can be an end product on its own. However, storyboarding is often used as a preliminary step to video sketching. It helps teammates decide what the video needs to include in order to convey their ideas effectively. Usually, a storyboard is accompanied by a script that verbally describes the actions or dialogue necessary for someone to understand each frame.

→ **People:** Remote teammates
→ **Duration:** 1 week minimum.
→ **Technology:** Paper and pencil, shared spreadsheet, still camera or phone camera
→ **Other resources:** Drawing or collaging materials (optional)

→ *Throughout the process, refer to the discussion guide at the end of this activity.*

Phase 1: With remote teammates

1. **Revisit:** This activity begins with the assumption that you have already developed your concept (see Project Generator, 6.2, for more information about how to do this) and that you have already successfully completed several of the earlier trust-building activities together.

2. **Draft a narrative:** Working together, create a narrative about your team's concept based on your North Star objective. The narrative should explain the conceptual framework of your idea, including how you propose to engage your chosen audience. Your team may have a specific product, service, or experience in mind—or may simply want to raise awareness about a topic of shared interest. What are ways that you can work together to showcase your team's unique ideas and perspectives?

3. **Cultural insights:** Take care to represent multiple cultural perspectives in the narrative. For example, teammates could work in parallel on two different storylines and later combine those storylines into one final piece that showcases your two distinct cultural viewpoints or contexts. Or you could work all together on one narrative with a single setting, but take care to acknowledge all teammates' cultural perspectives throughout the process.

4. **Draft a storyboard:** One teammate should create a shared document and insert a table with at least eight equally sized cells. Individually, come up with eight distinct actions to help communicate the project idea from beginning to end. Moving from left to right, and from the top of the table to the bottom, fill in the cells according to your narrative. The first square in your table should correspond to the first step (or scene) that you need to take to communicate your concept. Another approach is to have each member of the team fold a piece of paper into eight equal parts, write inactions or steps, photograph them, and send them to one another for discussion.

5. **Discuss:** Share your draft plans with each other. Work with your teammate so that you are taking both storyboards into account and determine which combination of actions you will incorporate into your final approach. Talk about each step, and make notes in a shared document for each square—or write your notes in the individual squares. Come to a consensus about the narrative.

6. **Visualize:** Figure out the particular visuals you will use to demonstrate your team's narrative. Consider using still images, such as collage, photography, or illustration. For example, perhaps one teammate is especially strong at drawing or photography and can create a cohesive set of images for each cell of the storyboard. Depending on the skills of your team, you could also consider creating information visualizations or other illustrated digital graphics; non-photographic images can help communicate your idea or entertain your viewers, as necessary, in order to communicate your concept. (Think, too, about how you would superimpose or integrate your digital graphics into photographic images).

7. **Create a script:** Collaborate on a script based on your initial narrative. Even if your video does not require dialogue, a script is useful for organizing your thoughts, communicating direction, and explaining each scene of the storyboard. You can either embed your script in the storyboard or write it in a separate document. It is important that the writing process be collaborative, so if you are using a shared document, work in it together to create textual elements that explain your concept in interesting and relevant ways,

for audiences in both cultural contexts. (For your selected audiences, recall the Fictional Character Exchange (4.5) as a way to bring them to life!)

    a. **Voice:** Discuss whether you need voice(s), voice-over, or dialogue to help your viewers connect the dots or whether the video speaks for itself.

    b. **Text:** Does it make sense to integrate text and/or captions in the video? If so, what language(s) will your team use?

    c. **Music:** Will you add any music to the video? Music can go a long way and add distinct cultural flavors.

8. **Critique & Revise:** Meet as a team to work through the Critique guidelines (Chapter 5) in order to improve the writing in the script and strengthen the storyboard. Work together to tighten the language and refine the execution of the related visuals. If you can, share your work with people outside of the collaborative team to receive feedback and address any gaps in understanding.

9. **Finalize:** Polish your script and storyboard to the best of your team's ability, with attention to strong visuals and good writing. This step is especially important if the team does not plan to execute a video, as the storyboard will be your team's final format for showcasing your shared concept.

DISCUSSION GUIDE

- What is your team's big idea, and how will you visually convey this idea? Is the idea valid in both cultures?
- What are the best locations for showing your idea? Why?
- Will your idea be relevant or useful in different geographic locations?
- How do you think people in different cultures will perceive your idea?
- What are the guidelines for showing/sharing recognizable faces in your culture? In your teammate's culture?

b. Activity

Collaborative Video Sketch

This phase is more challenging and requires a higher degree of communication and pre-established trust between teammates. Unlike some of the other approaches outlined in this chapter, creating a concept video is more time-and technology-intensive. The instructions for this activity assume that your team has already successfully completed several trust-building activities and developed your concept together (see Project Generator 6.2a).

As you get ready to create a video, account for typical pre-production activities, such as scouting locations, recruiting people (actors, voices, other helpers), and creating a shot list. Within your team, this phase is also an opportunity to discuss a range of location options and what the different cultural contexts might offer the narrative. Take risks and be experimental; you have nothing to lose!

→ **People:** Remote teammates
→ **Duration:** 2 weeks minimum; more time is recommended
→ **Technology:** Variable, but might include one or more of the following: video camera, still camera or phone camera; image editing software (to add proposed ideas to static images); image sequencing software (e.g., tools for creating short movies, slideshows, or animated GIFs); audio editing software; messaging apps capable of sharing images and video
→ **Other resources:** People (actors), microphone (for voice overs), and music (sourced with copyright in mind)

→ *Throughout the process, refer to the discussion guide at the end of this activity.*

Delegate

Phase 1: With remote teammates

1. **Check in:** Communication is vital throughout this process. Work together to establish team guidelines and agree on communication channels for regular updates, such as a combination of messaging, videoconferences, status updates in a shared document, and so on. These guidelines and channels are particularly critical when exchanging any in-progress video files through cloud-based sharing services in order to avoid confusion, frustration, and unnecessary duplication of work, which can happen as the result of lags in file syncing.

2. **Review:** Consult your storyboard and consider what you can do as part of *pre-production* (while shooting your still images) versus *post-production* (during or immediately before the process of threading all of your stills together into a final video).

3. **Capture images/video:** Think about capturing a variety of shots for your video in order to generate visual interest. Consider combining wide-angle shots that capture a large area, close-up shots that focus on a particular detail, and everything in between. Consider relevant tools: This phase can be accomplished through a series of still images, shooting live video with a phone, or other more advanced video-capturing techniques.

4. **Delegate:** Interweaving your team's collection of images (whether still or moving) can be accomplished in a variety of ways, depending on the skills and interests of each individual teammate (see Goal & Role Tracker 6.3). One approach is for teammates to work on their own, but in parallel, on two (or more) different aspects of the storylines, and then combine those pieces into one final video. Or you could work together on one video while trading off responsibilities. The latter approach is a great way to take advantage of potential time differences between remote teammates. Another approach is to assign the task of *editing* to a single individual, while other teammates are responsible for additional tasks, such as writing.

5. **Video Sketch:** Use basic video-editing software to combine your collection of still and moving images (many free mobile and desktop applications exist). This step might involve:

   a. Shooting a well-planned live video directly on a phone or camera (this option is especially good if no editing tools are available or if no teammate has editing in their skill set)

   b. Using hobby or professional motion design software, if available

   c. Editing together still images to create a stop-motion piece (stop-motion means shooting one still image at a time and making gradual changes to each still image) and saving your piece as a GIF

6. **Communicate & Update:** When your portion has reached a stopping point, share your progress with your teammates. One approach is to play the in-progress video on the computer and capture a recording of it on your phone so that you can share it with teammates via your preferred messaging app. This option is a quick way to communicate updates to teammates who are waiting for shared working files to update, and can help prevent confusion during the creation and editing process.

Feedback & finalize

Phase 2: With remote teammates

7. **Critique & Revise:** Meet as a team to work through the Critique guidelines (Chapter 5) in order to improve the video. Tighten pacing, sequencing, and sound components. If you can, ask for feedback from people outside the team. This helps demonstrate how well the video communicates your concept.

8. **Finalize:** Polish your Video Sketch to the best of your team's ability, paying attention to strong visual storytelling and cultural context. Ultimately, your aim is to capture your viewers' imaginations and invite them into your team's concept.

9. **Celebrate:** Even if the final video sketch does not meet your original expectations, the experience of working together as a team provides valuable practice in teamwork, critical thinking, and intercultural learning. As a multi-layered project, this particular activity enables you to understand how short-term and long-term goals can support creative ideation.

DISCUSSION GUIDE

• Does it make sense to show your team's idea in more than one cultural context?

• What aspects may be intriguing, distracting, or confusing to viewers from a different culture?

• If needed, how can you sensitively approach people about acting for your video sketch?

• Recall your team's collective goals. How does your video sketch address those?

6.6

Public Display:
Celebrate outcomes with the wider community

Publicly sharing the outcomes of your intercultural collaboration can be impactful and meaningful for your teammates and your communities. This activity encourages you to celebrate the peaks and valleys of your teamwork by sharing your ideas and outcomes with your communities. During your collaboration, you may have gathered external feedback (e.g., Outside Input 5.5). However, the Public Display activity is different; it focuses on generating conversation about the outcomes of the collaboration instead of gathering feedback to refine work-in-progress.

Gathering information and feedback from outside the team is essential. If your team is working on contextually specific ideas and interventions, getting feedback from local people in the applicable locations will help your idea evolve, particularly if they have expertise in your topic area. Moreover, sharing your work with an external audience makes your team accountable to an audience outside yourselves. It can give you an important sense of accomplishment and serve as a celebration for your hard work.

Don't be put off by this activity's name! Like the other activities in this book, this does not require expertise in public presentations, exhibitions, or performances. The scale and formality of the Public Display are up to you. Whether you share with five, fifty, or five hundred people, the quantity is not the point. The purpose is to engage people outside the team in your conversation about what the team has accomplished or learned together.

Extend ideas to local and global publics

One of the advantages of collaborating across cultures is the opportunity to consider different global audiences and perspectives. When teammates from different cultures explain and share the outcomes of remote collaboration with their communities, it extends the team's ideas to local and global publics. Ultimately the responsibility to engage with new ideas and tackle global problems extends beyond your team—all of us must participate to make our world a better place.

Present accessible ideas

Considering how to make your work comprehensible and accessible to audiences outside the collaboration, from either culture, will force your team to analyze your work through a new lens. The team must assess whether your work effectively communicates your intentions across cultures. Consider particular audiences and locations for your Public Display, and then reflect on how the work visually communicates—and whether or not it will (or should) communicate verbally at all.

Mobilize community interest

By talking publicly about your team's ideas, you take a first step toward beginning discussions with other people who have the potential to encourage their thinking about their own outlooks, lives, and habits in a different way. By drawing community members into conversations about your North Star objectives and insights drawn from your intercultural collaboration, you may also initiate new partnerships. People who share your values and concerns may be excited to connect with you to help bring your team's ideas to fruition. In this way, the goal-setting introduced at the beginning of this chapter may come full-circle.

The bigger-picture advantage of sharing your work with the larger community is that it heightens awareness about intercultural work among the general public, shining a spotlight on the value of diverse perspectives and on the significance of our increasing interconnectedness. We hope that this awareness, in turn, encourages others to explore the possibilities of intercultural learning, communication, and collaboration.

Benefits & outcomes

- Share and celebrate your work with people outside the collaboration
- Cultivate community connections, both local and global
- Mobilize interest in your topic and promote intercultural collaboration
- Consider the possibility of extending your work into new projects

Activity

Public Display

Sharing the outcomes of your collaborative project with a larger audience can have real benefits. Not only does your team have an opportunity to celebrate the completion of a project, but you have the opportunity to share the intercultural learning endeavor itself with friends, family, and community members. Depending on the kind of project that you produced, a presentation or exhibition in a public venue can be a wonderful opportunity for all members of the intercultural team to shine—as well as to receive feedback and think about extending the work into new projects.

→ **People:** Local and/or remote teammates
→ **Duration:** Variable, from a few hours to several days or weeks
→ **Technology:** Variable, but might include black and white or color printer, projector and screens, computers/displays, and mobile devices, depending on the nature of the venue and project outcomes
→ **Other resources:** Public venue for presentation, space and vertical or horizontal surfaces appropriate for displaying the work; cameras or phones for documentation

---

Tips

- **Select a venue:** Have a conversation with your team about how your various local contexts affect the reading and interpretation of your collaborative outcomes. Think about how visitors may interpret the work differently depending on the context.

- **Share your intercultural learning:** In addition to sharing your ideas with an external audience, you also have the opportunity to share what you have learned from intercultural collaboration. This raises the profile of intercultural teamwork and highlights its benefits for your particular discipline, field, or sector. Talk with your team about how to identify people within each culture who are interested in your North Star objective. Decide how you might debrief with your team after each Public Display event.

- **Acknowledge the "we:"** When discussing shared work, focus your language on the notion of the *collective*, rather than the *individual*. Focusing on "I did this" or "I did that" can make teammates feel they are not being acknowledged for the collaborative aspect of the work. Acknowledging the team helps everyone feel valued for their contribution, ideas, and signature skills.

> • **Make connections:** The Public Display can help you connect with other people whose views resonate with your team's shared values, such as sustainability. This is an opportunity to establish new partnerships in your community; if these partnerships help bring your team's ideas to fruition, that will enable your team to continue working together.

Organize

Phase 1: With local and/or remote teammates

1. **Plan:** Review the team's Shared Calendar, Goal & Task, Roles & Actions.
2. **Locate:** Work together to choose a potential venue for sharing the collaboration outcomes with relevant community members (e.g., somewhere on campus, in the workplace, or at other locations in the community). Your team might also decide to exhibit the work across your two locations, with one in each cultural context.
3. **Select Options:** With your local and/or teammates, discuss the various local venue options for sharing collaboration outcomes and come to a decision.
4. **Event Plan:** Organize an event around the public presentation, exhibition, or display. Invite people outside of the collaboration to attend.
5. **Brainstorm:** With your team, come up with a range of creative ways to share and display your collaborative outcomes in your chosen public venue in order to spark interest from invited guests and unexpected visitors.
    a. What aspects of the collaboration are you excited to share with others? Why?
    b. What aspects do you feel hesitant to share? Why?
    c. As a result of this collaboration, what is something positive you have learned about
        • Your teammates' culture(s)?
        • Your project or topic?
        • Yourself?
    d. What would be the most engaging way for someone outside of the collaboration to learn about the work you have been doing?
6. **Sketch:** Create sketches to show how you might share your team's work in the allocated space.
7. **Get Feedback:** Present your display ideas to your teammates for feedback and determine what changes you need to make before the presentation or exhibition.
8. **Actualize:** Work together with your team to actualize the presentation plan; create visual or written panels for display, finalize concepts or prototypes to share, prepare print or digital visuals that are reflective of your collaborative work process or outcomes, and/or create appropriate language translations of your materials for all presentation contexts.

Implement & evaluate

Phase 2: In public space

9. **Implement:** Install the outcomes in the selected display space.
10. **Document:** Take photographs of each installation to share with your teammates.

Phase 3: With teammates

11. **Reflect:** Meet with your teammates to discuss the experience and share feedback and outcomes. Use the discussion guide.

DISCUSSION GUIDE

- What did you learn from this experience? How did the local venue impact what you were able to share with the audience? If you did it over again, what would you change, add, or remove?
- What components of the display were most intriguing to the audience? Why?
- How does sharing the team's work with an external audience affect how you feel about the team's work together?
- What did you do to establish meaningful connections with guests? Did you make any connections that might prompt new work?

References

De Bono, Edward. 2010. *Lateral Thinking: Creativity Step by Step.* New York: Harper Collins.

Ernst-Slavit, Gisela, and Margaret Mulhern. 2002. "Bilingual Books: Promoting Literacy and Biliteracy in the Second-Language and Mainstream Classroom." *Reading Online* 7 (2): 1096–1232.

Gaither, Sarah E., Jessica D. Remedios, Diana T. Sanchez, and Samuel R. Sommers. 2015. "Thinking Outside the Box: Multiple Identity Mind-Sets Affect Creative Problem Solving." *Social Psychological and Personality Science* 6 (5): 596–603. doi:10.1177/1948550614568866.

Gratton, Lynda, and Tamara J. Erickson. 2007. "8 Ways to Build Collaborative Teams." *Harvard Business Review* 85 (11): 100–109, 153.

Hill, Linda A., Greg Brandeau, Emily Truelove, and Kent Lineback. 2014. *Collective Genius: The Art and Practice of Leading Innovation.* Boston, MA: Harvard Business Review Press.

Leonard-Barton, Dorothy. 1995. *Wellsprings of Knowledge: Building and Sustaining the Sources of Innovation.* Boston, MA: Harvard Business School Press. https://books.google.com/books?id=0oUoAQAAMAAJ.

Locke, Edwin A., and Gary P. Latham. 2002. "Building a Practically Useful Theory of Goal Setting and Task Motivation: A 35-Year Odyssey." *American Psychologist* 57 (9): 705–17. doi:10.1037/0003-066X.57.9.705.

Mills, H., N. Reiss, and M. Dombeck. 2008. "Types of Stressors (Eustress vs. Distress)." www.mentalhelp.net/stress/types-of-stressors-eustress-vs-distress/.

OPSI. 2018. "Innovation Is a Many-Splendoured Thing." *Observatory of Public Sector Innovation* (blog). September 6, 2018. https://oecd-opsi.org/innovation-is-a-many-splendoured-thing/.

Pauker, Kristin, Colleen Carpinella, Chanel Meyers, Danielle M. Young, and Diana T. Sanchez. 2018. "The Role of Diversity Exposure in Whites' Reduction in Race Essentialism Over Time." *Social Psychological and Personality Science* 9 (8): 944–52. doi:10.1177/1948550617731496.

Pellicer, Alejandra. 2004. "The Orthographic Contrast between Two Languages: Mayan and Spanish." *Written Language & Literacy* 7 (1): 35–48. doi:10.1075/wll.7.1.05pel.

Sawyer, R. Keith. 2008. "Creativity, Innovation, and Obviousness Business Law Forum: Nonobviousness - The Shape of Things to Come." *Lewis & Clark Law Review*, 2: 461–88.

Sawyer, Keith. 2017. *Group Genius: The Creative Power of Collaboration*. New York: Basic Books.

Selye, Hans. 1976. "Stress without Distress." In *Psychopathology of Human Adaptation*, edited by George Serban, 137–46. Boston, MA: Springer US. doi:10.1007/978-1-4684-2238-2_9.

Stokes, Patricia D. 2005. *Creativity from Constraints: The Psychology of Breakthrough*. New York: Springer Pub. Co. http://public.eblib.com/choice/publicfullrecord.aspx?p=423619.

Suzuki, Shunryu. 2010. *Zen Mind, Beginner's Mind: Informal Talks on Zen Meditation and Practice*. Boston, MA: Shambhala Publications.

Tharp, Bruce M., and Stephanie M. Tharp. 2018. *Discursive Design: Critical, Speculative, and Alternative Things*. Design Thinking, Design Theory. Cambridge, MA: MIT Press.

UNESCO. 2003. "The Power of Culture for Development." In *Proceedings of the Workshop, 11–12 November 2002, Ferrara, Italy*. Vol. 7. Paris, France: United Nations Educational, Scientific, and Cultural Organization. https://unesdoc.unesco.org/ark:/48223/pf0000132988.

———. 2010. "The Power of Culture for Development." Paris, France: United Nations Educational, Scientific, and Cultural Organization. www.lacult.unesco.org/lacult_en/docc/The_Power_of_Culture_Development.pdf.

Wei, Meifen, Cixin Wang, Stacy Y. Ko, Shuyi Liu, and Raquel Botello. 2019. "Bicultural Stress and Perceived Benefits among Asian Americans: The Roles of Cognitive Flexibility and Making Positive Sense of Adversity." *Asian American Journal of Psychology*, April. doi:10.1037/aap0000158.

EPILOGUE

Throughout *Drawing from Differences*, you have worked collaboratively with your team to build trust and understanding using hands-on activities to communicate your thoughts, improve your ideas, and prompt dialogue. We hope these new thought processes, competencies, and tools enhance your understanding of the role of visual and physical artifacts in team building. By sharing your ideas in this manner, you have also learned the power of communicating and collaborating across cultures to drive big-picture thinking and generate ideas.

We challenge you to take your new tools a step further by confronting *wicked problems*. Design theorist Horst Rittel defined wicked problems as complex and confusing "social system problems" involving a wide range of stakeholders with dissimilar values (Rittel and Webber 1973; Buchanan 1992). Wicked problems are global challenges, including environmental and cultural degradation, social justice issues, and resource scarcity. These problems are neither concrete nor straightforward, and some might say that their complexity prevents any real solution. But we believe that harnessing diverse perspectives empowers humans to carve brighter paths toward sustainability, cultural preservation, and equity.

Businesses, academia, and organizations must do their part to increase awareness and engage with these social system problems. In these multi-layered environments, people can also learn to approach traditional systems in new ways through intercultural collaboration. We are excited to see higher education begin to inspire future professionals with sustainability and social transformation initiatives to drive positive change (Emans and Murdoch-Kitt 2018). Together with our model for intercultural collaboration, we hope students, professionals, and citizens of the world will integrate these concepts into their current landscape and use them for the common good.

There is much to celebrate in the work we can all do together.

And in the world, there is still much work to be done.

References

Buchanan, Richard. 1992. "Wicked Problems in Design Thinking." *Design Issues* 8 (2): 5. doi:10.2307/1511637.

Emans, Denielle, and Kelly Murdoch-Kitt. 2018. "Intercultural Collaborations in Design Education." In *Routledge Handbook of Sustainable Design*, edited by Rachel Beth Egenhoefer. London; New York: Routledge.

Rittel, Horst W. J., and Melvin M. Webber. 1973. "Dilemmas in a General Theory of Planning." *Policy Sciences* 4 (2): 155–69.

INDEX

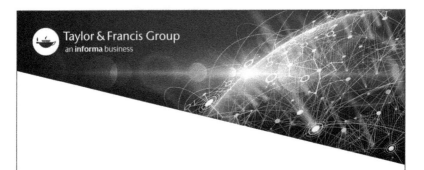

For Product Safety Concerns and Information please contact our EU
representative GPSR@taylorandfrancis.com
Taylor & Francis Verlag GmbH, Kaufingerstraße 24, 80331 München, Germany

www.ingramcontent.com/pod-product-compliance
Ingram Content Group UK Ltd.
Pitfield, Milton Keynes, MK11 3LW, UK
UKHW020931180425
457613UK00012B/320